# The Educational Morass

## Overcoming the Stalemate in American Education

Myron Lieberman

Rowman & Littlefield Education
Lanham, Maryland • Toronto • Plymouth, UK
2007

Published in the United States of America
by Rowman & Littlefield Education
A Division of Rowman & Littlefield Publishers, Inc.
A wholly owned subsidary of The Rowman & Littlefield Publishing Group, Inc.
4501 Forbes Boulevard, Suite 200, Lanham, Maryland 20706
www.rowmaneducation.com

Estover Road
Plymouth PL6 7PY
United Kingdom

British Library Cataloguing in Publication Information Available

**Library of Congress Cataloging-in-Publication Data**

Lieberman, Myron, 1919–
  The educational morass : overcoming the stalemate in American education /
Myron Lieberman.
    p. cm.
  Includes bibliographical references and index.
  ISBN-13: 978-1-57886-622-9 (hardcover : alk. paper)
  ISBN-13: 978-1-57886-623-6 (pbk. : alk. paper)
  ISBN-10: 1-57886-622-7 (hardcover : alk. paper)
  ISBN-10: 1-57886-623-5 (pbk. : alk. paper)
  1. Public schools—United States. 2. Educational change—United States. I.
Title.
  LA217.2.L538 2007
  371.010973—dc22                                    2007007849

∞™ The paper used in this publication meets the minimum requirements of
American National Standard for Information Sciences—Permanence of Paper
for Printed Library Materials, ANSI/NISO Z39.48-1992.
Manufactured in the United States of America.

This book is dedicated to Myrl and Ruth Herman, Robert and Doris Holtzman, Earl and Lila McGovern, David G. Salten, and John Wilson, good guys who never wavered along the way.

# Contents

# Foreword

**W**hen one undertakes the writing of a foreword for an important book, one is inclined to begin by taking note of earlier writings the author has produced. In the present instance, that's a challenging task simply because Myron Lieberman has written so much for so long. His first book was published in 1956, and he has authored or coauthored eighteen books since then. But there's more than books. Lieberman has written a wide variety of professional and popular articles, columns for print media, special reports on nearly every phase of collective bargaining in education, and numerous proposals for education reform projects to be undertaken by at least a dozen universities and think tanks.

Myron Lieberman has now brought forth in America a new book that goes beyond his earlier works in its breadth and scope. The book, as he writes in his introduction, is about elementary and secondary education (K–12) in the United States, and indeed it is. But Lieberman's range extends to the widest array of related issues. He takes the reader into regions of interest, such as the real cost of public education, the role of media in education policy, alternative routes to a competitive education system, and the absence of accountability among the most prominent public intellectuals who advise the public on educational issues. One of the author's abiding interests in his long career in education has been educational employment relations, including collective bargaining by teachers and the role of teacher unions. Dr. Lieberman has been a major figure on the teacher union scene: He ran for the presidency of American Federation of

Teachers (AFT) in 1962, and he has represented school boards in six states in their contract negotiations with the unions in their school districts. This man has had firsthand experience in educational employment relations that, to my knowledge, is unmatched in this country, past or present.

Along with others who have spent time laboring in the educational vineyard, I am continually beset by questions about both educational policy and practice that have no ready answers. What, for example, are the facts about merit pay for teachers? If it hasn't been tried, as the author asserts, why not? Why do well-meaning and seemingly well-planned education reforms so often fail? When I was a high school science teacher a few decades ago, there were no teacher unions, so wouldn't teachers be better off without unions today? Lieberman says mathematics and science teachers would be; teachers with talents that command a premium in the marketplace are bound to be disadvantaged by representation from a union in which most members do not command a premium. This is a much more important issue than merit pay as well as pay for performance, which Lieberman regards as usually impractical in large-scale educational employment outside of a market system.

In a chapter that challenges the positions of both the public school establishment and conservative orthodoxy, Lieberman argues that there is no substantive difference between public sector bargaining and political action and that the legislative efforts to distinguish them have provided school district labor unions with enormous advantages in the policy-making process at all levels of government. Minimally, his argument identifies several issues that were not considered in the expansive phase of public sector bargaining and that constitute a strong argument for limitations on it.

If there are taxpaying citizens who are not interested in the true costs of educating the nation's children, they have escaped my notice. *The Educational Morass* shows that government statistics on the subject often fail to include several costs that would double the expense set forth in government reports on the subject. Lieberman shows that there is almost as much confusion over the costs as there is over educational achievement, a sobering thought that is widely overlooked.

Readers of Myron Lieberman's prose are likely to discover a writing style that is direct, candid, and occasionally off-putting. He does not try to soften his message or avoid blunt criticism of the leading conservative public intellectuals on education issues. In short, Myron Lieberman writes his mind just as I've heard him speak it many times. That's one of the reasons—an important one—that his messages are usually clear and unambiguous, and that's why Dr. Lieberman stands as good a chance as anyone presently on the scene in education to set in motion some of the reforms American K–12 education so badly needs.

J. Stanley Marshall
President, Florida State University, 1969–1976
Founding Chairman, James Madison Institute

# Acknowledgments

I am indebted to a very large number of persons, none of whom has seen the final draft or evinced agreement with all of it or, in a few cases, with any of it. To avoid any erroneous attribution of views, I have expressed my appreciation privately and wish to emphasize that I am solely responsible for the content, including any errors.

# Introduction

This book is about elementary and secondary education (K–12) in the United States. I regard such education as a highly ineffective service and, for reasons to be explained, unlikely to achieve significant improvement in the absence of heavy external pressure, which is not in sight. The reasons for these conclusions and what can be done about it are the core of the book.

An analysis of all the important issues in education would require an encyclopedic volume that includes several topics about which I know very little. The topics that are discussed are intended to explain various obstacles to raising the quality and lowering the real costs of K–12 education. These objectives appear to have eluded our educational system. Showing why this is and what may be done about it is a daunting task, but it does not require an analysis of every important educational issue. In any case, I believe that the following analysis is adequate for my objectives and hope that it is also sufficient for whatever objectives readers bring to it.

Education is a morass because several groups have veto power, but no interest group, or coalition of interest groups, controls all of the factors essential to effect either a major reform or a different system. Public education is a highly decentralized public service, buffeted by national, state, and local interests and reported by media that are not up to the task of describing the situation realistically. Understandably, given my outlook, the following pages are highly critical of both liberal and conservative leaders and the think tanks in the business of public enlightenment and those in positions of leadership in public education. Educational literature is re-plete with scholarly discussions of "accountability," but the discussions stop well short of identifying anyone who should be held accountable for the educational morass in which we find ourselves.[1] The argument here is that although the extent of accountability in public education is vastly ex-aggerated, the absence of it among its critics may be a more serious prob-lem in the long run.

In trying to show the pervasive influence of interest groups, I have relied mainly on the role of the National Education Association (NEA), the Amer-ican Federation of Teachers (AFT), and the American Federation of Labor and Congress of Industrial Organizations (AFL-CIO). It is not my position that everything about teacher unions is bad or that there would be immedi-ate improvement if teacher unions were abolished. Improvement might ma-terialize promptly on some issues, but some conservative analysts have gone from completely ignoring the unions to attributing everything negative about public education to them. For instance, conservatives tend to attribute the absence of merit pay to union opposition, but there is no merit pay in the states in which there is no collective bargaining. In fact, there is no merit pay even where teacher union bargaining is prohibited and in countries in which educational achievement far exceeds our own.

In taking account of interests, there is no assumption that individuals and groups always seek to act in accordance with their economic interests; fur-thermore, individuals and organizations are often mistaken or unsure as to where their economic interests lie. Quite frequently, their noneconomic in-terests take precedence over their economic interests. I do not regard teach-ers as either more or less self-serving than most other interest groups. Al-though teacher and teacher union interests, as they perceive them, deeply affect what does and does not happen in public education, my analysis agrees that other factors influence their conduct.

In emphasizing the role of interests, there is no implication that a pol-icy is contrary to the public interest because it provides economic benefits to its sponsors. Business leaders oppose higher taxes on corporations; this fact does not mean or imply that their opposition is unjustified. Similar considerations apply to teachers and teacher unions. The interests of ac-tors may alert us to be skeptical of the policies they propose, but the de-sirability of the policies depends upon their consequences, not the motives of the parties who promote or oppose the policies. Individuals are often mistaken about what is in the public interest; they are less often mistaken about what is in their own interest, but it happens. Furthermore, interests are much broader than financial rewards; hence, the absence of financial interests is not equivalent to the absence of any interest. That said, I strongly agree with Vilfredo Pareto's observation that men find it easy to convert their interests to principles.[2]

There is a widespread assumption that objectivity requires teachers, journalists, and policy analysts to conceal their personal views on the issues under discussion. This assumption is a major fallacy. The way to avoid bias is to be forthcoming about one's views and relationships to matters being discussed, so that others are more alert to possible biases in the analysis. Consequently, I have no hesitation in stating my view that our nation needs a three-sector industry: public schools, nonprofit schools, and for-profit schools. That said, I am not and have never been a proponent of the school-choice plans that have been in effect since 1990. I have not opposed them, but for reasons discussed in the following chapters, I have never regarded them as likely to bring about significant improvement.

## *CONSERVATIVE* AND *LIBERAL* DEFINED

As used in this book, *conservative* and *liberal* are umbrella terms that cover a wide range of political, economic, and cultural orientations. On education, the common thread that ties conservatives together is the conviction that school choice and much greater utilization of private schools would be in the public interest. Denominational groups that sponsor their own schools (Catholics, Orthodox Jews, Lutherans, and Christian fundamentalists) are conservatives as I use the term, but so are groups that support a free market in education. As used here, libertarians are also included even though they are typically not social conservatives; quite the contrary. The mainstream of the Republican Party is included; obviously, there is a great deal of overlap between this group and the others cited.

It should be emphasized that conservatives as previously defined are not necessarily the only supporters of a specific conservative educational objective. For instance, opinion polls show that inner-city black parents are supportive of school choice, but this group is not conservative in a political or cultural context. On noneducational issues, *conservative* denotes a qualified preference for market over government solutions to social problems, greater reliance on religious organizations, affirmation of traditional family values, increased support for national defense, opposition to tax increases, and a skeptical attitude toward the efficacy of government. Each of these characteristics has definitional problems of their own, and some disagreement among conservatives on specific issues is the rule, not the exception. I acknowledge the definitional problems, but no other term is less problematic in referring to the groups that share broad areas of agreement on the topics I have cited.

Similarly, I use the term *liberal* to denote a broad array of groups that typically disagree with the cited conservative positions. Like *conservative*, *liberal* applies to groups whose members often disagree with each other on a variety of issues. It is, therefore, the case that I apply the terms *conservative* and *liberal* in ways that do not always reflect the views of organizations or individuals who characterize themselves, or are characterized by others, as conservative or liberal. The alternative would be to try to explain all the exceptions and nuances that divide scores of organizations and groups on scores of issues; such an effort would complicate the discussion to an intolerable degree. If there are fifty conservative organizations, the fact that five differ on issue A and a different five on issue B and so on does not invalidate use of *conservative* to characterize the organizations or individuals as a group. In any event, that is the assumption that guides the following pages.[3]

## THE PUBLIC SCHOOL ESTABLISHMENT

At various points, this book refers to the "public school establishment" or the "public school lobby." The appendix is intended to clarify these references. All too often, an impression is created that the NEA and AFT are the "public school establishment," but it is a much larger and more influential group. It should be obvious that when a group with the membership and resources of the public school establishment is united in pursuit of an objective, it is a very formidable force.

In an editorial concession made to avoid a much longer book, this one does not have much to say about the AFT, even though in some ways the AFT has been a more important and more interesting organization than the NEA. Nevertheless, there is no doubt that the NEA is the larger and more influential of the two unions. Furthermore, it cannot be overemphasized that the merger agreement between the two unions failed to pass in the NEA primarily over the refusal of a majority of NEA delegates to become affiliated with the AFL-CIO. No educational or political issues held up the merger despite the widespread perception, especially among conservatives, that the AFT is very different from the NEA. Actually, as former AFT president Albert Shanker once commented, it may be that the AFT's historic mission was to unionize the NEA.

## DEMOCRACY: A POINT OF VIEW

This book was not written to support a point of view about "democracy," but it supports one of the major views of its practical meaning. This view holds that we do not live in a society in which citizens deliberate on public policies and eventually settle on the policies that are in the public interest. Instead, it is a society in which interests drive coalitions that are more or less effective in persuading others that their interests and principles are served by the coalitions' interests and objectives.[4]

This view of democracy contrasts sharply with the participatory theory of government, which holds that the people rule by participating in policymaking—the more citizen participation, the better. The argument in this book assumes as well as demonstrates that "rule by the people" is impossible. A full and fair opportunity for the people to choose their rulers is the sine qua non of a democratic society; within very broad limits, what governments do often depends more upon the political efficacy of the contending parties than on the merits of their proposals from a public interest point of view.

I wrote the analysis that follows not to support any particular position on the defining characteristic of a democratic society; this issue emerged after I had written most of the analysis without any expectation of discussing its implications for democracy as a system of government. However, readers interested in the nature of democracy as actually practiced will find considerable evidence on the subject in the following pages. One point in particular stands out, and this is the importance of the resources, strategies, and tactics used in efforts to gain public support for policies that are alleged to be in the public interest. This dimension has been largely neglected in education, but it is an important topic of this book. The analysis of policy independently of the resources, strategies, and tactics employed in achieving or implementing it underlies a great deal of the futility of the controversies over educational policy in the United States.

## THE COMPLEXITY THAT LIES AHEAD

An interest group approach to K–12 education does not deny the role of other factors leading up to our educational situation in early 2006. The decrease in the number of school districts from 130,000 in 1930 to 14,465 in 2003 obviously facilitated the emergence of a collective teacher voice.[5] The increasing share of financial support borne by the states and the federal government also weakened the focus on local issues. Education was only one of several state and local public services to become unionized after 1960, and the teacher unions frequently joined other public employee unions on various issues. Social and cultural issues have intensified in most social institutions and organizations, and their influence is not to be denied.

The issues that are considered in this book are intended to illustrate the reasons significant improvement in K–12 education is ordinarily not within our reach under our existing system for providing it. Issues not considered that would weaken the argument do exist, but they are far overshadowed by the issues not considered that would strengthen it. For example, comprehensive analyses of education in the Bush II administration or the No Child Left Behind Act (NCLB) are not provided. One reason is that the act must be reauthorized or extended in 2007, and its future would be in doubt even if Republicans had not lost control of Congress. Also, the references to the act throughout the book provide a better context for assessing its educational sophistication and influence. Finally, the notes at the ends of the chapters list several publications that would provide more detailed analyses of NCLB.

## A PERSONAL NOTE

In one respect my qualifications to write this book are unusual. Few, if any, are as familiar with both the leadership of the teacher unions and the leadership of conservatives in education. From 1956 to 1979, I was an advocate in the teacher union movement, including my candidacy for the presidency of the AFT in 1961–1962, when I received one-third of the convention votes after an inept campaign. From the mid-1960s to the late 1980s, I served as the labor negotiator for school boards in six states and once on behalf of a teacher union. Until 1977, my service as a negotiator was performed as a moonlighting professor, and I continued to be employed as a consultant by the NEA and AFT. This comity with the unions ended in 1979, when I published a widely publicized article that argued that collective bargaining in public education as it had emerged was a policy mistake.[6] My viewpoint changed as a result of my service as a labor negotiator for school boards in Rhode Island, New York, New Jersey, California, and Arizona before I had any interaction with conservative public intellectuals on education or conservative foundations.

In 1987, I moved to Washington, where I enjoyed excellent opportunities to meet conservative educational policy leaders and explore their views on educational issues. I was also well situated to observe the major conservative think tanks and the U.S. Department of Education. My Washington experience convinced me that conservatives cannot bring about significant improvements in K–12 education without basic changes in their agenda and strategy.

Whether or not the criticisms of individuals, ideas, policies, persons, and organizations in this book are justified, they are based on the belief that criticism is essential for progress. In educational literature, criticism of conservatives by liberals, and of liberals by conservatives, is rampant and mainly useless because the criticisms are interest oriented, not truth or agreement oriented. The opposing parties never get together to work out a test or trial that they agree would resolve their differences; the contrast with scientific research and policy based upon it could not be more stark. That factual and policy analysis is spurred by interests is not bad per se; this book is the result of my interests. The problem is that interests frequently undermine the procedures and data that are essential to valid empirical and policy conclusions.

One way for authors to guard against any such development is to be explicit about their own interests and beliefs, and I have tried to do this in the following pages.

One additional point is relevant to the impracticality, real or alleged, of some of the recommendations made in the following chapters. Recommendations that cannot be implemented within a few years may nevertheless provide the basis for evaluating incremental actions. Are the latter bringing us closer to a more desirable state of affairs? Absent any idea of the ideal state of affairs with respect to an issue, incremental change will more often be undesirable change. Furthermore, unexpected opportunities calling for drastic change sometimes arise. It is better to have drastic changes thoroughly vetted before they are implemented. I regard most of the changes recommended achievable in three to five years in at least a few states or school districts, but the results in some cases may not be available for sometime after that. Regardless, there are valid reasons to consider them objectively.

# NOTES

1. The conservative effort to hold John Dewey's educational ideas responsible for the deficiencies of contemporary education more than fifty years after his death is an exception. Dewey was president of the American Psychological Association (1899) and the American Philosophical Association (1905) and a founder and first president of the American Association of University Professors (1915). He was recently characterized as the nation's most eminent philosopher of law in Richard A. Posner, *Law, Pragmatism, and Democracy* (Cambridge, MA: Harvard University Press, 2003), 97–129. Apparently, spelling out the ideas that led to the ruination of American education did not take up much of Dewey's time.

2. Vilfredo Pareto (1848–1923) was an Italian economist and sociologist widely regarded as one of the founders of sociology as a discipline.

3. For an excellent discussion of the deficiencies in ideological and political categories such as "conservative" and "liberal" and examples of other terms used to categorize large ideological and political groups, see David Boaz and David Kirby, *The Libertarian Vote*, Cato Policy Analysis 580 (Washington, DC: Cato Institute, October 18, 2006), available at www.cato.org/pubs/pas/pa580.pdf.

4. For an extended discussion of these issues, see Jürgen Habermas, *Between Facts and Norms: Contributions to a Discourse Theory of Law and Democracy*

(Cambridge, MA: MIT Press, 1996); Richard A. Posner, *The Problematics of Moral and Legal Theory* (Cambridge, MA: Harvard University Press, 1999); and Lance D. Fusarelli, *The Political Dynamics of School Choice: Negotiating Contested Terrain* (New York: Palgrave MacMillan, 2003).

5. *Digest of Education Statistics, 2004* (Washington, DC: U.S. Department of Education, 2005); Thomas A. Lyson, "The Importance of Schools to Rural Community Viability," in *The Role of Education: Promoting the Economic and Social Vitality of Rural America*, ed. Lionel J. "Bo" Beaulieu and Robert Gibbs (Mississippi State, MS: Southern Rural Development Center, January 2005), 23–27.

6. Myron Lieberman, "Eggs I Have Laid," *Phi Delta Kappan* (February 1979), 415–419.

# Part 1

## CONVENTIONAL REFORMS RECONSIDERED

It is obviously impossible to consider in depth all of the reform proposals that are currently set forth by various individuals and organizations. Chapters 1 through 4 review several futile reforms that nevertheless receive a great deal of serious media and professional attention. Chapter 5 emphasizes cost issues, a dimension that is frequently overlooked in analyses of reform proposals.

The reform issues in Part 1 are important in their own right, but they also illustrate the widespread lack of agreement on educational priorities. Unlike many other conservatives who write about public education, I believe the phrase *failing public schools* is a substantive and tactical mistake. There are some reforms that would result in significant improvement, but as chapters 6 through 8 show, there is very little chance that reforms strongly opposed by the public school establishment will materialize until conservatives adopt different programs and strategies to implement them.

# 1

## The Achievement Gap and Other Perennials

**P**ublic education is a complex enterprise that renders valid generalizations about it inherently arbitrary. However, "arbitrary" does not necessarily mean "without valid reason," and I have tried to explain my reasons. Readers will have to decide for themselves whether they are "arbitrary" in a pejorative sense. Inasmuch as reforms opposed by the public school establishment are more difficult to implement, I begin with the reform proposals that it supports.

Several education policy analysts regard the most important educational problem in the United States to be the substantial achievement gap between black and Hispanic pupils on the one hand and white and Asian pupils on the other.[1] Stanford University professor Linda Darling-Hammond has proposed what is essentially the public school establishment's remedy for this gap. According to Darling-Hammond,

- The quality of teachers is an extremely important factor in student achievement, but students from disadvantaged minorities are much more often taught by less-qualified teachers.
- Pupils from disadvantaged minorities have fewer educational resources of all kinds.
- Minority students are more often assigned to tracks that do not lead to successful preparation for college.
- Disadvantaged minorities receive fewer health and social services, such as guidance counselors and social workers.

- When formal education is fully equal, blacks and Hispanics achieve as well as white and Asian students.[2]

Darling-Hammond's conclusion that schools can compensate fully for substantial differences in home and neighborhood environments is untenable. The differences between the effects of parents who encourage reading, emphasize the importance of education, feed their children adequately, do not allow television to replace school work, and foster good work habits (and many others conducive to high achievement) and those of parents who do none of these things have never been substantially eliminated by any system of education.

The evidence that formal schooling is not likely to compensate for negative, nonschool factors is quite strong. As Nobel laureate James J. Heckman points out,

> Family environments are major predictors of adult cognitive and noncognitive abilities. . . . Although much public policy discussion focuses on the failings of schools, a major finding from the research literature is that schools and school quality contribute little to the emergence of test score gaps among children. By the second grade, gaps in ranks of test scores across socioeconomic groups are stable, suggesting that later schooling has little effect in reducing or widening the gaps that appear before students enter school.[3]

Heckman's analysis contrasts sharply with that of both liberals like Linda Darling-Hammond, who claim that good teachers can eliminate the achievement gap, and conservatives, who reflexively identify "failing public schools" as the cause, but the truth of the matter is much closer to Heckman's analysis.


## SALARY INCREASES FOR TEACHERS

Probably the most frequent establishment reform suggestion is to raise the talent level of teachers by paying them higher salaries. The argument is that although teacher quality is the most important determinant of pupil learning, teaching does not get its share of the best and the brightest. Consequently, education lacks its share of outstanding individuals who can provide the ideas and inspiration to raise the achievement levels of U.S. pupils. This is a rather vague rationale, but because it is so rarely challenged and receives the enthusiastic support of teachers and their unions, let us consider it next.

How much more would be required to pay teachers to achieve a significantly higher talent level in public education? The Teaching Commission, an organization founded by Louis Gerstner Jr., former CEO of IBM, has proposed raising the salaries of public school teachers by 10 percent, with the better half to get a 30 percent raise.[4] The average teacher salary in 2004–2005 was $47,750.[5] Teacher fringe benefits, especially health and other types of insurance and retirement contributions, averaged about 20 percent of total compensation for a total average teacher compensation of approximately $56,102 for the 2004–2005 school year.[6] The Teaching Commission did not discuss the number of teachers, but putting private school teachers aside, the nation employed an estimated 3,000,000 public school teachers on a full-time basis in 2005–2006.[7] How much more would these teachers have had to be paid in order to achieve the goals of the Teaching Commission?

Roughly speaking, it would require $33.6 billion annually to implement the Teaching Commission's salary recommendation. How will the government get the additional $33.6 billion to pay teachers? It would come from taxes, loans, or inflation. All of these methods would be counterproductive for the economy as a whole; they would make it more difficult to pay the salary increases. One cannot redistribute $33.6 billion this way without having negative effects on the economy. Furthermore, if teacher salaries were increased by $5,600 and $16,800, the pressure to increase class size would be irresistible. But the same individuals and interest groups that urge higher salaries are also opposed to increasing class size, even though fewer teachers would increase the feasibility of paying higher salaries.

In many districts, NEA or AFT affiliates represent both teachers and support personnel; an effort to pay teachers 10 or 30 percent more without a large increase for support personnel would be followed by strikes and mass withdrawals from the union by the support personnel and perhaps legal action for union failure to represent support personnel fairly. Also, teacher salaries would rise above the salaries of lower-level administrators, such as principals and department chairs. Even if it is a good idea to have teacher salaries exceed management salaries, such a change would weaken the talent level in the management ranks.

For the sake of discussion, assume two unlikely developments: first, that all fringe benefits are included in the raise, and second, that the teacher raise does not require any salary increases among administrative and support personnel.

Paradoxically, raises of $5,600 and $16,800 in average teacher compensation would actually slow down the infusion of higher talent because a much smaller percentage of teachers would retire. If teacher salaries were increased by the amount suggested, most of the additional money required would go to the school district personnel already employed for a considerable period of time. Many teachers are members of retirement systems that base pensions on the final year of teaching or the average of the final three years. Teachers participating in retirement systems of this kind are likely to delay retirement for as many years as necessary to take advantage of large salary increases. In any event, there are simply too many teachers to increase their salary levels much higher than they are.

Actually, teacher unions are exacerbating teacher salary problems with their emphasis on the incorporation of early childhood education (ECE), the education of three- to five-year-old children, in the public school system. The Teaching Commission's recommendations are unrealistic for at least two other reasons. One is that overpayment of teachers is as important as underpayment; if we stop the overpayments, we would have enough to attract a higher talent level. Second, to urge the expenditure of $33.6 billion to raise the talent level of teachers is unacceptably vague: to raise the talent level how much in what fields, with what differences in student outcomes? The advocates of higher teacher pay as a much-needed reform have no idea as far as the record shows.

## MERIT PAY AND "PAY FOR PERFORMANCE"

Merit pay is a system of compensation in which teacher compensation is based at least in part on individual performance. Paying teachers of certain subjects more than others is not merit pay; neither is compensation for teachers collectively based on pupil performance. These may be desirable policies in their own right, but to have merit pay, the compensation system must allow paying teacher A more than teacher B, who teaches the same subject in the same school and has the same length of service and academic credit. If merit pay is paid to teachers collectively, it will be paid to some teachers who do not deserve it; the larger the group, the more nonmeritorious teachers will receive merit pay.

If these problems are not kept in mind, they will result in failure to resolve the incentive problems that merit pay is supposed to resolve. This is evident from the 2000 California legislation that provided $100 million for merit pay. The funds were allocated on a school basis, based on collective improvements in test scores. Depending on the extent of improvement, the amount allocated was $5,000, $10,000, or $25,000 per teacher in the recipient schools, but the actual distribution was to be negotiated by the school board and teacher union in each district in which one or more schools were awarded merit pay.

With one exception the unions and school boards negotiated agreements that divided the merit pay equally among the teachers in the meritorious schools. The exception was the Los Angeles Unified School District (LAUSD); there, the United Teachers of Los Angeles (UTLA) refused to bargain at all on the distribution. The legislation provided that in case of disagreement between the school board and the union, the award to the school was to be distributed to teachers on the basis of length of service. Consequently, some teachers who would have received $10,000 in an equal division among all teachers received less than $4,000. They filed an unfair labor practice charge against UTLA for not representing them fairly and lost, unjustifiably but legally.

The critical point here is that neither the statutory solution nor the negotiated equal division allowed any difference in compensation based upon individual performance—and it defies common sense to assume that there were no average or poor teachers in the recipient schools. Nonetheless, the legislative scheme was referred to as "merit pay" in the media. Apparently, the media could not afford the additional one or two sentences required to point out that the distribution of "merit pay" contradicted the rationale for it in Los Angeles.

About 99 percent of the nation's public school teachers are employed under individual or union contracts or board policies that do not include merit pay. About 75 percent are employed under school board or union contracts for one to six years. In order to effectuate merit pay, school boards would have to insist upon it in the new contracts over adamant union opposition; few school boards believe the battle is worth the effort, especially since they have lived without it for a long time. The over-whelming majority of school boards get their advice from school admin-istrators who are also opposed to merit pay; the administrators do not want the task of identifying the merit teachers, especially because their judg-ments will be carefully scrutinized and severely criticized by the unions and teachers who were not awarded merit pay.[8]

In recent years, several conservatives have advocated "pay for per-formance" by paying teachers on the basis of increases in student test scores. This basis is assumed to avoid the subjectivity problem in merit pay, but it is unlikely to be widely adopted. First, many nonteacher factors affect student test scores. To attribute test scores, positive or negative, solely to teacher performance is unrealistic. Even the *Wall Street Journal*, the conservative flagship, has spread confusion on the issue. Commenting on the 2000 NEA convention, the *Journal* editorializes,

> The really significant event at this convention was the rank-and-file's hos-tility to tying teacher pay to student performance, which is to say, the teacher's ability to teach. How radical. . . . Most parents, in fact, don't quite realize just how much the NEA rank-and-file remains stuck in the mind-set of an industrial union. And for this reason, as go steel and textiles, we sus-pect, so go the teachers.[9]

Three years later, a lead article in the *Journal* was devoted to "pay for performance" for doctors. After pointing out that several health insurers had recently launched pay-for-performance plans for doctors and that "some doctors" resisted the plans for reasons very much like the reasons offered by teacher critics of merit pay, the article includes the following:

> "For 50 years, doctors have been reimbursed for their times and costs, with-out respect to how well they performed their job," says Steve McDermott, chief executive of Hill Physicians, San Ramon, Calif., one of the largest independent-physicians groups in the U.S., with more than 2,200 doctors. The group is participating in the California initiative and has its own bonus program that can pay doctors as much as $100,000 a year. "As a nation, we spend $1.7 trillion on health care, but we have no performance measures to tell us the return on investment."[10]

Not surprisingly, the *Journal* did not reconsider its editorial about teacher opposition to pay for performance.

The pay-for-performance approach also has two "cut score" problems. First, student achievement will often lie on a continuum. Separating this continuum into categories like "proficient" or "inadequate" or "needs improvement" is likely to result in situations in which small differences in achievement lead to large differences in how they are rewarded. These situations inevitably generate morale problems among teachers who are not "paid for performance."

## MERIT PAY AND PROFESSIONALISM

In 1994, Chester E. Finn Jr. wrote, "Uniform salary schedules that treat everyone alike, whether good, bad, or mediocre, have no place in any true profession."[11] The concept of "professionalism" arose in situations in which the recipients of services were not in a position to evaluate the competence or the integrity of the producers. For example, patients are frequently unable to evaluate the services of physicians, hence it is easy for doctors to take advantage of patients in various ways. Furthermore, you cannot employ physician B to watch over physician A, who will be operating on you. B would not accept, A would refuse to operate with B present, and the vast majority of patients could not afford the cost of monitoring their physicians. Consequently, the protection of patients lies primarily in the enforcement of codes of ethics adopted by physicians. This situation differs sharply from one in which the employees work for long periods of time for the same employer. In this situation, which is applicable to education, the employer can assess the competence of employees.

During the past decade, more and more doctors have been employed by health maintenance organizations (HMOs). As this happened, doctors began to unionize and bargain collectively with the HMOs over their fees, which are the same for the same procedures, "whether good, bad, or mediocre"; Medicare and Medicaid pay hundreds of thousands of doctors the same amount for the same services without regard to quality of service. According to Princeton professor Uwe E. Reinhardt, one of the nation's leading authorities on medical economics,

> Although health policy wonks and policy makers have for years talked about tying the payment of physicians and hospitals to quality indicators, so far it has been mainly talk. At this time virtually no physicians have

their payments tied to such indicators and, if they do, it is as part of an experiment.[12]

Apparently, Finn was not aware that physicians are not "true professionals" according to his criteria.

The foregoing comments illustrate conservative illusions about merit pay. In Cincinnati, the teacher union agreed to try a merit pay plan with the right to opt out of it after a trial period. The union did opt out in May 2002 by a vote of 1,892 to 73. In my view, any plan that called for teachers to be evaluated on thirty-six different criteria, as Cincinnati's did, was lucky to get seventy-three votes.

A pervasive problem with merit pay is that for every teacher awarded it, several others will regard themselves as more deserving. Consequently, when they don't get it, they will scrutinize the administrator's assessments, something that the administrators want to avoid. The administrators much prefer to blame the union for the absence of merit pay, especially if their school boards want it.

Let us assume that principals are to decide who is to receive merit pay, subject to an appeal to the superintendent. The majority of principals will not want the assignment. First, they know that regardless of who receives the merit awards, other teachers will probably feel more deserving and be resentful toward the principal. Second, the award process will require a lot of work. Inasmuch as principals realize that their decisions are likely to be challenged, they will assume that their evaluations will come under intense scrutiny—something they, like most of us, wish to avoid. Exceptions notwithstanding, the awards are likely to affect the principals' relationships with their faculties adversely.

The strongest evidence that school management shares the responsibility for the absence of merit pay is its absence in the thirteen states that have not authorized collective bargaining in their school districts. A few states, such as North Carolina, actually prohibit it. The NEA and AFT have state and local affiliates in these states, but in the absence of a bargaining law, they tend to be much weaker than their counterparts in the bargaining-law states. Nevertheless, there is no merit pay in the nonbargaining states, nor is there any serious effort by school management to promote it.

It is often assumed that school administrators, especially principals, would base their recommendations on observations of classroom teaching. However, the number of teachers in a particular school varies from one to over two hundred; the number obviously affects who can observe and evaluate teachers, the time allotted to this assignment, and the duties that would have to be dropped to allow for adequate observation, assessment, meetings with teachers, and related paper work.

There is very little classroom observation of teachers; the costs of such observation quickly become prohibitive. Consequently, there are many opportunities for teacher shirking, and incentives are desirable to forestall such an outcome. However, compare the teacher situation with that of insurance salespeople, who also work with minimal direct supervision. Insurance salespeople are paid by commission, that is, by performance. In education, however, justified outrage would be the reaction to pay for performance that did not take pupil and family and neighborhood differences into account. How to do this is an unresolved quandary.

Those implementing merit pay would also have to come to grips with pervasive comparability questions. How much learning in music in the third grade is as meritorious as how much learning in twelfth-grade physics? Central High School in St. Paul, Minnesota (where I went to school), enrolls Hmong students who lack a written language and are experiencing severe difficulties in adjusting to life in Minnesota. In this situation, pay based on test scores would be sheer guesswork.

The unions would like the teachers to regard the union as the party responsible for increases in teacher compensation. Obviously, merit pay contradicts this position. Nevertheless, bargaining is partly about the distribution of employee benefits, and the employees should have something to say about how money spent for their welfare should be distributed. Allowing management to decide the distribution unilaterally is inconsistent with this principle; it would also be an unfair labor practice unless a good faith effort was made to negotiate the distribution with the union. If the union refuses to accept merit pay after negotiations and impasse procedures, management is legally authorized to implement merit pay. Teachers often refuse to accept it if the merit pay is a small amount.

There is no merit pay in several countries whose students consistently outperform U.S. students in mathematics and science.[13] In fact, in South Korea, a nation whose students consistently outperform U.S. students in science, mathematics, and computer competence, 3,741 teachers returned their merit pay in 2001; about 86.4 percent of South Korean teachers were opposed to it on the grounds that (1) evaluation is impossible; (2) it will evoke conflict; and (3) it will result in lower morale among teachers who don't get it. The Korean federal government published its system of merit pay in 2001 for government officials in 2001, whereupon government officials went on strike. At the same time, merit pay has declined in government employment in Western democratic countries that started with high hopes for it.[14]

In the private sector, unions play an important role in the allocation of economic benefits of monopoly. They play a much more restricted role in competitive industries because the exigencies of competition limit the benefits of adversarial approaches to employment issues. This is why cooperative relationships between unions and management in the private sector are not models that are likely to be followed in public education. Merit pay can be appropriate in public education, but the benefits minus the costs cannot bear the weight that conservatives reflexively ascribe to it. Nevertheless, the Bush administration plans to spend $100 million annually for five years to support "experiments" in pay for performance. With over 14,000 school districts in the country, one might think that the Bush administration has better use for its resources than to promote policies that have such poor prospects and that should be resolved locally in the first place. Interestingly enough, the U.S. Department of Education awarded merit pay to 66 to 71 percent of its employees from January 2003 to April 2005.[15] For all I know, the department employees responsible for the pay-for-performance program were awarded merit pay for their plan to waste $100 million annually for five years.

In view of the known obstacles and the uncertain benefits, there is little chance that any but cosmetic plans for merit pay will be implemented in the public schools. The plans that are implemented may make matters worse instead of better; administrators have not been brought up in a system in which merit pay was utilized, and most are not prepared, technically or attitudinally, to implement it.[16]

## CLASS SIZE REDUCTION

For several reasons, smaller class size is a high-priority union objective. Economists have a different take on the issue. If class size is reduced without a corresponding gain in student achievement, educational output per person-hour, that is, educational productivity, is also reduced. The teacher and teacher union reaction is that concepts like productivity and output per person-hour are not applicable to education—an interesting commentary on the economic sophistication of teachers.

Data from Florida illustrate the problem. A Florida class size initiative passed by a narrow margin in 2002. The initiative limited class size by 2010–2011 to eighteen in prekindergarten through third grade, twenty-two in grades four through eight, and twenty-five in grades nine through twelve. Beginning in the 2003–2004 school year, class sizes must be reduced by two pupils per year until they meet the 2010–2011 standards specified in the initiative.[17] Table 1.1 shows the impact of the initiative on the number of public school teachers in Florida. The increases shown in table 1.1 must be supplemented in future years to reach the 2010–2011 standards.

Average salary for teachers in Florida for 2004–2005 was $41,578. Even if the average salary remained constant for the next two years, this would require an estimated additional outlay of $770,149,294 over a three-year period to fund the increase in teachers required by the class size initiative; however, this figure does not include benefits. National 2004 estimates by the Bureau of Labor Statistics show that fringe benefits including insurance, retirement and savings, and legally required contributions make up 20.2% of the total compensation to teachers.[18] When benefits are included, a conservative estimate of the cost of employing 18,523 additional teachers to reduce class size exceeds $965,000,000. This huge

**Table 1.1.　The Impact of Florida's 2002 Class Size Initiative on the Number of Public School Teachers in Florida**

| Year | Total Number of Teachers | Total Increase from Previous Year | Annual Increase Due to Class Size Initiative | Annual Increase Due to Enrollment |
|---|---|---|---|---|
| 2004–2005* | 155,576 | 7,601 | 4,324 | 3,297 |
| 2005–2006** | 160,698 | 5,402 | 2,378 | 3,024 |
| 2006–2007** | 175,933 | 14,955 | 11,821 | 3,134 |

*Actual
**Estimated
*Source: Teacher Projection Report,* Florida State Department of Education: www.firn.edu /doe/evaluation. Accessed July 21, 2005.

additional cost may be leading to more union members, but it is undoubtedly having a negative effect on teacher compensation in Florida.

Florida voters did not understand the enormous costs of the initiative until the initiative had passed. One of the measures taken to pay the costs of implementing the initiative was to encourage high school students to graduate a full year earlier than they normally would. Inasmuch as it usually costs more per pupil to educate secondary than elementary pupils, reducing the time in secondary schools was a win-win situation for students and the Florida school districts. The question to be asked is, why did it take the sudden need to find large savings to discover and act upon the savings made possible by earlier graduation from high school? Similar savings are possible in every state. This is the kind of improvement that would be identified and implemented much sooner in a competitive education industry.

Class size reduction is expensive. It is unlikely that any benefits of it would be the same regardless of grade level or subject. Even if clarifying information becomes available, the policy answer is still elusive. If class size is reduced, more teachers will be needed, and the additional teachers may be of lower quality and depress whatever educational gains were made possible by smaller classes. Theoretically, class size reduction may be worth the additional cost if only a few school districts implement the reductions, but statewide reductions may be counterproductive.[19]

## MATHEMATICS AND SCIENCE TEACHERS

Education analysts frequently lament the perennial shortages of mathematics and science teachers. Most proposals to have teacher salaries are market driven; if you have to pay more to get good mathematics and science teachers, pay them more. Until recently, however, this remedy was adamantly opposed by the teacher unions. In 2002 the AFT adopted a resolution approving salary differentials for "agreeing to teach in hard-to-staff and/or low-performing schools."[20] The resolution did not urge or require AFT locals to negotiate such arrangements; it merely said that locals would not be violating AFT policy if they did so. The NEA's policy is "The Association opposes providing additional compensation to attract and/or retain employees in hard-to-recruit positions."[21]

Why are the teacher unions so opposed to higher teacher salaries in fields characterized by perennial shortages? First, the teacher unions, like unions generally, are political organizations. That is, although their objectives are largely economic, the union organizational structure is based upon one person, one vote, in a democratic framework. In education, agreements reached through collective bargaining must ordinarily be ratified by majority vote in the local union—and union majorities are opposed to paying a small group substantially higher salaries than the majority receives.

In practice, the unions have other reasons for avoiding salary differentials. If differentials for mathematics and science teachers are accepted, they are likely to be proposed in other subjects. This will exacerbate internal conflict within the union over who should be paid more and who should be paid less. These conflicts are very likely to be highly divisive issues within the union, best avoided if at all possible. Despite teacher polls to the contrary, school management has usually encountered teacher opposition to salary differentials for teachers in difficult-to-staff schools and subjects.[22]

Furthermore, the unions have always opposed differentials, whether for merit or for groups of teachers by subject, on the grounds that the differentials are merely excuses to keep down the salaries of most teachers. In addition, the unions need the shortages of mathematics and science teachers to prove that teachers are not being paid enough. The illogic of paying all teachers more if a small number must be paid more is ignored in collective bargaining and in union publications generally.[23] Clearly, school management is not as concerned about the national implications as it is about the immediate local pain that will result from efforts to pay salary differentials to teachers in short supply. Interestingly enough, school districts in states without a bargaining law have not addressed the problem either, which suggests that school management shares responsibility for the problem.

Another possibility is for the state legislatures to appropriate differentials for mathematics and science teachers. Unfortunately, the state teacher unions are likely to oppose salary differentials for teachers in short supply for certain subjects, and state school board associations are usually very weak employer organizations. An ongoing legislative problem would be that the differentials would have to be adjusted from time to time and place to place. The states could adopt automatic ways of adjusting the differentials, but this solution would have problems of its own.

The optimal state-level solution in the bargaining-law states would be for the legislatures or state labor boards to take science and mathematics teachers out of the teacher bargaining unit. This would mean that science and mathematics teachers would choose their own representative (not necessarily a union) to bargain for them. In this way, the science and mathematics teachers would not be part of a larger bargaining unit in which their legitimate interests are always subordinated to the majority's. One problem with this solution is that in most districts, the number of mathematics and science teachers is too small to sustain a viable organization; whether these teachers would prefer no union representation remains to be seen because the teachers might or would lose union protection on other issues. A third possibility would be legislation allowing school districts to contract out mathematics and science instruction, regardless of the provisions of any collective bargaining contract negotiated after a certain date.

All of the suggested solutions fail to address the underlying problem, which is that science and mathematics teachers should be considered a different occupational group, not a subgroup of K–12 teachers. The talents and skills required are of a different order. Professors of neurosurgery and history are not in the same profession simply because they teach in the same university. Putting them on the same salary schedule would result in a dearth of neurosurgery professors, even if we substantially overpaid history professors. Similarly, once we lump science and mathematics teachers together with all other teachers, we ensure the shortages of the former and must resort to solutions that cannot be as effective as getting it right in the first place.

To be sure, in some districts, there are efforts to pay science and mathematics teachers more while avoiding a collision with the teacher unions. These efforts include more generous preservice credit, allowing qualified mathematics and science teachers to teach additional periods for additional pay, or treating these teachers as "consultants" or "independent contractors" so that they are not employed pursuant to teacher salary schedules.

The consequences of the shortages are too complex to estimate precisely, but they are undoubtedly very substantial.[24] Teacher unionization did not create the problem, but it is the major obstacle to a viable resolution of it in most districts.

## THE POWER OF PRINCIPALS TO HIRE AND FIRE TEACHERS

Brookings Senior Fellow Diane Ravitch advocated that principals be accorded the power to hire and fire teachers.[25] Their recommendation is dubious on its face.

In 2000, there were over 92,000 public schools, ranging in size from 423 one-teacher schools to almost 1,400 with an enrollment of 1,000 or more students. The mix also includes special education, alternative, and other schools not classified by grade span. To recommend an administrative framework covering over 92,000 schools in 14,928 school districts is a foolhardy undertaking; it is practically impossible to know the optimum delegation of authority over personnel in more than 92,000 schools, and it is arrogant to assume that one does know this.

Clearly, in many districts, principals have de facto authority over who is hired and fired, and the personnel director and superintendent and school board routinely accept a principal's recommendations. This means that it is impossible for outsiders to know where the power to hire and fire really lies; the formal structure does not necessarily tell us.

The time required for principals to become experts on the legal and arbitral developments relating to tenure and dismissal must also be considered. In most contracts, the principal is the first step in the grievance procedure. The grievant can usually appeal the principal's decision to the district superintendent and, if necessary, to binding arbitration. The Ravitch recommendation would make the principal's decision the final instead of the first step before the grievance goes to arbitration. This change would be extremely advantageous to the unions but disadvantageous to principals. Under the existing system, most grievances are withdrawn or settled before being submitted to arbitration. If principals are the final step before arbitration, which they would be as the final decision maker, the principals will be forced to undertake extensive preparation that is ordinarily not necessary under the existing system. Interestingly enough, the National Association of Secondary School Principals (NASSP) does not have a policy on principal authority over teacher employment and dismissal.

The National Association of Elementary School Principals (NAESP) has been conducting surveys of elementary school principals every ten years since 1928. In the 1998 survey, 45 percent of the respondents indicated that they had "primary responsibility" for teacher selections; another 21.8 percent reported that the responsibility was shared with others in the school (presumably teachers); and another 29.2 percent reported that their responsibility was shared with the district office. About 10 percent of urban principals, 36.6 percent of the total, reported having little authority for selecting teachers.[26] This was undoubtedly due largely to collective bargaining contracts and district policies that mandated seniority in filling teacher vacancies. Over 64 percent reported supervising at least ten support staff. Although nothing was covered in the survey on principal authority over or time devoted to support staff, it is apparent that the problems of inadequate principal control over staff are largely in urban schools. The larger the school, the more likely that the principals had to share responsibility for staff selection and supervision. In the absence of persuasive data—or any data for that matter—principal authority over staff appointments appears to be a secondary, not a major, educational problem, where it is a problem at all.

## THE DURATION OF COMPULSORY EDUCATION

At what age should parents have the right to choose the work option instead of the schooling option for their children? After all, if parents know best what is in the best interests of their children, why does this not apply to whether their children should be in school or working?

Up to the age limit, the only competition is between public schools and private schools, whose charges vary a great deal. A lower compulsory age limit would drastically alter this situation on two essential conditions: (1) that our labor laws not restrict employment of fourteen- to sixteen-year-olds much differently from the restrictions on older persons and (2) that students who leave school early be allowed to return without penalty, perhaps with a credit toward their expense of continued education. The potential benefits include

- Greater equality of opportunity. The gap between the lifetime earnings of early leavers and high school and college graduates would be greatly reduced.
- Student attendance and performance would be greatly improved by the prospect of early employment.

- The costs of education would be greatly reduced by the smaller cohorts at the secondary level, which is much more costly than the prior levels.
- Higher education would come under strong pressure to demonstrate its economic value compared to the lifetime earnings of workers who entered the labor market four to six years before college graduates.
- The social security system would benefit from the influx of workers at an earlier age.
- Secondary schools would be much more purposeful institutions. They would no longer be institutions in which the college-bound would treat their senior year as playtime while others were forced to remain in an institution that was not able to educate them effectively. However, a substantial number of the academically abler students would probably take advantage of the early-leaving option.
- The suggested policy would help to remove the stigma associated with "dropouts."[27]

The public school establishment will strongly oppose this version of school choice. The striking fact is how little conservative attention is paid to it. The absence of such attention reflects the power of the public school establishment and higher education to preempt the educational reform agenda, and the failure of conservative leadership to advocate schooling options that would have immediate practical and political benefits.

Black and Hispanic leaders will probably oppose policies that allow the reduction of time students are required to stay in school. They will argue that such a policy will lead to a two-tiered society: one class whose children go on to college and get good jobs and careers and another class that is destined to work in dead-end jobs during their entire careers. The fact that the decisions will be made by parents will be ignored, as will be the personal and social cost to young people who are not going to school and not working. Instead of facilitating the integration of young people into adult society, the focus has been on helping young people graduate from high school and attend college. It is an open question who benefits from this emphasis.

The increases in the number of students taking advanced placement (AP) courses is evidence that acceleration of secondary school graduation would appeal to a large number of students. In 2004–2005, more than one million students enrolled in AP courses, many for college credit. The college graduation rate for students taking two or more AP courses was 76 percent, whereas only 33 percent of the students who did not take any AP courses graduated from college.[28]

Initially, elite private schools offered many AP courses to support their reputation as schools for high achievers. In recent years, however, these schools have replaced AP courses with alternatives that enable their students to graduate with distinction. When AP courses began to weaken instead of strengthen student enrollment in precollege courses, the private schools dropped AP courses—the stated reason, of course, being the welfare of the students.[29]

Consider some of the benefits of ending compulsory education at age fourteen (for example) instead of sixteen or higher, *in conjunction with freedom to enter the labor force on a regular full-time basis at that time*. There is no intellectual or physical reason to maintain compulsory education at higher age levels, especially since there is substantial duplication of curricula at the secondary and college levels.

Most of the legislation on the duration of compulsory education was introduced at the behest of unions for protection against low-wage "child labor"; it had very little to do with the maturation of young men and women. "Adolescence" was not the cause of most of our protective labor laws; instead, it was a result of it. Prior to the extension of compulsory education to teenagers, they were regarded and regarded themselves as young adults, not as "adolescents." And why is it that the proponents of school choice, after proclaiming that parents know what is best for their children, do not also argue that parents know best whether the work or the formal schooling option is the most desirable for their children?

The benefits of less time in school would be apparent immediately. Adding years to the work life of citizens who do not attend college would help substantially to equalize their lifetime earnings with the income of college graduates. Earlier entry into the labor force would result in larger pensions for young people who do not go on to college, and there would be significant increases in the national output of goods and services. Some labor shortages, including shortages of teachers, would decline. The change would also help to dissipate the fallacious assumption that learning takes place in schools but not in private employment. We could also anticipate some reduction in crime and incarceration.[30]

The major supporters of reducing the duration of compulsory education to fourteen or fifteen might be high school teachers in the inner cities. These teachers frequently have to cope with student violence, including violence against teachers. Along with vandalism and other disruptive behavior, the violence renders it impossible to educate students who are in school to learn. The measures taken to cope with these problems are expulsions, security personnel assigned to schools, and devices to check the entry of weapons and drugs into the schools. These measures are expensive and are not adequate to provide a safe learning environment.[31]

There are three major objections to lowering the compulsory age limit to fourteen or fifteen. One is that immature students should not have the option of dropping out of school and neglectful parents letting their children do so; the decision is too important to allow immature youth to make it. This argument ignores reality. In learning, the student has to do most of the work; if students won't or can't do it, there is no point to keeping them in school where they prevent others from learning.

The second major objection to the proposed policy is that there will be a mass exodus from school by youngsters who are not prepared for any kind of employment. This leads to the third objection; the outcome would be an outbreak of juvenile crime. A mass exodus is very unlikely because most students and parents believe that a high school diploma is essential for either employment or higher education. Who would hire the dropouts? There are several unskilled and semiskilled occupations for which workers are in short supply that are currently filled by immigrants or holders of green cards. Government subsidies to employers might make it worthwhile for employers to employ dropouts, and contact with the world of work and employers' refusal to subsidize idleness might bring about positive attitudinal changes. In any event, the constant reiteration of the claim that the problem is lack of educational resources or lack of sensitivity or racial discrimination is no longer credible.

What about an upsurge in crime if students can leave school at age fourteen or fifteen? Inasmuch as teenagers are already the demographic group with the highest involvement in criminal activities,[32] perhaps it is time to question the policies that have led to this outcome. More of the same policies will lead to more of the same consequences.

In an analysis of school violence, Jackson Toby suggests that the solution is to make high school attendance voluntary. In support of this policy, Toby points out that this is the policy in Japan, where most of the violence occurs at the junior high school level; even at this level, there is less violence because most students want to prepare for high school. At both junior and senior high school levels, teachers are much more able to control their classes. Seven percent of Japanese students exercise their option not to attend high school, and this fact is the main reason Japanese high schools are so much safer than their junior high schools. Making high school voluntary would not completely eliminate violence and disruptive behavior; probably nothing would. Nonetheless, it is possibly the best solution to several serious problems that have not been satisfactorily resolved for a very long time.

The teacher unions will oppose any move to lower the duration of compulsory education, as will the unions of employees who will be concerned about a flood of young hires who might drive wages down in their occupations. The organizations of disadvantaged ethnic minorities, such as the NAACP, are also likely to be a source of opposition. These organizations may regard the change as a threat to the social and economic mobility of their ethnic group. Charges of racism and the evils of taking advantage of innocent youth will feed the punditry grist mills, along with fallacious statistics on the economic benefits of higher education. Nevertheless, early college high schools (ECHS) may achieve some progress on this issue. The Early College High Schools Initiative was launched in 2002 by the Bill and Melinda Gates Foundation, the Carnegie Corporation of New York, the Ford Foundation, and the W. K. Kellogg Foundation.[33] These foundations committed $40 million to launch seventy small schools that would combine high school and the first two years of college in less than the six years conventionally required to graduate from high school and earn two years of college credit. By December 2004, 46 early college high schools were operative, with over $120 million in support, and 180 early college high schools were under development. Potentially, ECHSs can achieve the following:

- Reduce precollege education by at least one full year
- Ease the transition from high school to college

- Generate student incentive to complete high school and early college work at a much faster pace and higher achievement levels
- Reduce the need to apply for college and financial assistance

By 2004, thirty-eight states had enacted policies on dual enrollment (high school and college). The legislation varied on target population, funding, course content, faculty, and several other criteria. In states without dual enrollment legislation, policies on the various criteria were left up to individual schools and colleges.[34] In addition to significant savings and higher achievement, dual enrollment may lead to reforms in teacher certification and school finance. Nevertheless, it underscores a basic flaw that pervades education in the United States—the failure to improve the prospects for pupils who do not choose or wish to enroll in college. The failure is only one manifestation of the bias against going to work unless and until an educational organization certifies your eligibility to do so.

## NOTES

1. See Abigail and Stephen Thernstrom, *No Excuses* (New York: Simon and Schuster, 2003) for a recent summary of the dimensions of this gap. The phrase *achievement gap* may have been a strategic mistake because the policy objective should be to raise achievement across the board, as we do in health care.

2. Linda Darling-Hammond, "What Happens to a Dream Deferred? The Continuing Quest for Equal Opportunity," paper presented at the annual meeting of the American Educational Research Association in San Diego, CA, April 12, 2004. The research on which Darling-Hammond based her conclusion has come under severe criticism by Grover Whitehurst, the director of the Institute of Education Sciences in the U.S. Department of Education.

3. James J. Heckman, "Catch 'Em Young," *Wall Street Journal*, January 10, 2006, A14. Heckman later modified this position by asserting that early childhood education followed up by parental and school support and encouragement led to positive results that were well worth their costs. See James J. Heckman, "Beyond Pre-K," *Education Week* (March 21, 2007), 40.

4. Louis Gerstner Jr., *Teachers at Risk* (New York: The Teaching Commission, 2004). In addition to Gerstner, who served as chairman, the commission included three former governors, a former secretary of the U.S. Department of Education,

university presidents, and others, including Barbara Bush. Although the commission did not explicitly propose the 10 and 30 percent, it utilized these percentages to illustrate its message that it is essential to raise the salaries of all teachers along with an even larger increase for the most proficient half. The commission was terminated in March 2006.

5. NEA Research, *Rankings & Estimates: Rankings of the States 2004 and Estimates of School Statistics 2005* (Washington, DC: National Education Association, May 2005), 76.

6. The most commonly utilized health insurance plan in Michigan school districts in 2004–2005 cost public school districts $15,834 per covered employee; however, health insurance was only one of five to fifteen fringe benefits provided Michigan teachers. Michigan's spending on benefits was reportedly second among the states in 2004. "Study Says Benefits Costs Strangle Districts," *Michigan Education Report* (Spring 2005), 8.

7. The 3,000,000 figure is between the middle alternative projections of 2,985,000 and the high alternative projection of 3,033,000 rounded out for ease of computation. Debra E. Gerald and William J. Hussar, National Center for Education Statistics, *Projections of Education Statistics to 2008*, NCES 98-016 (Washington, DC: U.S. Department of Education, 1997), 72.

8. See Myron Lieberman, *Privatization and Educational Choice* (New York: St. Martin's Press, 1989), 14–19.

9. "Without Merit," *Wall Street Journal*, July 10, 2000, online.wsj.com/article/SB963184079331481976.html, accessed April 9, 2007.

10. Laura Landro, "To Get Doctors to Do Better, Health Plans Try Cash Bonuses," *Wall Street Journal*, September 17, 2004, 1.

11. Chester E. Finn Jr., "What to Do about Education," *Commentary* (October 1994), 36.

12. Uwe E. Reinhardt e-mail message to author, December 30, 2003. Reinhardt's statement was confirmed by an article in the *Wall Street Journal* that pointed out that "in most cases, doctors generally receive the same payment from insurers, regardless of how the patient fares." The gist of the article was that insurers have *begun* to pay doctors *partly* on the basis of performance, as evidenced by such measures as preventive care and follow-up treatment. The article points out that doctor pay for performance is new and that many doctors are concerned about the criteria for it. The head of a California physicians group is quoted as saying, "As a nation, we spend $1.7 trillion on health care, but we have no performance measures to tell us the return on investment" (Landro, "To Get Doctors to Do Better," 1).

13. Aubrey H. Wang, Ashaki B. Coleman, Richard J. Coley, and Richard P. Phelps, *Preparing Teachers around the World* (Princeton, NJ: Educational Test-

ing Service, 2003), 42. A study that is superficially supportive of merit pay by treating salary differentials for difficult-to-staff locations or subjects as merit pay is Susan Scalafani and Marc S. Tucker, *Teacher and Principal Compensation: An International Comparison* (Washington, DC: Center for American Progress, 2006).

14. David Marsden, *A Theory of Employment Systems* (New York: Oxford University Press, 1999), 148–176.

15. Information provided by Office of Management, U.S. Department of Education. On October 23, 2006, U.S. Secretary of Education Margaret Spellings announced a grant of $5,510,860 to the Ohio Department of Education to support pay for incentive plans in Cincinnati, Columbus, Cleveland, and Toledo. The grant was the first from the Teacher Incentive Fund (TIF), a $99 million fund "to support programs that develop and implement performance-based teacher and principal compensation systems, based primarily on increases in student achievement, in high-need schools." Although the other approved grants were expected to be made before the November 7 elections, only half of the funds were committed prior to a new competition. Unfortunately, the TIF program reveals every deficiency in incentives discussed in this chapter. See "Secretary Spellings Announced $5.5 Million Grant to Ohio to Reward Effective Teaching," U.S. Department of Education Press Release, October 23, 2006.

16. In July 2006, the Bush administration made $99 million available to try out merit pay plans and another $10 million to Vanderbilt University to study them. One might suppose that these actions should have preceded support for merit pay.

17. Article IX, Section 1, Florida State Constitution.

18. U.S. Department of Labor, Bureau of Labor Statistics, "Employer Costs for Employee Benefits—2004–2005" (June 16, 2005), table 3, www.bls.gov/ncs/ect/home.htm, accessed March 21, 2007.

19. Michael F. Addonizio and James L. Phelps, "Class Size and Student Performance: Framework for Policy Analysis," *Journal of Educational Finance* (Fall 2000), 135–156.

20. AFT resolution adopted at the 2000 AFT Convention, available at www.aft.org/about/resolutions/2002/compensation.htm, accessed March 21, 2007.

21. NEA Resolution F-9(h), adopted at 2002 Representative Assembly.

22. In 2004, the UFT agreed to allow 10 percent of New York City's schools to pay more to teachers of difficult-to-staff subjects, contingent upon an across-the-board increase for all teachers.

23. See Myron Lieberman, "Are Teachers Underpaid?" *Public Interest* (Summer 1986), 12–28.

24. Eric Hanushek, "Lost Opportunities," in *Our Schools and Our Future*, ed. Paul E. Peterson (Stanford, CA: Hoover Institution Press, 2003), back cover.

25. Diane Ravitch, "Let Our Schools Hire and Fire Teachers," *New York Times*, July 15, 1995, 19.

26. James L. Doud and Edward Keller, *The K–8 Principal in 1998* (Alexandria, VA: NAESP, 1998), 12–13, 15.

27. For an exchange between Jackson Toby, who supports early-leaving options, and Chester E. Finn Jr., who opposes them, see Jackson Toby, "Of Drop-Outs and Stay-Ins: The Gershwin Approach," *Public Interest* (Spring 1989), 3–13; Chester E. Finn Jr., "Dropouts and Grownups" and reply by Toby, *Public Interest* (Summer 1989), 131–136.

28. Del Stover, "Advanced Placement Classes Are Growing in Popularity," *School Board News*, August 24, 2004, 8.

29. Anne Marie Chaker, "Some Private High Schools Drop AP Courses," *Wall Street Journal*, November 23, 2004, online.wsj.com/article/SB110116734597 581331.html, accessed April 9, 2007.

30. See Lewis M. Andrews, *The Early Graduation Reward Plan* (Hartford, CT: Yankee Institute for Public Policy, 2004) for an analysis of how an early graduation plan could be beneficial in Connecticut.

31. Jackson Toby, "The Politics of School Violence," *Public Interest* (Summer 1994), 34–56.

32. Myron Lieberman and Charlene K. Haar, *Public Education as a Business* (Lanham, MD: ScarecrowEducation, 2003), 148–153.

33. For an excellent summary of the project, see Nancy Hoffman and Joel Vargas, *Integrating Grades 9 through 14: State Policies to Support and Sustain Early College High Schools* (Boston: Jobs for the Future, 2005).

34. Melinda Mechur Karp, et al., *State Dual Enrollment Policies: Addressing Access and Quality* (Washington, DC: U.S. Department of Education, 2004), 1, 15.

# 2

## Charter Schools

In statistical terms, charter schools are the major educational reform of the twenty-first century. The number of charter schools has increased from the first charter school in 1992 to approximately 4,000 in the 2006–2007 school year and appears set for additional but slower growth in the next few years. During 2006–2007, 4,000 charter schools enrolled one million students, approximately 2 percent of public school students in kindergarten through the twelfth grade.

From a legal point of view, charter schools are defined in the state legislation that establishes them. In the professional literature, charter schools are tax funded; governed by parents, teachers, nonprofit organizations, or private companies; and responsible to a local or state chartering authority, which may be a school board or university.[1] Charter schools are released from some of the restrictions on public schools. There is an informal understanding that the states will allow charter schools as long as the schools demonstrate results equal or superior to those of the public schools.

The foregoing definition of charter schools has both the advantages and disadvantages of vagueness. The definition does not specify either the achievement level that justifies charter renewal or the state regulations that will not be applied to charter schools. The upshot is that political influence among governors and state legislatures plays a critical role in the development and operations of charter schools.

## DIFFERENCES AMONG CHARTER SCHOOLS

Charter schools differ from regular public schools, but in what ways and to what extent vary considerably. Important differences may include the following:

- The educational rationale
- Who can issue charters
- The requirements for getting a charter
- The state funding formula for charter schools
- The term of the charter
- Pupil eligibility for charters
- Bargaining rights, if any, in charter schools
- How charter schools are governed
- The terms and conditions of employment
- Appeal procedures for rejection and termination of charters
- Certification requirements for charter school staff
- Limits on the number of charter schools

This list is not exhaustive. Each of the above differences can be a critical factor in the emergence, the operation, or the effectiveness of charter schools. It is practically impossible to delve into all of the differences, which are changing constantly; hence some oversimplification is inherent in the following discussion. Aided by a team of researchers, Dick M. Carpenter found fifty-five types that could be categorized in 1,163 charter schools.[2] Table 2.1 shows the breakdown according to Carpenter's typology.

Only Arizona permits schools for profit to be chartered; in some cases, however, the charter schools contract with for-profit companies to manage the schools.[3]

**Table 2.1.  Charter School Typology with Distribution by Subtypes**

|  | *Open Enrollment* | *Targeted Student Population* |
|---|---|---|
| Traditional: 268 (23.1%) | Math-science: 10 (.8%) <br> Core knowledge: 57 (4.9%) <br> Back-to-basics: 133 (11.4%) <br> College prep: 48 (4.1%) <br> International baccalaureate: 2 (.1%) <br> Edison: 10 (.8%) | Back-to-basics/at risk: 4 (.3%) <br> College prep/alternative: 1 (.0%) <br> College prep/at risk: 2 (.1%) <br> College prep/gifted: 1 (.0%) |

| | Open Enrollment | Targeted Student Population |
|---|---|---|
| Progressive: 337 (29%) | Multicultural: 12 (1.0%) | Ethnocentric/alternative: 1 (.0%) |
| | Ethnocentric: 13 (1.1%) | Dual language immersion/at risk: 1 (.0%) |
| | Dual language immersion: 33 (2.8%) | Progressive/special education: 1 (.0%) |
| | International/global: 5 (.4%) | Progressive/at risk: 1 (.0%) |
| | Progressive: 46 (3.9%) | Project-based/at risk: 2 (.1%) |
| | Multiple intelligences: 19 (1.6%) | Experiential/alternative: 1 (.0%) |
| | Constructivist: 8 (.6%) | Experiential/gifted: 1 (.0%) |
| | Problem-based: 5 (.4%) | |
| | Project-based: 26 (3.0%) | |
| | Experiential: 26 (2.2%) | |
| | Montessori: 53 (4.5%) | |
| | Paideia: 1 (.0%) | |
| | Waldorf: 14 (1.2%) | |
| | Environmental: 7 (.6%) | |
| | Technology: 9 (.7%) | |
| | Arts: 42 (3.6%) | |
| Vocational: 143 (12.3%) | Vocational: 34 (2.9%) | Vocational/alternative: 27 (2.3%) |
| | Technical: 1 (.0%) | Vocational/at risk: 38 (3.2%) |
| | School-to-work: 2 (.1%) | Technical/alternative: 6 (.5%) |
| | Entrepreneurship: 10 (.8%) | School-to-work/alternative: 10 (.8%) |
| | Business: 3 (.2%) | School-to-work/at risk: 11 (.9%) |
| | | Entrepreneurship/at risk: 1 (.0%) |
| General: 342 (29.5%) | General: 110 (9.4%) | General/alternative: 81 (6.9%) |
| | Conversion: 43 (3.6%) | General/special education: 22 (1.8%) |
| | | General/at risk: 86 (7.3%) |
| Alternative Delivery: 73 | Home study: 57 (4.9%) | Home study/at risk: 2 (/1%) |
| | Virtual: 9 (.7%) | Virtual/alternative: 1 (0%) |
| | Hybrid: 3 (.2%) | Virtual/at risk: 1 (.0%) |

*Source:* Dick M. Carpenter II and Chester E. Finn Jr., *Playing to Type? Mapping the Charter School Landscape* 2006 (Washington, DC: Fordham Foundation), 11.

## THE CHARTER SCHOOL CONCEPT

The founder of the charter school movement is Ted Kolderie, a prominent education policy analyst in Minnesota and then nationally.[4] In 1992, Kolderie outlined the benefits of charter schools as follows:

- It is very difficult to change schools from within. Parents and others should have the opportunity to establish new schools that can compete with the public schools.

- Charter schools can empower parents, especially parents who cannot move or afford private schools, through choice.
- The states have an obligation to provide choices for the disadvantaged.[5]

Kolderie's rationale emphasized equity as much as competition. Like other charter partisans, however, Kolderie did not spell out the conditions required for competition to be effective. His rationale was that charter schools would offer choices, and the more choices, the more competition and the more pressure to improve public schools would result.

Initially, the charter school movement was dependent on local school boards to charter and monitor charter schools. This posed a conflict of interest inasmuch as the school boards would lose the revenue that goes to the charter schools; also, the demand for charters was being interpreted as evidence of the shortcomings of the public schools. Whatever the reason, several states expanded the charter authorizers to include universities, state charter boards, and nonprofit organizations; Louann Bierlein's study shows that 561 authorizing entities had chartered 1,832 charter schools in 2002, but another 1,800 charter schools, most of which were probably chartered by local school boards, were not included in the survey.[6]

## UNION POSITIONS ON CHARTER SCHOOLS

By and large, the education establishment is opposed to charter schools, but as usual, the NEA and AFT do the heavy lifting politically and in the media. Former AFT president Albert Shanker initially appeared to be sympathetic to the charter school concept, but as the idea picked up momentum, Shanker repeatedly expressed his opposition to it. In one of his influential columns in the Sunday *New York Times*, he argued that "many" viewed charter schools as the adoption of "elements of free enterprise" in education. Allegedly, these misguided individuals "see a parallel with a popular business practice: giving branch offices substantial authority to manage their own affairs."[7] As chapter 11 points out, the leading advocates of a free market in education do not support charter schools; quite the contrary. In any event, and except for a few highly publicized exceptions, the NEA and AFT are opposed to the expansion of charter schools.

## THE AFT STUDY OF CHARTER SCHOOLS

In July 2002 the AFT released its comprehensive study of charter schools. The study raised seven main questions and twenty-three subsidiary questions and reached conclusions on all the main and most of the subsidiary questions. Not surprisingly, the overwhelming majority of answers were unfavorable to charter schools. The conclusion of the study as a whole is as follows: "The AFT concludes that policy makers should not expand charter school activities, until more convincing evidence of their effectiveness and viability is presented."[8] Of course, this recommendation was predictable in view of AFT opposition to state legislation that would establish or expand charter schools or remove union-inspired restrictions on their ability to succeed.

The AFT study says nothing about the per-pupil cost in charters compared to public schools, a comparison that would demonstrate that charter schools cost much less per pupil than public schools with comparable students, without any loss in achievement. Nevertheless, the AFT study does include a few valid criticisms, all of which mattered less than the negative but unstated effect of charter schools on union membership.

Despite national union opposition to charter schools, the United Federation of Teachers (UFT), the AFT's New York City affiliate, applied for and received approval to launch a charter school in 2005. The UFT already represented five of the twenty-six charter schools in New York City, but none had been established by the UFT itself. Undoubtedly, the UFT took this step to bolster its efforts to organize teachers in all of the city's charter schools, which may increase considerably in the next few years. Obviously, if the union's charter school is "successful," as it will be no matter what actually happens, the UFT will try to persuade teachers and parents that unionized charter schools are best for students, parents, and teachers.[9]

The UFT's approach to charter schools contrasts sharply with those of the national bodies of the NEA and AFT, especially the NEAs. The UFT avoided the impression that it was reluctantly getting involved in an "experiment"; instead, it raised millions in private funds and an impressive list of congratulatory messages, led by Hillary Clinton's. In this connection, the UFT's motivation—enhancing its ability to organize charter school teachers—is or should be irrelevant to assessing the outcomes.

Dentists and physicians try to minimize pain and suffering in order to gain or retain patients, but we do not dismiss these outcomes because the professionals had a pecuniary stake in it; the latter is an incentive to the wider social objective. Similarly, the UFT's stake in the outcome qua union should not affect our assessments of the educational and fiscal consequences of its charter schools. The consequences are what they are, whatever the motivations of the parties who brought them about. However, just as the anticharter stance of the NEA and AFT lead them to exaggerate the negative and minimize the positive aspects of charter schools, the UFT now has a huge stake in conveying the impression that its charter schools are highly successful. Will it ignore the costs and exaggerate whatever its charter schools may achieve? Its parent organization, the AFT, has disseminated several unwarranted criticisms of charter schools, hence principle may not govern UFT assessments. In any event, a competent, unbiased assessment of the UFT's efforts would be very helpful, but whether such an assessment will be available remains to be seen.

Like the AFT, the NEA initially adopted a wait-and-see attitude toward charter schools. Then in 1996, the NEA announced that it would sponsor six charter schools, later increased to ten, under union-approved conditions to evaluate the usefulness of charter schools; however, only four charter schools actually opened. One of them, Kwachiiyoa, was the lowest performing of San Diego's 121 schools, even when compared to schools that enrolled students of similar socioeconomic backgrounds. In 2002–2003, Kwachiiyoa was subjected to state intervention because of the low achievement levels of its students.[10]

NEA policy on charter schools was adopted in July 2003. Why anyone would want to start a charter school that met the conditions set forth in the NEA's resolution on the subject is a mystery, but that is the point of the conditions. NEA's state affiliates are less inhibited in their opposition to charter schools. An analysis of a proposed charter school law by the Tennessee Education Association was headed "What is wrong with charter schools? A short course follows on the crime of mugging the children and taxpayers of Tennessee."[11]

The NEA and AFT initially opposed charter schools because it is much more difficult to organize charter schools than school districts.[12] Now that charter schools employ a significant number of teachers, the NEA and

AFT have decided to launch an aggressive effort to organize them. The California Teachers Association (CTA) budgeted $250,000 in 2003–2004 to organize charter schools with matching funds from the NEA, which budgeted $1.75 million over a three-year period for this purpose. The NEA also stipulated that the CTA would share the lessons learned with other NEA affiliates also interested in organizing charter schools.[13] Nevertheless, organizing charter schools is the NEA's and the AFT's second-best alternative; "best" is no charter schools. Thus in 2004, the NEA contributed $500,000 to defeat Referendum 55, a Washington state initiative to establish charter schools in that state. The Washington Education Association (WEA) contributed $200,000, and the AFT $55,000; altogether, the three unions contributed 88 percent of the $856,000 contributed to the opposition committee, with the balance coming largely from local WEA affiliates and school administrators.[14]

## KINDS OF CHARTER SCHOOLS

Essentially, there are two kinds of charter schools. One group consists of schools established pursuant to somebody's vision of what a school should be. The vision may be a school devoted to a particular pedagogy, such as a Montessori school. Or it may be a school devoted to certain kinds of students, such as the disabled or low achievers. All such schools may be deemed "start-up" schools; they constitute about 75 percent of all charter schools.

The second category is conversion schools. These are existing schools, public or private, that decide to become charter schools. This is usually done in accordance with a statutory provision governing conversions. About 25 percent of charter schools are conversion schools.

Conversion schools have some important advantages over start-up schools. They have facilities, whereas most state charter laws provide no funding or inadequate funding for buying, building, or leasing facilities. Furthermore, start-ups require funding for planning, legal counsel, and recruitment of officers and staff, but such funding is often inadequate or nonexistent. In the conversion schools, these matters are usually resolved at the outset pursuant to a statutorily enacted procedure.

## FINANCIAL SUPPORT FOR CHARTER SCHOOLS

Financial support for charter schools varies considerably.[15] Some states have more than one system for charter school finance. The variations exist with respect to the sources of support (federal, state, local, private), the criteria for support (the state formula for distribution or a percentage thereof), who is covered (for example, elementary, middle, or senior high school), and what is covered (for example, is transportation covered by the school districts?). Two districts may receive the same amount per pupil, but one may be required to pay for several costs that are paid by school districts elsewhere. Consequently, charter schools with lower revenues may be better off than charters with higher revenues because the former may have several costs, such as transportation, absorbed by the district.[16]

State support for charter schools is usually a percentage of the per-pupil cost of public schools. A study of the issue concluded that of seventeen states including the District of Columbia, only Minnesota allocated at least as much per pupil to charter schools as to their public schools. However, amounts usually do not include capital outlay, debt service, and interest; hence charter school expenditures per pupil are sometimes much less than the expenditures in public schools.[17] As a result, financing capital outlay and start-up costs have been among the most difficult problems faced by charter schools. Note also that charter schools are responsible for several activities that are conventionally handled by school district central offices: payroll and infrastructure costs are illustrations.

In recent years, several states and the District of Columbia have taken action to alleviate the facility and start-up problems of charter schools. Also, from 1994 to 2006, the U.S. Department of Education provided more than $1 billion in grants to charter schools. Twenty-seven of the forty states with charter school laws provided some assistance on facilities in 2005. The assistance varied from allowing charter schools to utilize available public buildings to low-cost loans for facilities construction or lease. About ten states and the federal government provide annual grants for charter school planning, design, and implementation. In addition, twenty-eight states and Puerto Rico provide technical assistance to charter schools. There are also several nonprofit technical assistance centers for charter schools established with foundation support. The upshot is extremely diverse state funding; at one extreme, there are charter-friendly states like Arizona, Michigan, and California, and at the other extreme, states such as Iowa and Tennessee that provide no assistance for facilities or start-ups.[18] On charter school financial issues, there is no substitute for examining the specifics of each state's funding formula.

## WHO CHARTERS CHARTER SCHOOLS?

As previously noted, authorizing agencies that were not anticharter materialized in several states. With the path cleared, or at least not confronted by insurmountable obstacles, the number of charter schools increased rapidly. The biggest obstacles to expansion were the legislative limits on the number of charters, the shortfall in start-up funds, and the exclusion of for-profit companies. These anticompetitive features of state legislation on charter schools were due largely to the opposition to charter schools from public school organizations, especially the NEA and AFT.

Although united in opposition to charter schools, public school organizations have different reasons for their opposition. Naturally, all dislike the idea that they should have to compete for students. School administrators are concerned about the fact that they may not know until the beginning of school how many students opted for charter schools; inasmuch as school districts are funded so much per pupil, this uncertainty leads to problems in staffing and budgeting. The main but unstated teacher union objection is that teachers in charter schools are much less likely than regular school teachers to be union members. To minimize their losses and perhaps identify a cadre of prounion teachers who can assume union leadership roles, some state teacher unions are offering "associate memberships" to charter school teachers.

In Minnesota, the charter school law provides charter school teachers with the option to unionize and bargain collectively. Also, to counter union objections to charter schools, the Minnesota charter school law includes the unique provision that after three years, a majority of the boards of directors of charter schools must be teachers in the school. Although Minnesota has chartered over one hundred charter schools since 1998, there has been only one case (as of March 2007) in which the teachers in a charter school have elected to unionize and bargain collectively.[19]

The fact that charter schools must ordinarily be authorized by a state agency works to the detriment of charter schools in two ways. First, as applicants take note of the approvals, there is a tendency to conform applications to those already approved, especially among applicants under time pressures. The other problem is that the weakness and failures of charter schools are regarded as the failures of the chartering authorities. In order to protect themselves against criticism, the chartering authorities establish rules and requirements that limit the innovations that charter schools can adopt.[20]

Characterizing high levels of parent satisfaction in charter schools as their most important outcome suggests that charter schools are not ameliorating the low-achievement problems. They may have other benefits, but up to the summer of 2006, superior academic progress was not among them. The highest levels of satisfaction with public schools are found among minority parents who would presumably be the most dissatisfied with their public schools.[21] The high levels of parental satisfaction with charter schools may be due more to the low expectations of the parents than to the superior outcomes in the charter schools. The fact that public school students show no significant test-score superiority over comparable charter school students is favorable to charter schools because they are funded at considerably lower levels than regular public schools; however, the preoccupation with test scores of comparable pupils has obscured this important fact.

## INNOVATION

The statements of purpose in charter school legislation, charter boards, and charter schools often refer to "innovation" as an objective of charter schools. According to Chester E. Finn Jr., Bruno V. Manno, and Gregg Vanourek, charter schools are "seedbeds of policy and educational innovation."[22] As chapter 3 elaborates, most innovation of any consequence results from research and development that is funded in a search for profits. Charter schools are overwhelmingly nonprofits that spend nothing to create and disseminate innovations, and their record is barren of any innovations that have been widely adopted; there does not appear to be a single innovation of any significance originating in charter schools. The reasons for this conclusion are as follows:

- The conservative leaders of the charter school movement are frequently leaders of the "back to the basics" approach to classroom instruction, with a mindset that regards deviations from this approach as "fads."
- Many charter schools are Montessori or core knowledge or other already established kinds of schools. The more such genres are adopted, the less innovation there is likely to be. Some charter schools copy the practices, such as school uniforms, that characterize elite private schools.
- The idea that there is a large group of teachers with great ideas but held back by authoritarian administrators is part of the folklore of education. No doubt there are teachers with great ideas, but the culture and structure of public education do not foster their emergence. In the for-profit sector, successful innovations reduce the number of workers required, or make it possible to get by with a lower talent level, or improve the quality or quantity of the service. Furthermore, there is a market system that ensures that successful innovations will reach consumers promptly. These developments flow naturally from the fact that private industries are for profit.

In public education, the pupil-to-teacher ratio has decreased from 17.9 in 1987–1988 to 15.8 in 2003–2004,[23] and the teacher unions are doing their utmost to reduce class size as much as possible. Inasmuch as funding is assured and there is no competition for students, there is little interest in innovations that increase educational productivity; not surprisingly, educational productivity has been declining while productivity has been increasing elsewhere in our economy. *Innovation* is merely a buzzword with respect to charter schools, as it is in public education generally. If the U.S. Department of Education terminated the Office of Innovation and Improvement (OII), only its grant recipients would know the difference.

Dubious commentary about charter schools comes from a variety of sources. Seymour B. Sarason, a retired professor of psychology at Yale University, has offered the following thoughts on the subject:

> For example, although teachers are by far the largest group in schools, their ideas, attitudes and experience play little or no role in formulating proposals for reform. Teachers are asked or mandated to implement reforms for which they had no input.[24]

No input? With local, state, and national teacher unions employing 7,000 staff members and collecting over $2 billion annually in dues? With school boards legally required to bargain over any change in the work rules? With contracts routinely providing union rights to consult on matters of mutual interest? With monthly school and department faculty meetings? With the right to attend and often to enjoy special rights of access at school board meetings?

> The funding of charter schools should in no way be at the expense of existing school systems. . . . The state should reimburse the system so that it cannot claim that the charter schools are being supported at the expense of existing schools, a claim which if not respected will *predictably* create an adversarial gulf between the two with the consequence that the existing school systems will be unreceptive to whatever the outcomes of charter schools are; and we should not be surprised if they seek to undermine them. . . . Any other funding policy is self-defeating.[25]

This recommendation is like saying "Don't experiment with gasoline-fueled vehicles without getting the approval of parties who make their living from horse-drawn carriages." Giving teachers or any public employees the right to block changes deemed contrary to their interests is the problem for, not the solution to, improvement.

## CHARTER SCHOOL PROBLEMS

To be a significant reform, charter schools will have to expand. In order to expand, they will need funding to pay for their start-up costs. After receiving assistance from the states most likely to provide it, slower growth in the future is probable. If charter schools can't show a profit and can't appeal to investors for their start-up costs, from what source will the funds come for planning, land acquisition, office space and supplies, architects, legal assistance, and other start-up costs? Unless this question can be satisfactorily answered, charter schools are not likely to have a significant impact on U.S. education.

Charter schools depend on volunteers, but the inner cities have the lowest incidence of volunteers of any urban areas.[26] Furthermore, the volunteers—often at the management level—frequently lack experience on depositing revenues promptly, maintaining clear minutes, avoiding conflicts of interest, maintaining financial records, seeking bids (especially on large purchases), and getting competent legal advice before entering into agreements that can lead to large liabilities. It can be difficult to help these volunteers, some of whom try to conceal their lack of sophistication about utilizing financial institutions, such as banks, or professional services, such as accounting.

Charter schools often experience problems of continuity when the founders move on or out. Inasmuch as the schools were not founded as for-profit entities, the successive directors and managers often lack the dedication of the founders. The most successful charter schools appear to be the ones that have employed a management company to manage the school under a lay board of directors, but it is always possible that a knowledgeable agent will take advantage of its not-so-knowledgeable employers. Regardless, even if a small number of nonprofit charter schools are successful in terms of raising achievement or lowering the costs, they will lack a dissemination incentive comparable to the profit motive. This is evident from the fact that charter school pupils ordinarily achieve about the same results as comparable pupils in the public schools but at a much smaller cost per pupil. As is pointed out on pages 98 through 107, the government statistics on the per-pupil cost of public education substantially understate its real cost. Perhaps because they are afraid of criticism for advocating charter schools as a budget-cutting measure, the supporters of charter schools do not emphasize their greater efficiency, even if their test scores are not superior to the scores of students in public schools. From a policy point of view, the lower costs of charter schools are an extremely important fact, but it has not been helpful politically. Furthermore, the charter school advocates want equal funding at the public school level, not funding at the much lower level that reflects their greater efficiency.

Chester E. Finn Jr. points out some additional problems facing charter schools:

- Lack of national leaders, as illustrated by the lack of White House and congressional interest in the idea, and also excessive concern over "the bad apples"
- Exploitation of charter school failures by opponents of charter schools

- State limits on the number of charter schools
- The split among charter school advocates on whether the market provides adequate accountability or whether charter schools must be regulated more like conventional schools
- The split among charter school advocates on whether to act like a trade association that defends every charter school, or as a reform movement that disavows charter schools that do not meet high standards[27]

In addition to these problems, charter schools frequently face another set of obstacles resulting from the systems for approving and regulating charter schools. For instance, approval of a charter school plan sometimes leaves little time to staff the school. Sometimes facilities are not completed on time, or delays render it difficult to assure parents that the school open on time. Furthermore, opening a charter school, like opening any new school, usually involves a host of practical problems that cannot be anticipated. Needless to say, the critics of charter schools ignored these obstacles in criticizing the performance of charter schools.

## SUMMARY AND CONCLUSIONS

The supporters of charter schools report only facts favorable to charter schools, whereas their opponents report only facts critical of charter schools. Because there may be some outcomes that are favorable and others that are unfavorable, proponents and opponents alike may be reporting accurately, but their policy prescriptions may be unwarranted. The partisans rarely discuss ways and means to reduce their factual disagreements in order to move jointly to agreed-upon policies. On the contrary, when one of their factual arguments is shown to be fallacious, they simply find another reason to maintain their policy positions.

Controversies over the effectiveness of charter schools provide many examples of the double standards relied upon by supporters and critics of charter schools. A prominent example is the conflict over a front-page article in the *New York Times* on charter schools.[28] The article reports the findings of an AFT study of educational achievement in regular public and charter schools. Relying on test scores from the National Assessment of

Educational Progress (NAEP), the AFT alleges that students in charter schools have lower achievement on average than comparable students in public schools. The article evoked a huge outcry over bias in the *New York Times* and the AFT study. For example, a full-page advertisement in the *Times* points out that NAEP test scores do not track the progress of the same students over time; they reflect the achievement of different groups at various grade levels. When the dust settled, it was clear that the pro–charter school critics of the *Times* article were right on the basic issue. It was equally clear that they had frequently violated the same standards in criticizing public schools.[29]

Inasmuch as there is a widespread perception that public education is not as effective as it should be, the public school establishment is under strong political pressure to come up with "reforms" of one kind or another. Charter schools meet this political necessity, as evidenced by the fact that they often have bipartisan support or avoid all-out opposition by liberal coalitions dominated by the public school establishment.[30]

Charter schools do present options. The options may be practically useless to the overwhelming majority of students, but they enable politicians to claim support for school choice while retaining teacher union support. Because charter schools are public schools, they are usually subject to the public school regulatory apparatus—not completely, but enough to avoid drastic breaks from the status quo. Over time, charter schools can be organized, thereby stemming any losses in union membership.

Why do the school choice forces enthusiastically support charter schools? Some support anything labeled "school choice," and charter schools offer "choices." Some need to show "progress" to their funders. Some see school choice as a linear concept; the more choice, the better, regardless of specifics. Still others grasp an opportunity to get a share of government largesse, some for the first time in their lives. All sincerely believe that their charter schools will improve matters, but they do not subject their reasons to critical analysis.

In most states, charter schools have been a political compromise between the public school coalition and the school choice or voucher coalitions. The public school coalition has defeated efforts to enact vouchers inclusive of private schools; the school choice coalition can claim that it has expanded school choice. For this reason, charter schools are attractive to politicians under pressure to do something that satisfies both coalitions.

Nevertheless, a successful political compromise is not necessarily a successful educational compromise.

The charter school movement should be assessed according to experience with charter schools in states that have made a good faith effort to maximize their success. There is little point to evaluating the performance of charter schools in states in which they must be chartered by school boards and are underfunded, required to operate under union or district collective bargaining contracts, limited to a very small number of charters, required to employ only certified teachers, and otherwise faced with unnecessary obstacles as they emerge and function. The issue that matters is how charter schools have functioned in states such as Arizona, which has adopted the most positive framework for charter school authorization, funding, and regulation. This is not to pass judgment on the adequacy of Arizona charter school legislation; rather, on a comparative basis, it is the most charter school friendly. What conclusions about charter schools can be drawn from charter school experience in Arizona and other charter-friendly states? The answers to this question appear to be as follows:

- Charter schools have not generated any breakthrough in educational achievement.
- Charter schools have demonstrated that the public school levels of educational achievement can be reached, at least in certain grades and subjects, at a much lower per-pupil cost than is the case in conventional public schools.
- The requirement that public schools employ only certified teachers is counterproductive. However, waiving the requirement for all schools may have very different outcomes than waiving the requirement for a small number of charter schools, which can pick the low-hanging fruit among the individuals qualified but not certified to teach.
- The diverse nature of charter schools is a strong indication that for-profit schools would quickly identify niches leading to a significant market share if charters are allowed on the same basis as nonprofit and government schools.
- Charter schools are often initiated by parties with little or no experience in handling large financial transactions or accounting for financial operations. It is essential to remedy this weakness without undue interference with educational operations.

- Union policy statements to the effect that the unions support or will not oppose charter schools that meet certain conditions are basically statements of opposition to charter schools because the conditions are prohibitive.
- Charter schools have stimulated changes in regular school districts, but the changes are not very significant. It is fallacious to conclude from the few districts that are marginally affected that competition from charter schools is leading to significant changes in public education.

Supposedly, the rationale for charter schools provides autonomy in operating schools in exchange for the obligation to achieve satisfactory results. In practice, however, the levels of achievement required to maintain charter status are not defined in charter school legislation. Furthermore, although charter renewals vary from two to fifteen years, the standards for renewal are not spelled out. Presumably, charter schools must be accorded some time to be fully operational, but how much time is not specified in charter legislation.[31]

The upshot of this vagueness is that a great deal of discretionary power rests with the chartering authorities. When charter school legislation is enacted, the chartering boards tend to interpret the requirements to be a charter school liberally, but it is inevitable that critics will sometimes achieve control of the renewal process. When that happens, we can expect considerable controversy over how much, if any, improvement is required to maintain charter status. Of course, many charter schools seek renewal of their charter status regardless of performance.

To realize whatever potential they may have, charter schools must get beyond the need to ward off continuing efforts to restrict their freedom and limit their growth. This can sometimes be achieved, especially with strong gubernatorial support.[32] However, there is a danger that charter schools will be perceived mainly as a way to accommodate disadvantaged minorities. Paradoxically, in their efforts to demonstrate that they are not simply options for the affluent, charter schools are enrolling higher percentages of minority students than the public schools.

To achieve the potential benefits of charter schools, for-profit companies must be allowed to establish charter schools in their own right. This may not be the only way to get the research and development that leads to continuous improvement, but it has been the way that led to this result in most industries. One reason is that for-profit schools can take advantage of scale, especially for schools experiencing severe difficulties. Stand-alone schools do not have an experienced source of support to which to turn in case of severe difficulties. Charter schools that are part of a chain have such a source of support. Management of a chain of charter schools has a stake in the performance of each school; it will ordinarily have both the incentives and the resources to help struggling charter schools.[33]

Finally, charter schools, especially those for profit, must have the confidence that charter schools will not be suddenly wiped out by a legislature or by other public officials. Very few will invest in an industry that is continually fighting for its right to exist. As long as this risk exists, investors will avoid charter schools. To be sure, there appear to be several very successful charter schools that deserve praise and support; it is an open question, however, whether their success generates more or less pressure on public schools to reform.

Nevertheless, charter schools are likely to survive their limitations. First, it will be difficult for their political supporters to concede their limitations, which are substantial. Second, charter schools have led to institutions, such as state and national organizations of charter schools, that have some ability to represent their members in legislative and other forums; they have achieved lift-off, albeit to a low altitude. Also, charter schools provide significant opportunities for for-profit providers to contract with charter school boards and gain valuable experience in operating schools. The upshot is that despite their limitations, it is too early to dismiss charter schools as just another superficial reform.[34] Charter schools are a structural innovation, and like innovations generally, they cannot be expected to work perfectly, or even at all, in their first trials. Most early carmakers failed to produce viable cars, but it would have been a major blunder to rely on this fact to predict the demise of the automobile industry.

## NOTES

1. See also the NCES definition, nces.ed.gov/nationsreportcard/glossary.asp#c, accessed March 26, 2007.

2. Dick M. Carpenter II and Chester E. Finn Jr., *Playing to Type? Mapping the Charter School Landscape* (Washington, DC: Fordham Foundation, 2006).

3. In the fall of 2003, the inspector general (IG) of the U.S. Department of Education ruled that for-profit charter schools are not public schools.

4. The AFT claims that former AFT president Albert Shanker launched the charter school movement in a speech to the National Press Club in 1988, but Kolderie had been promoting the idea long before then. See AFT, *Do Charter Schools Measure Up? The Charter School Experiment after 10 Years* (Washington, DC: American Federation of Teachers, 2002), 9. The AFT's claim illustrates the exaggerations that permeate Shanker's legacy.

5. Kolderie was a journalist who became interested in educational issues in the early 1980s. Although he did not leave a voluminous paper trail, his involvement in the charter school movement in Minnesota and nationally is set forth in Ted Kolderie, *Creating the Capacity for Change: How and Why Governors and Legislators Are Opening a New-Schools Sector in Public Education* (St. Paul, MN: Education Evolving, 2006).

6. Louann Bierlein, *Charter School Authorizing: Are States Making the Grade?* (Washington, DC: Fordham Foundation, 2003).

7. Albert Shanker, "Charter Schools," *New York Times*, June 24, 1994, source .nysut.org/weblink/index.asp?DocumentID=689&FolderID=592&SearchHandle =0&DocViewType=ShowImage&LeftPaneType=Hidden&dbid=0&page=1, accessed April 9, 2007.

8. AFT, *Do Charter Schools Measure Up?*, 7.

9. Ellie Spielberg, "Summer of Activity Preceded Opening of UFT Charter School," UFT website, September 8, 2005, www.uft.org/news/teacher/in_news/ charter_school, accessed September 19, 2005; Joe LoVerde, "DA Votes to Form Panel to Study Feasibility of UFT-Run Charter School," UFT website, May 5, 2004, www.uft.org/news/05_05_04_da_vot/index.html, accessed September 19, 2005.

10. Mike Antonucci, "They Left Us in the Cold," *EIA Communique*, August 4, 2003, 1, www.eiaonline.com/archives/20030804.htm, accessed April 9, 2007.

11. Bryan K. McCardy, *The 2001 Edition of Tennessee's Charter School Legislation: An Analysis and Commentary* (Nashville: Tennessee Education Association, 2001), 1.

12. See David Kirkpatrick, U.S. Freedom Foundation, *School Report 696*, September 21, 2006.

13. "NEA Set to Spend $1.75 Million to Organize Charters," *EIA Communique*, December 15, 2003, 2, www.eiaonline.com/archives/20031215.htm, accessed March 21, 2007. The EIA report quotes "a high-ranking NEA official" telling the NEA board of directors that the organizing campaign "might slow the growth of charter schools."

14. Mike Antonucci, "NEA Is Largest Contributor to Charter School Opposition in Washington State," *EIA Communique*, October 18, 2004, 1, www.eiaonline.com/archives/20041018.htm, accessed April 9, 2007.

15. See F. Howard Nelson, Edward Muir, and Rachel Drown, *Venturesome Capital: State Charter School Finance Systems* (Washington, DC: U.S. Department of Education, 2000), funded by Contract ED 98-CO-0029 between the department and the AFT Educational Foundation.

16. Nelson, Muir, and Drown, *Venturesome Capital*, 48–52.

17. For a discussion of the amounts involved, see Myron Lieberman and Charlene K. Haar, *Public Education as a Business: Real Costs and Accountability* (Lanham, MD: ScarecrowEducation, 2003), 37–55; and Nelson, Muir, and Drown, *Venturesome Capital*.

18. Charters also receive a significant amount of support from private philanthropies.

19. Telephone call to Minnesota State Department of Education, March 23, 2007.

20. See Carol Ascher and Arthur R. Greenberg, "Charter Reform and the Education Bureaucracy: Lessons from New York State," *Phi Delta Kappan* (March 2002), 513–517.

21. Terry M. Moe, *Schools, Vouchers, and the American Public* (Washington, DC: Brookings, 2001), 43–121.

22. Chester E. Finn Jr., Bruno V. Manno, and Gregg Vanourek, *Charter Schools in Action: Renewing Public Education* (Princeton, NJ: Princeton University Press, 2000), 70.

23. NEA Research, *Rankings and Estimates* (Washington, DC: National Education Association, 2005), ix. Class size is a different concept but generally moves in the same direction as the pupil-to-teacher ratio. In 2002, the difference was reported as nine or ten students in K–3.

24. Seymour B. Sarason, *Questions You Should Ask about Charter Schools and Vouchers* (Portsmouth, NH: Heinemann, 2002), 30.

25. Sarason, *Questions You Should Ask*, 32.

26. Stephanie Boraas, "Volunteerism in America," *Monthly Labor Review* (August 2003), 3–11.

27. Chester E. Finn Jr., "The Challenge of Charter Schools," *Hoover Digest* 3, (2002), 80–82.

28. Diana Jean Schemo, "Nation's Charter Schools Lagging Behind, U.S. Test Scores Reveal," *New York Times*, August 17, 2004, 1.

29. Martin Carnoy, Rebecca Jacobsen, Lawrence Mishel, and Richard Rothstein, *The Charter School Dust-Up* (New York: Teachers College Press, 2005).

30. For a persuasive discussion of this point, see Lance D. Fusarelli, *The Political Dynamics of School Choice* (New York: Palgrave MacMillan, 2003), 85–87.

31. These and other weaknesses in the charter school concept are pointed out in National Association of Charter School Authorizers, *Principles and Standards for Quality Charter School Authorizing*, adopted by the membership on May 14, 2004.

32. Jon Schroeder, *Ripples of Innovation, Charter Schooling in Minnesota, the Nation's First Charter School State* (Washington, DC: Progressive Policy Institute, 2004). The entire report makes this point.

33. Byron C. Hassel, "Friendly Competition," *Education Next* (Winter 2003), 8–15; Bruno V. Manno, "Yellow Flag," *Education Next* (Winter 2003), 16–22.

34. Lisa Snell, *Defining the Education Market: Reconsidering Charter Schools*, Cato Conference, September 28, 2004.

# 3

## Educational Research

**R**elatively little attention is paid to research in controversies over educational policy. For instance, *A Nation at Risk*, the most highly publicized educational reform document in our nation's history, did not include any references to educational research. In addition, there is a broad albeit not unanimous consensus that educational research has had little impact on teaching or other aspects of education. Although commentaries differ on why this is the case, professional educators often join in the severe but long-standing criticisms of educational research.[1]

Negative comments about educational research in the late 1960s and early 1970s led to the establishment of the National Institute of Education (NIE) in June 1972. Its sponsor, New York senator Daniel Patrick Moynihan, expected NIE to be similar to the National Institutes of Health, which conducts long-range studies on health issues. Nevertheless, one congressional opponent of NIE made a comment about it in 1971 that seems as relevant today as when the comment was made:

> This provision simply opens the Federal Treasury to the same educational researchers without any assurance that the quality of education would be improved.
>
> The Office of Education in the last 10 years has spent approximately $1 billion on education research. Most of this was contracted out to various educational research organizations. Under this bill all that would happen would be that a new organization, the National Institute of Education, would be created to do the same thing which is being done now. . . .

By defeating this amendment, the House will have an opportunity to reject the concept that the way to solve problems is to recast an old agency with a new name and increase its size and scope with the same people who run the old program, with additional waste of time and effort.[2]

The latest reorganization of the research activities of the U.S. Department of Education took place in 2001, when the Bush administration established the Institute of Education Sciences, headed by an executive director appointed for a six-year term to facilitate bipartisanship in the department's research program. This was a constructive change, but it does not address the basic criticisms of educational research that follow.

## EDUCATIONAL RESEARCH AND DRUG RESEARCH: A COMPARISON

In view of the broad consensus on the deficiencies of educational research, let us consider how it differs from research in the pharmaceutical industry, which is often cited to suggest the potential importance of educational research if it received comparable funding. Pharmaceutical companies conduct or finance a great deal of research.[3] Their research expenditures, accounting for billions annually, are made in anticipation of discovering drugs that will help millions avoid or overcome pain and disability or delay death. Because the researchers are searching for drugs that will be patented and widely utilized, their research focuses on drugs that can help large numbers of persons or dominate a market niche.

The following analysis does not ignore the criticisms of the pharmaceutical industry. Whether the companies charge too much or unjustifiably fail to make the drugs available in poor countries that need them desperately or do not publish the results of research with negative outcomes may be valid criticisms, but these issues do not change the fact that pharmaceutical research leads to valuable drugs.[4] Although government support plays a critical role in the development of some life-saving drugs, the following analysis reflects the most common pattern of research and development in the pharmaceutical industry.

Inasmuch as the companies must pay for the research out of their revenues, their research programs are scrutinized from several standpoints. The researchers must stay abreast of developments in medicine, the pharmaceutical industry, and relevant biomedical sciences. Because drugs lose their patents after twenty years, there is enormous pressure to discover new drugs that will compete successfully in the marketplace; however, before this can happen, the new drugs must be tested extensively and approved by the Food and Drug Administration (FDA). The approval process includes reviews of the research to ensure that it was conducted pursuant to rigorous standards. The process may require hundreds of millions of dollars and several years, and because rejections are not unusual, the researchers must be careful to meet the standards required for approval. Despite these costs, however, the outcome is a highly profitable drug industry because of its success in identifying drugs that extend life, ease pain and suffering, and eliminate or reduce disabilities. It should be noted, moreover, that reputable economists contend that the FDA has greatly escalated the costs of bringing drugs to market, and that more drugs would be available sooner at lower prices in the absence of the FDA.[5]

In contrast, most educational research is conducted by professors and is not proprietary. Because it is not proprietary, it is not likely to be a successful commercial product. The education research community sees the large research budget of the pharmaceutical companies and the impressive results. The common reaction is, "Give us this much money and we will generate comparable results in education." Unfortunately, everything between the money and the results in the pharmaceutical industry is ignored.

Hugh Burkhardt and Alan H. Schoenfeld illustrate the mindset in education:

> Consider the matter of tangible support. Just how important, in dollar terms, is the research enterprise in education?
>
> Organizations in applied fields where change is recognized as important (medicine, engineering, electronics) typically spend 5 to 15 percent of turnover on R&D, with about 20 percent of R&D expenditures on basic research and 80 percent on design and systematic improvement. Here is how education compares. The U.S. House Committee on Science (1998) wrote currently the U.S. spends approximately $300 billion a year on education and less than $30 million, 0.01 percent of the education budget, on education research. . . . This minuscule investment suggests a feeble long-term commitment to improving our educational system.
>
> We trust that the case has been made.[6]

Unfortunately, the case has not been made. Consider what is missing from their argument.

## WHO CHOOSES THE RESEARCH TOPICS?

The identity of the decision maker on the research to be conducted is a critical difference between research in the two industries. In academe, the decision maker is ordinarily a professor who is largely free to decide the research issues to be studied. One reason is that very few, if any, university employees are affected by poor research conducted by university faculty. A dean or a university business official may have to sign off on research proposals intended to generate external funding, but the choice of research topic is seldom the reason for a refusal to sign off. The business office will want to be sure that the proposal accords with institutional policies on overhead rates, released time, and employee benefits. The academic officials who sign off also need to know these things as well as the extent of replacement and support needs. Approval of the research per se is not involved or is ordinarily pro forma.

In the for-profit sector, the choice of research issue is more a company than an individual researcher decision. The expertise and recommendations of the researchers are accorded careful consideration, but so are the company and research budgets, the anticipated cost, the revenues if the research is successful, and what the competition is doing. In contrast, the costs of poor educational research are largely absorbed by taxpayers, not the researchers or their employers. In the for-profit sector, the cost and consequences of poor research materially affect other employees, officers, and owners of stock in the company. For this reason, research issues in the for-profit sector undergo a much more thorough vetting than is customary in educational research.

Universities are mainly concerned about the ability of educational researchers to attract external funding. Whether the funding is likely to have any impact upon practice is seldom a concern. Business failures due to poor research, or no research, are a frequent occurrence, but no university has gone into bankruptcy because its educational research never affected educational practice.

The U.S. Department of Education (USED) is the largest single funder of educational research and development; hence it will be helpful to consider how it manages the R and D process. When the USED reviews external research proposals, it usually employs three or more external reviewers for each proposal. The reviewers are often paid a small amount ($100–$150 per proposal in 2003) to evaluate requests for several million dollars. The reviewers are asked to answer several weighted questions, such as what is the quality of the research design, the competence of the research staff, and the potential impact of the research? The reviewers may have had no particular expertise in the field relevant to the research; however, multiple reviews of each proposal are submitted confidentially, and the decision to fund or not to fund is often made at higher levels that are not identified. The procedure is called "peer review" to give the impression that it is like the procedure followed by the National Institutes of Health in making awards for medical research.

Hundreds of millions are distributed according to this slapdash procedure. The procedure has emerged out of two considerations. First, both Republican and Democratic administrations are fearful of getting several angry losers for each grant winner. The department officials responsible for making the awards can point to the reviews to justify rejection or stack the reviewing panel with certain or probable supporters of the proposal when department officials wish to fund it. They can and sometimes do ignore the peer reviews altogether if they do not get the kind of reviews they want.

Most pharmaceutical research does not lead to successful commercial drugs, but the failures are paid for by the revenues from the successful drugs.[7] The failures in pharmaceutical research at least rule out certain possibilities because the research is described carefully; it has to be so that there will be no doubt as to what precisely has been tested. Thus if a drug does not demonstrate its utility in a trial, researchers can ascertain or gain useful clues on whether the failure is due to the dosage, the frequency of application, the stage of the illness, the physical condition of the takers, or some other factor. This kind of progress is not possible in most educational research because the relevant factors and conditions are not spelled out with sufficient precision.

To be sure, private, proprietary interests sometimes do affect the conclusions reached in pharmaceutical research. Justin E. Bekelman, Yan Li, and Cary P. Gross found strong and consistent evidence that industry-sponsored research tends to draw proindustry conclusions.[8] Nevertheless, bias of any kind in pharmaceutical research is much more likely to be exposed, and it runs the risk of career- and company-ending liabilities.

Basically, the for-profit and nonprofit dimensions reflect the differing incentives in the two industries. In the pharmaceutical industry, the major incentive is to conduct research that will enable the company to make a profit; to do that, however, the research must be helpful to end users. Educational research is evaluated largely by other professors but not primarily on the basis of its utility to teachers, most of whom will never read or hear about the research. In contrast, a great deal of educational research is devoted to policy positions on which the researcher has a relatively permanent position. For instance, on school choice issues, the outcomes of research are highly correlated with the policy positions of the researcher. The researchers have not adopted their policy positions because of their research results; instead, their research is intended from the outset to promote their policy positions.[9] The constant requests for funds to disseminate educational research contrast sharply with the criticisms of the pharmaceutical industry for spending too much on advertising, including company-sponsored conferences, sometimes on cruise ships.

## TEACHER INCENTIVES TO UTILIZE RESEARCH

Teachers lack the incentives to use or stay abreast of educational research. This fact adversely affects every aspect of such research. To see why, compare the situations of doctors and teachers relating to research. Doctors want to help their patients, but their interests in research are also strongly motivated by self-interest. A doctor who was not aware that a new drug had dangerous side effects could be subject to severe penalties, including loss or suspension of the freedom to practice and huge civil suits. In contrast, there are no penalties for failure to utilize research that would improve instruction. In many cases, utilization of research, not failure to utilize it, would have negative consequences for teachers. They would or might be required to change their course syllabi, tests, and teaching methods. They would or might be required to take additional training, which might or might not be available. The idea that teachers will utilize research because of their desire to help students is part of the folklore of education; however, if research makes the teachers' work easier, they are more likely to utilize it.

Teacher compensation is based partly upon the amount of academic credit earned after initial employment. In theory, the courses taken after employment could enable teachers to stay abreast of research in their subjects and how to teach them. In the real world, however, the teacher interest is in amassing as much credit as inexpensively and as soon as possible. The school board interest supposedly lies in making sure that the courses strengthen the teachers' ability to perform effectively. This conflict of interest is played out in collective bargaining, a forum in which the unions argue that teachers should decide what courses to take because teachers know best what will help them teach more effectively. School boards that naively accept this argument quickly discover that their teachers are being paid for courses to enter a different occupation, that are the least expensive or most convenient, that treat foreign travel as professional development, or that are required for acceptance into graduate school. The teacher incentives to take in-service courses vary widely, but they have only weak incentives to study research in order to improve their classroom instruction.

The reality is that policymakers use research to legitimate what they are doing. Research that challenges policies and practices is used mainly by those who want to change them.[10] As James S. Coleman points out,

> Policy research is also used when policymakers are divided on the relevant issues or when policymakers want to persuade public and legislative opinion that policy changes are needed. . . . On the other hand, policy research is ignored by policymakers who feel no pressure to legitimize their policies. Research also tends to be ignored, unfunded, or even defunded if it points in politically unpopular directions.[11]

Contemporary controversies over educational policy provide an inexhaustible supply of examples that support Coleman's analysis. For example, in controversies over charter schools, school choice, social promotion, high-stakes testing, and teacher certification, to name just a few, all of the contending parties cite research that allegedly supports their positions. Research that led partisans to change a policy position is relatively rare.

## DISSEMINATION

No aspect of research in education contrasts more sharply with pharmaceutical research than dissemination. Educational researchers constantly plead for more federal funding of "dissemination." A panel sponsored by the American Educational Research Association (AERA) asserts that "more effective communication of research findings to educators is a major shortcoming" and that "dissemination is at least as great a problem as quality of education research." Furthermore, AERA's Panel for the Improvement of Education Research (PIER) asserts that "dissemination is regarded as a central shortcoming of the federal research program."[12]

Educational research is not disseminated for several related reasons. First, teachers, the putative consumers, have extremely weak incentives to understand or utilize it. Second, the producers, mainly professors of education, have no incentives or resources to fund their research; they would not receive a profit or even be reimbursed for the costs of dissemination. Third, much of the research is not helpful to anyone. In contrast, doctors (for example) have strong incentives to utilize research; failure to do so could lead to lawsuits for damages and disciplinary action, including loss of license to practice medicine. At the same time, the pharmaceutical companies, having invested billions in research, must recoup it, and they can do so only if doctors know about and prescribe the new, effective pharmaceuticals.

Consequently, the pharmaceutical companies employ large numbers of sales representatives to call on doctors with samples and literature, pay doctors' expenses to professional conferences at which their drugs will be discussed, and advertise heavily in the press, on television, and in professional and lay journals. Actually, the pharmaceutical companies have been criticized for spending too much on dissemination, a striking contrast to the producers of educational research.

Lewis J. Perelman emphasizes the point that education is an industry in which the consumer does most of the work. Perelman also claims that unless research results in commercially viable innovations, and unless there is a marketing system in place to commercialize the innovation, the innovation will not be widely successful. "Demonstration" and "model" schools are successful only when potential adopters are not aware of the innovation. Perelman is especially caustic in his criticisms of the New

American Schools Development Corporation, an initiative of the first Bush administration intended to create a model school in each congressional district. Private sector research would not waste hundreds of millions on such overtly political considerations.[13]

## THE POLITICAL DYNAMICS OF EDUCATIONAL RESEARCH

Most conservative research and policy organizations do not accept or solicit government funds for their activities. For example, the Heritage Foundation, the American Enterprise Institute, and the Cato Institute, the three leading conservative policy organizations in Washington, do not apply for or accept government funding. Prior to the George W. Bush administration, this contributed to liberal domination of federally funded educational research. The fact that most educational research is conducted by professors of education in public institutions of higher education is naturally conducive to a liberal orientation in educational research; however, since the advent of the Bush administration in 2001, several conservative organizations have demonstrated no compunction whatsoever in requesting or accepting federal support.[14]

One argument for not accepting government funding is that researchers who accept such funding often end up dependent upon it. Another thought is that it is hypocritical to criticize government spending while seeking it for research. Obviously, this point of view narrows the competition for government funds for educational research. Research funded by government goes overwhelmingly to parties who support government programs, or minimally, who are not critics of the administration doling out the federal funds.

James L. Payne points out that expert witnesses who testified for the continuation of federal programs outnumbered opponents by a 16–1 margin. In fact, proponents of government-funded research frequently pay their expenses from government research funds to testify for the programs they are trying to keep alive or to expand. Meanwhile, even on some of the largest federal education budget items, there is no opposition testimony on the issues. Payne concludes that the way Congress votes reflects this huge imbalance in testimony on funding issues. In his view, as long as the supporters of more government funding testify before Congress and the critics do not, most members of Congress will continue to believe in the value of unproductive federal programs.[15]

## THE POLITICIZATION OF EMPIRICAL ISSUES

Research on how to teach reading illustrates a huge problem. Conservatives advocate phonics, a method that emphasizes sounding out the syllables from the letters in words. At the same time, a significant number of teachers advocate what is widely referred to as the whole language approach, in which the emphasis is on the meanings of words. The advocates of the whole language method do not deny the usefulness of phonics, but they insist that it is not the superior method for all children at all times. These definitions of the two camps are oversimplifications; however, my purpose here is not to resolve the dispute but to cite it as illustration of the primitive level of education research.

Several points about this situation deserve thoughtful consideration. First, billions of children have been taught how to read just in the United States. If we include pupils worldwide who have been taught to read English, the numbers are huge indeed. Consider also the thousands of professors who teach prospective teachers how to teach reading. How does it happen that the most effective way to teach children to read has become a political issue, with conservatives contending that phonics is the most effective way and liberals arguing for a whole language approach? Politics comes into play when it is essential to adjust competing interests; it is not supposed to be the environment in which we resolve empirical issues. In fact, it is remarkable that how to teach reading is still a controversial matter. What private for-profit enterprise would still be debating this issue after it has been addressed by thousands of researchers and expenditures in the billions?[16]

Regardless, the Bush administration has made improvement in reading its basic educational research priority. To disseminate helpful research on the subject, it has established a website entitled What Works. Teachers and parents concerned about the best way to teach reading can supposedly get the help they need from the website. Unfortunately, What Works relies upon the same incentives that have failed to achieve utilization of research in the past.

The Bush administration has required adherence to phonics be a condition precedent for receiving federal funds for reading development. This is the case even though a significant number of teachers and researchers advocate or use the whole language method. Regardless of which group is right, this is not the kind of issue that should be resolved through legislation. There is always the possibility that further research will show that what appears to be the right way is the not the right way or the best way after all. There is also the possibility that a new and better way may emerge, as often happens in medical research. To legislate the best way to treat cancer would be a huge mistake for obvious reasons; doctors would have to break the law to provide the best possible treatment for their patients—a position that doctors should not be in. Neither should teachers. If they are using second- or third-best methods, or even counterproductive methods, their employers or professional associations should put an end to the practice, but the best practice, whatever it is, should not be legislatively determined. Obviously, once that happens, changes in political control lead to changes in pedagogy, an inefficient system with great potential for doing harm.[17]

Note how unlikely it would be for this issue to remain unresolved in a competitive education industry. Assume that different schools and teachers had adopted different ways to teach reading. Assume also that some ways had demonstrated their superiority in practice. In that case, the superior schools would advertise their superior results, thereby forcing their competitors to come up with a better way or lose market share. Reading effectiveness would play a role similar to safety or miles per gallon in car sales. Because school management would have strong reason to utilize the most effective practices, it would make sure that the teachers used it.

## THE APPLICATION OF RESEARCH TO PRACTICE

At the risk of belaboring the issues, let us consider the reading research program of the Institute of Education Sciences (IES), the research component of the U.S. Department of Education. The program is a multiyear project to ascertain the best way to teach reading. Let us put aside our bafflement that this project should be necessary after billions of pupils have been taught to read in English and assume that regardless of who or what is responsible, the subject is too important to leave any major issues un-resolved. Let us further suppose that after centuries and billions in expen-ditures by various sources, the research identifies the best ways to teach pupils to read. What will be the sequence of events that leads teachers to use the methods that have emerged from the research?

If past experience is any guide, few teachers will read the research and fewer still will adapt their practice accordingly:

- Some teachers will be near retirement or are about to leave teaching in a few years. They have weak incentives to read research or change to any new methods.
- Some teachers may read the research but not fully understand it.
- Some teachers will challenge the research, for reasons good or bad.
- Some teachers will lack the instructional materials required to teach the best way.
- Some teachers may be more effective by continuing to use less-than-optimal ways and introducing more effective ways only in the earli-est grades.

What about the principals? All the reasons teachers may be reluctant to change, or unable to change, apply to the principals, who often know less about the issues than the teachers. Still, let us suppose that the superin-tendent and school board are determined to bring about improvement in reading. What then?

Many teacher union contracts leave professional development as a teacher option, not as a management right, unless it is provided during the regular school day. Most teachers receive favorable evaluations; there will be problems in requiring tenured teachers with favorable eval-uations to undergo professional development at the direction of the dis-trict. The teachers involved can recruit favorable witnesses and testimo-nials if a dismissal goes to arbitration or the courts. Furthermore, many children learn to read regardless of what methods the teachers use; hence the district may not be able to point to low reading scores despite the fact that its teachers continue to use less-effective methods of teach-ing reading. Also, there may be several professors in the area who are prepared, even eager, to challenge the district's edict. We must also con-sider the fact that the union contract may be in effect for several years, precluding district efforts to regain its authority over professional development for years to come.

All of these possibilities are realities in many districts. It is difficult to say how many until there is a careful analysis of district rights to require in-service training and that it be applied in classrooms. Unfortunately, whatever changes in the teaching of reading are called for by the results of the Bush administration's reading research program, the administration has not faced up to the problems of ensuring that the results are applied in classrooms.

## SPENDING ON EDUCATIONAL RESEARCH

The educational research community argues that the low level of financial support, especially federal support, underlies the low state of educational research. This argument is based on the fallacious assumption that funding for educational research consists mainly of federal expenditures for it. In 2000, there were about 27,000 full-time professors of education in the United States.[18] A 1998 study indicates that the education professoriate devoted 11.1 percent of its time to educational research.[19] As in most other disciplines, the faculty teaching load reflects the research expectations of the institution. In universities with strong graduate schools, faculties usually teach one or two courses per week, usually meeting once a week for two to three hours. At the other extreme, faculties in community colleges teach twelve hours or more per week, and significant research is not expected. When faculty released time (including its overhead costs) is taken into account, the expenditures for educational research are much greater than is acknowledged by the proponents of increased expenditures for it.

Conceptually, we should include the value of graduate student time devoted to doctoral dissertations in education as resources devoted to educational research. Historically, doctoral dissertations were supposed to be evidence that the student was capable of conducting research at a high level. However, as more and more doctoral students in education sought higher-level positions in school administration instead of academic careers, most graduate schools of education adopted the EdD (doctor of education) degree as an alternative doctoral degree for practitioners who did not necessarily benefit from proficiency in foreign languages.

The issue here is not the quality of the research in doctoral dissertations. It is the amount of resources devoted to educational research. Academics often characterize doctoral dissertations in their universities as "research" but do not count it as research in estimating the resources devoted to educational research. The inconsistency leads to substantial underestimates of the resources devoted to educational research.

Of course, some institutions offer a doctoral degree without a dissertation requirement, and in many others, characterizing the dissertations as "research" is quite a stretch. Furthermore, many dissertations are devoted to topics that do not affect K–12 public schools; however, many dissertations in fields other than education (for example, law, psychology, taxation, sociology, and economics) are devoted to public education issues.

In 1999–2000, 245 institutions of higher education awarded 6,830 doctoral degrees in education, the largest number awarded in any field.[20] Some dissertations apply partly to K–12 education and partly to other areas of education; unfortunately, there is no feasible way to quantify the total portion that should be allocated to K–12 education. With several doubts and reservations, it appears that at least three-fourths of the doctoral dissertations in education are devoted to public education.

Most doctoral candidates in education are midcareer teachers or school administrators, such as principals and assistant principals. Some are doctoral students full-time, but the most common pattern is part-time during the school year and full-time during the summer. It usually takes more than a year, and sometimes several years after a master's degree, to complete the requirements for a doctoral degree. In short, virtually every factor affecting estimates of the student costs is subject to significant uncertainty; hence estimates of the cost of student time may be substantially lower or higher than the actual cost. Regardless, the quality of doctoral dissertations is irrelevant to the actual cost. Just as we count the expenditures for poor teachers in estimating the costs of education, we must also count the expenditures for poor research in estimating the costs of educational research.

At any rate, let us assume that the value of doctoral student time is equal to the average teacher salary plus benefits for one full year and that average teacher salary plus benefits is $50,000. On this assumption, the cost of doctoral student time for one year would be $341.5 million, an amount large enough to justify a critical review of the dissertation role in educational research.

## RESEARCH CONTRIBUTIONS FROM PHILANTHROPIC FOUNDATIONS

The philanthropic foundations contribute significant amounts for educational research. Nonprofit testing and educational policy organizations, such as the Educational Testing Service (ETS), also budget for research and development, but there appears to be no systematic data on the amounts.

Textbook publishers, education policy organizations, and several for-profit learning and testing companies active in K–12 education, such as Edison Schools and Sylvan Learning Centers, also devote a significant portion of their resources to research and development. These costs include research and development expenditures for program development, better instructional equipment, textbooks, audiovisual aids, distance learning, bleachers, buses, desks, athletic gear, lockers, uniforms, gymnasium apparatus, school construction, and other products and services provided by the for-profit sector. Because some of these expenditures are devoted to products and services that are sold in noneducational as well as educational markets, their R and D costs cannot be allocated completely to K–12 education. We can surmise that total expenditures for educational research are several times as much as the amounts provided by the U.S. Department of Education, but whatever the actual amounts, they would not explain the low state of educational research. In any event, reliance solely upon federal funds to estimate the amounts spent for K–12 educational research results in huge underestimates of expenditures for it, a striking commentary on the quality of research by the self-designated experts on the subject.

Of course, the public school establishment is adamantly opposed to the inclusion of the costs of teacher education and educational research as a cost of public education. No effort is made to resolve the issue here, but taxpayers pay regardless of where the costs are allocated in government budgets. It is impossible here to list the different cost patterns in teacher education, but there is no doubt that taxpayer support of teacher education amounts to several billion dollars annually. Even public school teachers who attend private institutions of higher education receive federal or state aid of one kind or another.

Whatever the complexities, the government costs of educational research are allocated to higher education, not to public education. Bear in mind also that the expenditures for educational research include the cost of research on school administrators—principals, business managers, superintendents, supervisors of subject areas, and on nonteaching staff. No way of resolving the expenditure issues can do justice to all of the exceptions and nuances that come with the territory, but there are huge research expenditures, even if we cannot estimate them precisely.

## CONSERVATIVE RECOMMENDATIONS ON RESEARCH

Conservatives frequently demonstrate a pervasive naiveté about public education. To illustrate, consider the recommendations on educational research from the Heritage Foundation:

> Congress should always ensure that the federal government is spending America's educational resources on research-based programs that produce measurable achievement in the classroom. In 2002, Congress will reauthorize the U.S. Department of Education and its research and information dissemination department, the Office of Education Research and Improvement (OERI) that provides research findings and instructional materials to schools across the country. Research with the department's stamp of approval can have a strong effect on instruction and student achievement. In the past, OERI has made little distinction between quality research and educational fads. Congress should make sure that OERI's research is relevant, accurate, and objective.[21]

In the first place, Congress is part of the problem, not the solution. At the first hint that Congress is thinking about turning the spigot off, the educational researchers appeal to their representatives in Congress to prevent this from happening. No member of Congress likes to see constituents lose their jobs. "You haven't performed adequately, so I can't help you" would be a rare congressional reaction. In fact, members of Congress often strive to locate or retain federal research projects in their own states, regardless of other considerations. Interestingly enough, the Bush administration implicitly rejected the Heritage recommendation by restructuring the Department of Education to minimize congressional disruption of its research program.

Aside from showing a naive faith in Congress, the Heritage recommendation would rule out research on a host of matters, such as teacher pensions, school finance, civil rights in education, school construction, school board members and elections, contracting out support services, certification, and the feasibility of lowering the school-leaving age, to cite just a few that may not lead to "measurable achievement in the classroom." Congress would be foolish to block research that could save school districts hundreds of millions annually because there was no evidence that the savings would result in "measurable achievement in the classroom." How the districts would spend the savings would be irrelevant to the desirability of research on school finance. One would not look to "measurable achievement in the classroom" to assess the usefulness of research on the investment policies of state teacher retirement plans.

## CONCLUSIONS

Part of the explanation for the educational research debacle is that the antimarket culture of public education is alive and well in educational research. Consider the following statements by the National Academy of Education (NAE), a small organization with a high proportion of members from the most prestigious colleges of education:

> We believe that some researchers will be captivated by the creation of a new social arrangement for the conduct of educational research: deriving theoretical principles from solving real problems in education. For researchers eager to work on our most compelling educational problems, the excitement of working closely with practitioners in schools and classrooms, plus opportunity to join colleagues nationally to build generalizable understandings, tools, and insights, will provide ample incentives to participate. On the other hand, calls to privatize education through vouchers and some charter school proposals threaten the idea that public schools are a social good available to all students regardless of their parents' ability or willingness to pay.[22]

The absence of financial incentives to attract high-quality researchers might be interpreted as an innocent oversight, but the gratuitous one-sided criticism of vouchers and charter schools in a document on research priorities is another matter. Surely, it tells us something about the NAE that none of its 150 members appears to have challenged the substance or relevance of its antivoucher views. Nothing better illustrates the liberal mindset of the education professoriate than NAE's embrace of a bankrupt system of educational research, overlaid with the phony idealism that seems to thrive in education. This acceptance is especially remarkable coming as it does from a group whose members repeatedly and explicitly argue that our existing system of education is heavily biased against the poor and minorities. NAE members are drawn disproportionately from the prestigious colleges of education—the ones that train the most future professors, house the most widely read educational journals, and employ the most professors who are prominent in the media and professional journals—and it might be added, pay the highest salaries. To say the least, their gratuitous put-down of market incentives is suspect, especially when the utility of educational research is compared to research supported by for-profit enterprise.

"The goal of IES research programs is to provide scientific evidence of what works, for whom, and under what conditions."[23] Although this statement does not break new ground, its context included congressional dissatisfaction with the meager results of federally funded educational research in the past and the fact that the phrase "scientifically based evidence" appears 118 times in the No Child Left Behind (NCLB) Act. More importantly, the research projects funded by IES had the depth and duration that were so noticeably absent from federally funded research in the past. For instance, IES launched the following five-year studies in 2003:

- A study to assess reading outcomes in the primary grades that can be associated with receipt of Reading First Grants
- A study of the impact of professional development on teacher practice and student achievement in early reading
- A study of English immersion and transitional bilingual education programs

- An evaluation of the achievement gains of middle school entrants to charter schools

Obviously, these research projects may resolve some of the most controversial educational issues. Whether they do or not, the research is not likely to overcome the inadequate teacher incentives to stay abreast of research that would improve classroom practice.

## NOTES

1. Robert E. Slavin, "Design Competitions: A Proposal for a New Federal Role in Educational Research and Development," *Educational Researcher*, 26, no. 1 (January/February 1997), 22. Slavin, a professor at Johns Hopkins University, is one of the most prominent educational researchers in the nation.

2. Comments by Rep. William Scherle (R-Iowa), *Congressional Record*, 117, (November 4, 1971), 39274.

3. An article on Pfizer's purchase of Pharmacia Corporation stated the result would be a corporation with 2002 revenues of $60 billion and R and D expenses of $7.1 billion. "Pfizer to Buy Pharmacia for $60 Billion," *Wall Street Journal*, July 15, 2002, 1.

4. For example, see Katharine Grieder, *The Big Fix: How the Pharmaceutical Industry Rips Off American Consumers* (New York: Public Affairs, 2003). The book begins "Drug companies make something to protect us from pain and illness that safeguard our ability to keep our routines at work and at home."

5. Milton Friedman, letter to author, November 29, 2005.

6. Hugh Burkhardt and Alan H. Schoenfeld, "Improving Educational Research: Toward a More Useful, More Influential, and Better-Funded Enterprise," *Educational Researcher* (December 2003), 3.

7. News reports on the 2002 merger of Pfizer and Pharmacopia asserted that each company had at least ten drugs that had revenues of $1 billion or more annually.

8. Justin E. Bekelman, Yan Li, and Cary P. Gross, "Scope and Impact of Financial Conflicts of Interest in Biomedical Research," *Journal of American Medical Association*, 289, no. 4 (January 22–29, 2003), 454–465. About two-thirds of the institutions sponsoring pharmaceutical research held stock in start-up companies that fund research in proprietary drugs. The industry share of the costs of biomedical research has increased from about 32 percent in 1980 to 62 percent in 2000, while the government share has decreased.

9. Lois Weiner, "Research or 'Cheerleading?' Scholarship on Community School District 2, New York City," *Education Policy Analysis Archives*, 11, no. 27 (August 7, 2003), epaa.asu.edu/epaa/v11n27, accessed March 7, 2006.

10. The 2004 controversy over the AFT report on charter schools (in chapter 2) is a good example. The AFT is opposed to charter schools, and its research was intended to inflict the maximum possible damage to their existence. Supporters of charter schools dismissed the AFT study immediately.

11. James S. Coleman, *Foundations of Social Theory* (Cambridge, MA: Harvard University Press, 1990). Coleman's analysis explains why even good policy research is ignored by policymakers.

12. Gerald Sroufe, director of Government Relations, AERA, "Initial Comments on H.R. 4875," submitted to Rep. Michael Castle, chair, Subcommittee on Children, Youth, and Families; and Rep. William Goodling, chair, Committee on Education and the Workforce, July 24, 2000.

13. Lewis J. Perelman, *School Is Out* (New York: William Morrow, 1992), 252.

14. The Black Alliance for Educational Options (BAEO), Education Leaders Council (ELC), American Board for Certification of Teacher Excellence (ABCTE), National Council on Teacher Quality (NCTQ), and Center for Education Reform (CER) are conservative organizations that have received federal grants. In 2003, Chester E. Finn Jr. expressed concern that the ELC, an organization primarily of state superintendents of education who had withdrawn from the Council of Chief State School Officers (CCSSO), was losing its freedom to be critical of government policy because of its dependence on federal funds.

15. James L. Payne, "The Congressional Brainwashing Machine," *Public Interest* (Summer 1990), 4–6; James L. Payne, *The Culture of Spending: Why Congress Lives beyond Our Means* (San Francisco: ICS Press, 1991). Educational research was not included in Payne's studies, but his conclusions are clearly applicable to it.

16. This point takes for granted that there may be a "best way" for some pupils, a different "best way" for others, and "best ways" that are equally effective. Also, even for individual students, the "best way" may vary, depending on maturation, the nature of the problem, and the needs of the class.

17. The case for phonics is set forth in National Reading Panel, *Report of the National Reading Panel: Teaching Children to Read* (Washington, DC: National Institute of Child Health and Human Development, 2000). For a lengthy criticism of the NICHD, see Gerald Coles, *Reading the Naked Truth: Literacy Legislation and Lies* (Portsmouth, NH: Heineman, 2000).

18. The basis for the estimate can be found in Myron Lieberman and Charlene K. Haar, *Public Education as a Business* (Lanham, MD: ScarecrowEducation,

2003), 126. The estimates in this book on the costs of educational research in higher education may have been too high due to excessive estimates of the research expenditures for the part-time faculty.

19. Linda V. Zimbler, U.S. Department of Education, National Center for Education Statistics, *Background Characteristics, Work Activities, and Compensation of Faculty and Instructional Staff in Postsecondary Institutions: Fall 1998*, NCES 2001-152 (Washington, DC: U.S. Department of Education, 2001), 40.

20. U.S. Department of Education, *Digest of Education Statistics 2001* (Washington, DC: U.S. Department of Education), 320. The study defined "doctor's degrees" as "the highest academic degree and requires mastery within a field of knowledge and demonstrated ability to perform scholarly research. Other doctorates are awarded for fulfilling specialized requirements in professional fields, such as education (Ed.D)."

21. Stuart M. Butler and Kim R. Holmes, *"Mandate for the Presidency"* (Washington, DC: Heritage Foundation, 2002), 142–143. Suggestions on how "Congress should make sure that OERI's research is relevant, accurate, and objective" would have been helpful. One way would be for Congress to stop appropriating earmarked research funds for designated institutions.

22. *Recommendations Regarding Research Priorities, An Advisory Report Presented to the National Educational Research Policy and Priorities Board* (New York: National Academy of Education, 1999), 42, 63–64.

23. Institute of Education Sciences, U.S. Department of Education, *New Education Research Programs*, undated memorandum, 1.

# 4

## Teacher Education and Certification

For over half a century, teacher education has been a highly controversial subject in American education. Although not the first of its genre, Arthur Bestor's *Educational Wastelands*, published in 1953, laid out the battle lines that have persisted into the twenty-first century and show no signs of abating.[1] The fact that controversies over "the facts" in teacher education have endured for well over half a century is a strong indication that conflicts of interest underlie these controversies.

### THE DEMOGRAPHICS OF TEACHER EDUCATION

Before I get into the policy issues, a few facts on the ground should be kept in mind. There were an estimated 3,564,000 teachers in 2004–2005 — 3,132,000 in public schools and 432,000 in private schools.[2] If there are no changes in the demand for teachers, about 210,000 new teachers will be needed annually; however, some vacancies would be filled by teachers returning to the classroom after leaving for one reason or another. It is estimated that 21 percent of the vacancies (45,000) are filled by newly minted teachers and 24 percent by teachers who had graduated from college but did not teach during the previous year.

In 2003, about 1,500 institutions of higher education had teacher education programs.[3] The institutions ranged in size from large state universities that graduate thousands of teachers annually to small denominational institutions that graduate only a handful destined for denominational schools. Sometimes teacher education is a minor program in a large research university; sometimes it is the raison d'être for the institution. These site differences often lead to differences over the content of teacher education programs.

## TEACHER CERTIFICATION: THE STATUS QUO

"Teacher certification" (sometimes referred to as "teacher licensure") refers to state authorization to teach in public schools. All states require certification to teach in public schools; only five states require certification to teach in private schools, a policy that is strongly opposed by private schools and their organizations. Thirty-one states do not require teachers in private schools to be certified, and the rest vary a great deal. Some require teachers to be certified if the school seeks state approval or accreditation. A few offer certification options, such as certification for state approval. Still others have different standards for certification of private school teachers or require certification if the school receives any public assistance. Schools that are not required to employ certified teachers often employ them regardless, so it is difficult to compare states on the basis of their certification policies.

On paper, teacher certification appears to be a straightforward process. A state agency, usually the state department of education, promulgates the requirements: so many credit hours in the liberal arts, so many in the subjects to be taught, and so many in teaching methods, including practice teaching. Institutions of higher education structure their teacher education programs accordingly. In practice, however, things are not so simple. Inasmuch as most of the issues have arisen in other occupations, let us begin with a brief discussion of their resolution elsewhere.

All states require a license to practice in certain occupations, but many occupations are licensed by one or more states but not all. Ostensibly, the purposes of the requirements are to protect the public from incompetent practitioners, but the weight of scholarship on the issue is that licensure does not achieve this objective and may even function to reduce the quality of service. Because some critics of teacher certification have also adopted this position, let us see how it could happen.

The eligibility of an individual to work in an occupation involves probabilities, not certainties. Theoretically, certification increases the odds that the service providers are competent. Assume that one hundred persons take a test to be certified as physics teachers. Assume also that there is a continuum; the persons who score the highest are much more likely to be competent teachers than persons who score in the middle or lower ranks, and those in the middle ranks are more likely to be competent than the individuals in the lowest ranks. Assume further that a score of 500 on the certification test is the midpoint of the grading continuum. A score of 500 means that the test taker has a fifty-fifty probability of competence. A score of 600 increases the probability of competence to 60 percent, and a score of 400 reduces the probability of competence to 40 percent.

This means that a score of 500 will necessarily eliminate some individuals who would be competent practitioners. The higher the required pass score, the more potentially competent teachers will be excluded. One issue is whether school districts should have the option of trying to beat the odds, based on their evaluations of the factors that reflect competence. The critical point is that the larger the number of candidates who are denied certificates, the larger the pool of denied candidates who would be good teachers.

We should approach certification issues skeptically; certification in most fields does not result in higher-quality practice.[4] Currently, most of the controversies over teacher education focus on the requirements for initial certification and pay relatively little attention to training after certification. The policy recommended here is that school districts should have much greater latitude in whom they hire as long as they can remedy any deficiencies after employment. Although most teachers would like to improve their skills and knowledge, the highest priority of most teachers lies in getting as much salary credit as possible in the shortest possible time with the least expense. The union's bargaining position is that the teachers know best what their needs are, and hence any courses teachers choose to take should receive salary credit.

Unfortunately, where the union position or anything close to it prevails, school districts provide salary credit for the least expensive and most convenient courses, courses taken for social reasons or to enter another occupation or to satisfy requirements for advanced degrees, often in a different specialization within the field of education, or courses required for certification to be an educational administrator.

On these issues, union dynamics are important. The union negotiator must satisfy as many of his constituents as possible. Obviously a contract that leaves the choice of courses for salary credit up to the teachers will maximize teacher support, so the union tries to negotiate provisions as close as possible to this outcome. The actual outcome depends on a number of considerations, especially management's bottom line on the issues. In practice, school management's positions are affected by several considerations, such as the presence of union-supported candidates on the school board and management's experience and assessment of its needs. Ideally, management would like to require prior approval for salary credit, but the tendency is for contracts and their implementation to move away from this ideal over time.[5]

School boards and school administrators thus face a dilemma. They can continue the status quo, which relies mainly on state certification to ensure teacher quality. However, if they rely on "professional development," especially course credit after initial employment, they must cope with teacher unions with a stake in restricting managerial prerogatives on salary credit. For various reasons discussed in chapter 7, many school boards do not cope with the problem very effectively.

Some conservatives propose to eliminate certification, but most argue for reducing the requirements in "pedagogy" (a pejorative among this group) and increasing the number of courses in the subjects that the teachers are going to teach. Pupils begin to take separate subjects in the sixth grade or about the time they enroll in middle school or junior high school. Prior to that time, elementary teachers usually teach all or most subjects to pupils who do not move from classroom to classroom. In some school districts, music and art teachers travel from classroom to classroom to provide instruction while the regular classroom teachers take a break, often naively referred to as a "preparation period." At any rate, teacher specialization usually occurs in or about the sixth grade.

Elementary teachers are required to teach reading, literature, history, mathematics, science, and geography, to cite a short list. Should one three-credit course on methods of teaching suffice for all of their requirements in pedagogy? Or should elementary teachers be required to take separate methods courses for each subject that requires a significant amount of their time? Over seventy years ago, an authoritative study of the professions had this to say on the subject:

> In the case of those professions for which training is or may be given in universities, there arises a problem relating to technical accomplishments. We are not referring to the acquisition of practical experience which will be discussed in what follows. The reference is to those routine technical accomplishments, such as the construction of dentures, without which no one is fit to receive a certificate of professional proficiency. If acquirements of this kind are all that a man needs, he should not come to a university. But if he comes to a university to pursue fundamental studies, should facilities be given to him to perfect himself in these acquirements also? It would seem that difficulties are often felt in regard to the technical accomplishments, which are necessary for the newer professions, and it is thought that there would be something derogatory to a university if provision for their acquisition was not made within its walls. But prolonged experience has not shown that there is anything unfitting about teaching of *materia medica* and other necessary elements of medical technique within universities. If that is so, there is no objection to dental students learning how to make dentures, or to students of accountancy learning bookkeeping in universities, provided that they come there in the first place to undertake a course of scientific study. The acquisition of these technical accomplishments is one thing if it is not based on scientific study, and quite another thing if it follows such study and is integrated with it.[6]

Everyone concedes that teacher knowledge of the subjects taught is essential. Note, however, that we can tell whether prospective teachers know their subjects by testing them in these subjects; that is all professors do in the institutions that prepare teachers. Instead of requiring a certain number of course credits in the subjects to be taught, why not simply require teachers to take a state test in these subjects? Actually, twenty-nine states require teachers seeking state certification to pass a test in the subjects to be taught, but the passing scores on the tests are widely acknowledged to be extremely low in states that rely on tests for this purpose.

Not surprisingly, many professors in the subjects to be taught oppose this approach. If such testing were adopted, everyone would know immediately which institutions and professors were preparing teachers in their subjects and which ones were not. To avoid any such accountability, professors in the arts and sciences oppose meaningful state tests to ascertain teacher preparation in the subjects to be taught; minimally, they are not activists for such tests. Interestingly enough, despite the frequent accusation that the underlying motivation for education courses is to ensure a market for professors of education, that same motivation is not attributed to efforts by liberal arts professors to substitute their courses for education courses.

Some states have delegated their authority over certification requirements to institutions of higher education; if a college says a graduate is qualified to teach, the state education department certifies the individual. Many colleges, especially small liberal arts colleges, would suffer severely if they could not enroll students planning to become teachers. Suppose, however, that it is proposed to eliminate or reduce the education requirements in the state certification requirements. What will replace the courses that are dropped? The resolution of this issue will depend on campus politics if it is not resolved by the state education departments or the state legislatures; anyone who believes that it will be resolved on the basis of what is best for pupils has probably had very little experience in how these issues are actually resolved in institutions of higher education.

At the federal level, conservative policymakers have sought federal appropriations to provide teachers with advanced training in specified subjects such as mathematics and physics. Much of the funding for these programs has been made available through the National Science Foundation (NSF) and the National Endowment for the Humanities (NEH), but their programs reach only a small fraction of teachers whose skill should be upgraded. A much better and much less expensive alternative would be to conduct an intensive campaign to persuade school boards to adopt more stringent requirements for salary credit. Such a campaign should educate school boards on the importance of the issue, perhaps with guidelines for what is adequate preparation in various subjects and model contractual language that would help school boards in bargaining with teacher unions. In addition to costing much less than federally sponsored courses for a handful of teachers, a school board campaign would facilitate a long-term solution to the problem instead of a one-shot solution for a handful of teachers, reach school boards that do not employ teachers who have enrolled in NSF programs, and provide model language for subjects not included in the NSF program. A school board campaign could also utilize the prestige and influence of national organizations of mathematicians and scientists to underscore the importance of the issue and perhaps bring their influence to bear in various school districts.

Teachers who participate in NSF programs are free to leave district employment as soon as the training is completed. This possibility discourages districts from providing large rewards for valuable in-service training. School boards should negotiate arrangements that maximize their ability to benefit from such training. For example, instead of paying relatively small amounts annually for in-service training, the districts could pay much larger amounts for a specified number of years of service after the training that is valuable to the district. Such arrangements could help to align teacher interests with school district interests.

In bargaining, the union negotiator is likely to insist that teachers should not be required to take any courses after initial employment. Supposedly, this is a matter for practitioners to decide in other professions; hence the same policy should apply to teachers. This argument overlooks the economic and legal pressures to stay abreast of research in other professions. For instance, if a drug turns out to have harmful side effects, doctors and pharmacists are responsible for learning this through publications, conferences, and meetings with pharmaceutical salespeople. Costly career-ending consequences and heavy personal liabilities may result from failure to keep up with research. Comparable pressures to stay abreast of research do not exist in education.

School districts vary enormously in the criteria utilized for salary credit. At one extreme, there are no criteria; whatever courses teachers take are approved for salary credit. In fact, a mini-industry has developed by providing teachers with bogus credit and even bogus degrees.[7] At the other extreme, the school districts retain the right of prior approval and apply reasonable criteria in giving or withholding approval.

In between, districts differ on how much academic work receives salary credit, the procedures for obtaining the credit, whether degrees per se or just the amount of coursework receives salary credit, whether there are restrictions on the kind of institutions whose courses are accepted for salary credit, and so on. Most school districts, however, do not accord salary credit the importance that it deserves.

## TEACHER EDUCATION IN THE NCLB ACT

More than any other in our history, the George W. Bush administration has taken an active role in teacher education. The NCLB Act signed by President Bush on January 8, 2002, required every teacher in districts receiving Title I funds to employ "highly qualified" teachers by the 2005–2006 school year; as a practical matter, this requirement applies to the overwhelming majority of U.S. school districts. "Highly qualified" means that a teacher must

- Hold at least a bachelor's degree;
- Hold full state certification or have passed the state licensure examination and hold a license to teach;
- Demonstrate competence in each academic subject to be taught. Both new and experienced teachers can meet the competence requirement through a "high, objective, uniform state standard of evaluation" (HOUSSE), which the states are allowed to establish on their own.[8]

The NCLB criteria have encountered several problems.[9] The state subject matter standards vary widely; there is disagreement over which courses should be counted as meeting the academic requirements; information to parents on the quality of their children's teachers varies widely; reviewing transcripts requires a great deal of time; and the lack of attention to classroom management is a troublesome problem in identifying "highly qualified teachers."[10]

## ALTERNATIVE CERTIFICATION

For several decades, conservatives have contended that there is a substantial pool of potentially qualified teachers who are unwilling to take the requisite courses in education to become certified. Eventually, the George W. Bush administration committed about $40 million to alternative certification. Instead of viewing alternative certification as the way to certify a small number of prospective teachers on an emergency basis, the Bush administration is trying to replace conventional certification with requirements that drastically reduce or exclude courses in education as a certification requirement.

Unfortunately, alternative certification has failed to attract a substantial number of qualified individuals, especially in mathematics and science. Individuals who have a bachelor's degree or higher in mathematics or science can usually earn much more in other occupations that utilize their talents. Alternative certification may make it easier for such persons to become teachers, but it does not eliminate the economic gap between teaching and other occupations that require academic majors in mathematics or science. The pool of individuals willing to forego higher salaries in other occupations in order to teach these subjects has turned out to be much smaller than conservative rhetoric assumes.

Nevertheless, alternative certification may be productive in subjects and grade levels in which individuals do not suffer any economic disadvantage by becoming public school teachers, and the amount of specialized knowledge required is not prohibitive. These conditions apply to teachers of some K–12 subjects, and probably to all in K–2, especially in school districts that employ music and art teachers to teach these subjects. Of course, K–2 (and preschool) teachers will be outraged by the suggestion that their work requires less specialized training than is required of other teachers, and the teacher unions support their position. Nevertheless, overpayment of some teachers is a major reason why school districts are unable to pay much higher salaries for potential teachers who command higher levels of compensation outside of teaching.

As of 2004, 44 states had 610 alternative certification programs that certified 35,000 teachers that year. Interestingly enough, most of the programs are administered by departments of education or their allies.[11] Over half (52 percent) of the programs are administered by institutions of higher education, 12 percent by a school district, 6 percent by a regional service center, 5 percent by the state department of education, and 4 percent by a consortium. Fifty-two percent of the programs were two years in duration, 32 percent one year, 12 percent three years, and 4 percent less than one year. Ninety percent of the participants taught full-time during the program, and this fact plus receiving a teacher's salary and benefits were cited as the most important reasons for choosing the alternate route. In addition to funding more extensive alternative paths to teaching, the

Bush administration has funded the National Center for Alternative Certification (NCAC), a source of information on alternative certification that
was terminated in 2006.[12]

## THE NATIONAL BOARD FOR
## PROFESSIONAL TEACHING STANDARDS

The National Board for Professional Teaching Standards (NBPTS) was
established in 1987 with funding from the Carnegie Corporation. Its
founders hoped to establish a board that would certify teachers who
served at a superior level of competence; the operative analogy was to the
boards that certify CPAs or the medical specialty boards that certify physicians who are experts in their fields.[13] NBPTS does not and was never intended to certify teachers as eligible to teach; the assumption was that it
would certify only teachers who had been teaching three years, as it turned
out. It was also anticipated that local unions would bargain for salary differentials for teachers certified by NBPTS and that state legislatures
would enact legislation providing such differentials. By 2006, NBPTS had
certified over 47,000 teachers in 50 states and 26 teaching fields. In a
number of states and school districts, the examination fees for NBPTS are
paid by the states or school districts.

NBPTS was established partly to meet the union objections to merit
pay. Inasmuch as NBPTS certification was by a national board, it eliminated the union objection that merit pay would lead to discrimination and
favoritism at the local level. Also, board certification enabled teachers to
retain the recognition of expertise when they moved to a different district.
In conventional merit pay, the distinction is lost when teachers move out
of the districts that awarded them merit pay. The entire process of obtaining NBPTS certification is voluntary; no stigma is attached to not seeking
NBPTS certification.

The individual most responsible for implementation of NBPTS was
AFT president Albert Shanker, and this is where NBPTS appears to have
gone off the tracks. As initially envisaged, NBPTS was to be controlled by
the subject matter organizations, like the American Chemical Society and
American Economic Association. Although conservatives had praised
Shanker repeatedly for his devotion to high standards, the fact of the mat-

ter is that under his leadership, NBPTS was organized under NEA and AFT control, not under the scholarly subject matter organizations.

After NBPTS had been operating for ten years, conservative education leaders began to pay attention to it and did not like what they saw. In particular, they alleged that NBPTS was relying upon low subject matter standards for certifying teachers. Consequently, in 2002, a group of conservative critics of "traditional college-of-education training" established the American Board for Certification of Teacher Excellence (ABCTE). ABCTE was launched in 2001 with a $5 million organizational grant from the U.S. Department of Education. It was followed up in 2003 by a $35 million grant over five years to provide beginning teachers with a "Passport," that is, a credential that would be accepted for certification in every state, and to establish a "master teacher" category, intended to compete with certification by NBPTS. The Passport has been the main focus of ABCTE. It is supposed to help implement the NCLB requirement of a "highly qualified" teacher in every classroom.

The Passport is achieved through two tests and a preservice teacher preparation requirement. The first test includes an essay examination and questions about student assessment, instructional techniques, and classroom management. It is followed by a subject area knowledge test, which tests the candidates on their knowledge of the subjects in which they seek certification. There is a preservice component to the Passport that gives candidates the opportunity to apply their knowledge and skills to classroom situations.[14] This appears to be a convoluted way of saying "practice teaching," the phrase commonly used to refer to a trial period of teaching before certification.

As of May 2006, five states (Florida, Idaho, New Hampshire, Pennsylvania, and Utah) had agreed to accept the Passport as a route to state certification, and 154 candidates had been certified, with more than 1,200 in the pipeline nationally after an intensive marketing campaign.[15] However, in some participating states, the holders of the Passport must satisfy additional requirements to be fully certified. It is impossible to predict how many potential teachers will seek a Passport, but it would have to be a much larger number to justify the $40 million in federal grants made to facilitate alternative certification and a master teacher program to compete with NBPTS. The teachers recruited through the Passport should be teachers who would not have entered teaching otherwise; the rationale for the grants is not served by the recruitment of individuals who would have become teachers anyway.

Unless a substantial number of states accept the Passport, it will be a marginal operation, especially as interstate reciprocity on teacher certification reduces the need for the Passport or something similar to it. The problem facing the American Board is that its standards must be high enough to avoid criticism, but the higher the standards, the smaller the number of teachers who will choose the Passport as the way to become certified.

The success of the Passport is also highly dependent upon the willingness of state education agencies to accept the Passport in lieu of their regular certification requirements, but the state superintendents of education and directors of teacher education and certification are generally not supporters of the Bush administration's educational program. The fact that California's licensing board refused to accept the Passport for certification in 2004 suggests that the five states that approved it are the low-hanging fruit.

## MASTER TEACHER CERTIFICATION

Master teacher certification by the American Board is an alternative to the NBPTS that began to certify teachers in 2004. It is based on the argument that NBPTS requires evidence of mastery of the subjects taught and best practices, whereas master teacher certification will require candidates to demonstrate such mastery by raising student achievement.

ABCTE claims that "increased student learning" will be an essential requirement for ABCTE certification. It is highly doubtful however, whether ABCTE can achieve this objective, at least in a way that will be accepted by state certification agencies or school districts. ABCTE's master teacher certification is seeking to replace the NBPTS program, which has already certified more than 47,000 teachers in all states and 26 teaching fields. These teachers are already receiving salary increments for NBPTS certification. In the bargaining law states that include most of the nation's teachers, NEA and AFT locals are not likely to bargain, or bargain very hard, for salary differentials for teachers holding ABCTE's master teacher certificate. One must wonder what the Bush administration was thinking when it financed a program that is so dependent on its opposition for implementation.

ABCTE no longer asserts its superiority over NBPTS. On the contrary, it asserts that "the Master Teacher credential offered by the American Board and the National Board certification are both valid and effective routes to professional recognition for great teachers."[16] ABCTE summarizes their differences as follows:

- ABCTE's master teacher certification costs $1,100; National Board certification costs $2,300.
- The time required for ABCTE certification depends on the amount of preparation time required "to score a distinguished mark on the content exam," which is said to be twenty to forty hours plus ten gathering and formatting data on student achievement.
- Focus on student achievement: ABCTE's master teacher candidates must demonstrate student achievement; NBPTS certification requires demonstration of mastery of effective educational practices.[17]

Except for the higher cost of NBPTS, teachers will probably prefer NBPTS instead of ABCTE certification. Even the much lower cost of ABCTE certification will not necessarily be in its favor because some states and school districts are picking up the cost of NBPTS certification. In the real world, teachers will have a choice between NBPTS certification, which already pays a differential in all states, and ABCTE certification as a master teacher, which may cost teachers less out of pocket but which pays a differential in only a few states. The Bush administration's commitment to ABCTE's master teacher certification is likely to be a large federal expenditure to identify a small number of master teachers.


## WHO SHOULD PAY TO IDENTIFY MASTER TEACHERS?
## A REALITY CHECK

By the end of 2005, the federal government had spent or committed at least $168 million since 1987 to identify master teachers, using this phrase to include NBPTS-certified teachers as well as those to be certified by ABCTE, starting in 2006. About $40 million had been spent or committed by the

Bush administration to ABCTE; the first $128 million in federal funds went to NBPTS. Clearly, the standards to be a master teacher have been resolved by political power; the 2005 Bush administration budget was the first since 1987 not to include funds for NBPTS and the first to include funds for ABCTE.

The situation raises this question: Should the federal government be supporting these procedures at all? Whatever portion of the $40 million to ABCTE is allocated to its master teacher project is virtually certain to be a low-return expenditure of federal funds. NEA and AFT locals represent about 70 percent of the nation's teachers. It is very unlikely that NEA and AFT locals will try to negotiate equal or better awards to ABCTE's master teachers than to NBPTS-certified teachers. Similarly, supporters of ABCTE's version are unlikely to persuade governors and state legislatures to award equal or higher stipends to ABCTE-certified teachers. Teachers aware of these probabilities are likely to choose NBPTS certification because it has much greater portability and established acceptance. It is only in Washington, where $168 million and still counting is not real money, that such expenditures with so little prospect to improve anything would be overlooked. Spending millions more on an underfunded plan to compete with NBPTS without widespread, prestigious scholarly support makes no sense at all to this observer.

## TEACHER EDUCATION AND "SOCIAL JUSTICE"

The National Council for Accreditation of Teacher Education (NCATE) is the accrediting organization for teacher education. According to NCATE's criteria for accreditation, a teacher education program must include attention to "professional disposition"; "social justice" is cited as an example of a professional disposition.[18]

Now whatever social justice means, it is not likely to be anything bearing on professional competence. To be sure, there is nothing necessarily wrong in requiring preparation for any profession to include attention to its social role and public policy issues, but prospective teachers are not better prepared to teach physics because they are educated about social justice, especially since the phrase means too many different things to different persons. How education affects and is affected by social justice could be a legitimate topic in programs of teacher education, but the content of many education courses and journals justifies their harshest critics. For instance, a recent article taken from the *Education Leadership Review*, a journal published twice a year by the National Council of Professors of Educational Administration (NCPEA), is entitled "Corporate Answers to Public School Problems." The summary at the beginning of the article concludes,

> Educational professionals must become the progenitors of accurate and professionally sound research that truly improves the academic life of youngsters. For without these actions, the political right will have reduced all that we know as being intellectual to a simple test-retest exercise.[19]

A subsequent excerpt asserts,

> Might it not be prudent to consider test burning, much like draft notice burning, as a next step in seeking the elimination of dependency on testing practices that benefit only a small portion of a vast democracy?[20]

The suggestion that it might be "prudent" to consider civil disobedience and violation of property rights to eliminate unwanted testing practices seems too bizarre to be taken seriously, but it would be a mistake to dismiss the above quotations as the rantings of a few far-out leftist professors. The authors have received degrees from colleges and universities. Their article has been "peer reviewed," that is, reviewed by other professors, presumably of educational administration. An editor and presumably some members of the journal's editorial advisory boards deemed the article worthy of publication in the journal even though it is obviously preposterous. For instance, the NCLB Act, which includes the requirement that all fourth- and eighth-graders be tested annually, received overwhelming bipartisan support in both the U.S. Senate and House of Representatives; the opposition to NCLB actually came from the "extreme right wing" members in the House of Representatives, such as Representatives Robert Schaffer and Tom Tancredo of Colorado. This underscores the basic point of the article; it is characterized by falsehoods and messianic stances that call into question the system that produced it.

The proponents of social justice education now have their own journal, a quarterly entitled *Equity and Excellence in Education*. The editor is a professor of social justice education at the University of Massachusetts, and a brochure lists articles such as

"No Poor Child Left Unrecruited: How NCLB Codifies and Perpetuates Urban School Militarism"

"The Necessity of Feminist Pedagogy in a Climate of Political Backlash"

"Shaping Democratic Identities and Building Citizenship Skills through Student Activism: Mexico's First Gay–Straight Alliance."[21]

It is difficult to say how prevalent such courses are in teacher education programs, but citing social justice as meeting the "professional disposition" requirement for accreditation indicates that they could be prevalent on a large scale.

Conservatives often criticize the liberal orientation of teacher education, but the remedies sought, substitution of courses in the liberal arts and sciences for education courses, would only make matters worse. Stanley Rothman, S. Robert Lichter, and Neil Nevitte have conducted the most comprehensive study (hereinafter, "the Rothman study") of faculty social attitudes and political identification.[22] Their study was based on a questionnaire sent to a random sample of 1,642 faculty members from 183 four-year colleges and universities. The institutions were selected to provide accurate proportions of the variety of U.S. colleges and universities.

The Rothman study shows the fallacy in the conservative recommendation that future teachers take more courses in the liberal arts and fewer in education as an antidote to liberal education courses; in most institutions, the preponderance of liberals is higher in the liberal arts courses that would replace education courses. The Rothman study also showed that a conservative point of view is a negative factor in academic employment. This is only to be expected except by those who cling to the illusion that higher education consists of open-minded scholars who judiciously assess candidates for positions on a professional basis.

The situation illustrates the practical difficulties facing conservative faculty in institutions of higher education. Few college or university departments hire anyone who is critical of the faculty choosing the potential faculty member. The emergence of conservative faculty organizations like the National Association of Scholars (NAS) is symptomatic of the marginal role of academic conservatives. Inasmuch as they cannot prevail in the national academic organizations, they have established conservative ones such as the NAS and state organizations affiliated with the State Policy Network (SPN). Intellectually, they are reduced to supporting affirmative action for conservative academics. One has to wonder how they can support a "liberal education" at all because it is so ideologically one-sided according to their own assertions.

## TEACHER EDUCATION: A CASE OF REGULATORY CAPTURE

Teacher certification is a case of regulatory capture, that is, control of regulation by the interests being regulated. In fact, the case for teacher certification is weakened by two considerations. One is the multiplicity of the certificates. In some states, more than one hundred different teaching certificates are issued. This contrasts sharply with practice in other professions. In law and medicine, for example, the states rely on one certificate; the holder can work in any specialty that he or she wishes. Malpractice considerations exert strong pressure on physicians to confine their practice to their specialized field, but these pressures do not apply to teachers. In effect, teacher certification is being utilized as an assignment tool, something that could be left to local discretion, as it is in other occupations. Ironically, rigid assignment to specific duties is a hallmark of unionism, but nowhere is it embraced more strongly than by teachers demanding to be treated as "professionals."

The second consideration is especially significant. Thousands of individuals teach school subjects in summer camps, but certification is not required as it is in other professions. For example, a substantial number of the teachers in summer camps are college students. Interestingly enough, nobody is making an issue of these uncertified teachers, perhaps because teachers own or operate many of the summer camps. Active duty members in our military services also teach school subjects, but there is no legal requirement that they must be certified.

The policy recommended here is that the states should adopt minimal requirements for initial certification but insist upon reasonable standards for salary credit after certification. Currently, however, there is little, if any, state regulation of salary credit, even though perhaps 20 percent or more of school district salary expenditures are based upon it.

In the bargaining-law states, the rules regarding salary credit are subject to bargaining, but many school boards are too weak to negotiate sensible rules on salary credit. One way to resolve the problem might be for the states to be more prescriptive on the issue. A better but more difficult-to-achieve alternative would be to render the rules governing salary credit a prohibited subject of bargaining. In any event, it would be highly desirable for every state to conduct a thorough study of the in-service courses that school districts are paying for; introducing a few facts about these courses might have a salutary effect on the controversies over it. Unfortunately, legislatures as well as school boards are more likely to be influenced by the political power of the teacher unions than by evidence that school districts are paying large amounts for courses that do not add to classroom competence.

In the primary grades, depth of subject matter, although always desirable, is seldom a problem. As grade levels rise and discrete subjects come into play, the emphasis in preparation shifts toward subject matter preparation. At the graduate level in universities, subject matter preparation is overwhelmingly dominant. Graduate students are expected to be mature individuals who can focus on the subject matter, regardless of professorial pedagogical differences.

There is no obvious point at which the transition to less emphasis on pedagogy is clearly marked, but the transition usually emerges as a significant problem in grades four to six. Because of the variations in student interests and talents, the preparation of teachers in the lower elementary grades is especially difficult; the student transition to adolescence is another factor that requires more attention to factors other than depth of subject matter. Especially from the sixth grade on, depth in subject matter preparation should be a given, but insistence that kindergarten and first-grade teachers have an academic major in the subjects they teach illustrates the ideological rigidity of conservative approaches to teacher education.

## CONCLUSION: THE UNITARY PROFESSION FALLACY

If the solution to the achievement gap is attracting more highly talented teachers, it appears that the gap will not be closed in the near future. Over

80 percent of public schools teachers are female, but teaching attracts a lower percentage of highly talented females than it did in the past. The reason is that teaching no longer benefits from the fact that it was by far the largest outlet for highly talented females.

Although the number of women college graduates has tripled between 1964 and 2000, the percentage who indicated that they would become teachers declined from over half in 1964 to 15 percent in 2000. If 1.0 represents the index of females in an occupation equal to the percentage of women in the labor force, the index went from 0.33 in medicine and 0.08 in law in the mid-1960s to 0.89 and 0.87 respectively in less than thirty years. Sean P. Corcoran, William N. Evans, and Robert M. Schwab concluded that from 1957 to 1992, "the likelihood that a female from the top of her high school class will eventually enter teaching has fallen dramatically."[23] In view of the fact that historically the percentage of female teachers has fluctuated around 80 percent, teacher talent is a concern, although somewhat mitigated by the increased availability of administrative positions to women.

Perhaps the single most harmful fallacy regarding teachers is that they should treated as members of the same profession. For instance, in collective bargaining, the kindergarten teachers, high school physics teachers, and junior high mathematics teachers are in the same bargaining unit, represented by the same union, and receive the same pay for the same college credit and years of experience. Although this practice preceded teacher union bargaining, bargaining solidified it and has rendered solutions practically impossible short of basic changes in our system of education.

To appreciate the implications of lumping all teachers together as a unitary occupational group, suppose doctors, nurses, laboratory technicians, and physical therapists were regarded as members of the same profession and the latter three groups outnumbered doctors four to one in their professional organizations. Suppose further that all the groups received the same amount of training and were paid solely on the basis of their academic credits and years of professional experiences.

Were these conditions to prevail, the latter three groups would be overeducated and doctors would be undereducated. If we wanted to raise the doctor's salaries to what doctors should be paid, we could do so only by raising the salaries of other medical staff to the same extent—a practical impossibility. Consequently, not many potential doctors would become doctors.

Now substitute high school physics teachers for doctors and early child-hood teachers for nurses, laboratory technicians, and physical therapists to get an idea of the actual situation in education. Mathematics and science teachers are far outnumbered by the others. Teacher union leaders cannot be elected to office by agreeing that mathematics and science teachers should be paid more than other teachers. Over half of our teachers are el-ementary teachers whose predecessors fought long and hard to eliminate salary differentials between elementary and secondary teachers; teacher union leaders cannot be expected to concede the differences in talent re-quired for various categories of teachers. In recent years, the imperative need to pay higher salaries to teachers whose talents are paid more outside of teaching has been widely recognized, but there is no agreement on how to overcome union opposition to this objective.

One reason is the lack of understanding of the basic problem. To un-derstand it, we have to analyze the 1961 teacher representation election in New York City and its aftermath. In the run-up to the election, the New York City Board of Education appointed University of Pennsylvania pro-fessor George Taylor to establish the rules governing the election. Taylor, perhaps the most prestigious expert on labor relations in the country, had to decide what positions would be covered, hence what teachers would be eligible to vote in the election. In labor terminology, he had to make a "unit determination."

At the time, the UFT was a comprehensive organization that included teachers from all grade levels. In contrast, there were several NEA affili-ates by grade level and subject, but no comprehensive organization. Thus the UFT argued for a single bargaining unit composed of all grade levels, but the NEA affiliates argued for three bargaining units: elementary, jun-ior high school, and senior high school. Part of the NEA's calculation was that even if it lost in the senior high school unit, it would win the election in the other two units.

Taylor ruled that there should be one comprehensive unit. When the election was held, the UFT won a decisive victory that triggered demands by large AFT locals elsewhere for representation elections in their school districts. Due to the publicity about the New York City election and Tay-lor's prestige, they also opted for comprehensive bargaining units. When state legislation authorizing teacher union bargaining was enacted in 1965 and thereafter, unit determination was resolved by bureaucrats in the state labor relations agencies, but they took for granted the desirability of comprehensive units.

This is the situation we face today. All teachers, regardless of grade level or subject, are in the same bargaining unit. Inevitably, unions bargain for what most members want, and most teachers want higher salaries for themselves, not higher salaries for subgroups whose talents pay more in noneducational employment.

The teacher unions can bargain for higher salaries for certain subgroups, but union negotiators don't like the idea. They are afraid of divisions within the union over who should be paid more and who should be paid less; hence they are disposed to keep the lid on. Also, they can cite the shortages of mathematics and science teachers to justify proposals for higher salaries.

The teacher unions did not create the problem, but they are the biggest obstacle to resolving it with one possible exception—school management. Even where unions are weak, as in the states that prohibit teacher union bargaining, school districts do not pay differentials to mathematics and science teachers. Of course, this is an indictment of school boards—one of several reasons to reconsider this overpraised governance structure.

Conceptually, there are several ways for individual districts to break the deadlock. First, school boards having severe problems recruiting mathematics and science teachers could bargain hard for adequate differentials; the fact that school boards have not adopted this solution illustrates how little power they have in dealing with the unions. Second, mathematics and science teachers could file a petition requesting a separate bargaining unit. This approach would work only in large school districts with a sizable number of mathematics and science teachers and teachers willing to say publicly that they should be paid more than their fellow teachers. Also the petition would have to be filed in a state with a labor board not afraid to overturn four decades of erroneous unit determinations. Still another possibility is for the district to contract out mathematics and science instruction to companies that could pay whatever it takes to get competent mathematics and science teachers. The district right to contract out the instruction would have to be negotiated with the union, but a determined district would normally have the right to implement the practice unilaterally if it had bargained in good faith on it through the impasse procedures and was able to withstand intensive union pressure to drop its proposed right to contract out.[24]

There are also various legislative solutions. The most feasible politically is legislative payment of differentials for mathematics and science teachers. This solution must resolve who is eligible and how much mathematics and science must be taught to receive payment. Because the solution is legislative, there would be some loss of flexibility, but this would be the easiest solution because it would not require a change in the bargaining laws.

The baby boom following World War II created a huge demand for elementary school teachers, and the demand led to higher salaries for elementary teachers, which led to more single salary schedules. Unionization and collective bargaining accelerated or solidified the change to single salary schedules, but it did much more than that—it rendered salary differentiation by grade level or subject practically impossible to achieve, at least in the short run. The short run ended a long time ago, and we now face a teacher compensation problem, a bargaining problem, a teacher education problem, and a teacher certification problem—all interrelated problems that constitute enormous obstacles to a more effective educational system. It should already be clear that these problems cannot be resolved without drastic changes in our educational system and the culture that sustains it. No coalition in sight appears cognizant of the basic problem, let alone prepared to deal with it.

In any event, the endless effort to ram majoritarian programs of teacher education down everyone's throats has resolved nothing except who has the most political support. This is precisely where the issue will be fifty years from now if the interminable arguments over teacher education continue to be resolved politically.

## NOTES

1. Arthur Bestor, *Educational Wastelands* (Urbana: University of Illinois Press, 1953); 2nd ed., 2000.

2. NCES, *Digest of Education Statistics, 2001*, NCES 2002-130 (Washington, DC: U.S. Department of Education, April 2002), 13.

3. C. Emily Feistritzer and David T. Chester, *Alternative Teacher Certification* (Washington, DC: National Center for Education Information, 2003), 12.

4. For example, see Morris M. Kleiner, "Occupational Licensing and Health Services: Who Gains and Who Loses?" Hearing conducted by the U.S. Federal Trade Commission and the U.S. Department of Justice, Washington, DC, June 10, 2003. Milton Friedman came to similar conclusions as a result of his study of medical licensure in the early 1900s.

5. See Myron Lieberman, *Understanding the Teacher Union Contract: A Citizen's Handbook* (New Brunswick, NJ: Transaction, 2000), 30–36.

6. A. M. Carr-Saunders and P. A. Wilson, *The Professions* (Oxford, UK: Clarendon, 1933), 379–380. By permission of Oxford University Press.

7. In May 2004, the Georgia Professional Standards Commission was investigating a dozen educators in five districts who had allegedly received graduate degrees from St. Regis University in Liberia—$995 for a master's and $1,500 for a doctorate. *Education Week* reported that the degrees were earned by describing their "life experiences." St. Regis is one of the diploma mills listed on the website of the Oregon Office of Degree Authorization, an independent state agency. Six teachers paid back the raises they had received and resigned.

8. U.S. Department of Education, *Improving Teacher Quality State Grants* Title II, Part A, "Non-Regulatory Guidance," www.ed.gov/programs/teacherqual/guidance.doc, accessed March 21, 2007.

9. Terry M. Moe, "The Qualified Teacher Charade," *Hoover Institution Weekly Essays*, October 13, 2004, www.hoover.org/pubaffairs/dailyreport/archive/2827866.html, accessed March 21, 2007.

10. See ASCD, "Does Highly Qualified Mean High Quality?" by Scott Emerick, Eric Hirsch, and Barnett Berry. *InfoBrief*, 39 (November 2004).

11. National Center for Alternative Certification, "Alternate Teacher Certification Successes Highlighted at NCAC 2nd Annual Conference," *Teacher Education Reports*, 27, no. 4, www.teach-now.org/newsdisp.cfm?newsid=62#1, accessed March 26, 2007.

12. The NCAC website is www.teach-now.org.

13. For my role in the establishment of NBPTS and my later criticisms of it, see Myron Lieberman, *The Future of Public Education* (Chicago: University of Chicago Press, 1960), 259–270; "Educational Specialty Boards: A Way Out of the Merit Pay Morass," *Phi Delta Kappan* (October 1985), 103–107; "Take the $25 Million and Run: The Case of the National Board for Professional Teaching Standards," *Government Union Review* (Winter 1990), 1–23.

14. American Board for Certification of Teacher Excellence (ABCTE), *A Higher Standard* (Washington, DC: ABCTE, May 11, 2006), 4. *A Higher Standard* includes demographic, educational, and geographic data on candidates for the Passport.

15. ABCTE, *A Higher Standard*.

16. ABCTE, *Prospective Candidates*, www.abcte.org/node/734, accessed February 18, 2006, 3.

17. ABCTE, *Prospective Candidates*, 4.

18. National Council for Accreditation of Teacher Education (NCATE), *Professional Standards for the Accreditation of Schools, Colleges, and Departments of Education, 2006 Edition* (Washington: NCATE, 2006), www.ncate.org/documents/standards/unit_stnds_2006.pdf, accessed March 26, 2007. On June 16, 2006, NCATE dropped "professional dispositions" as a requirement, but educational institutions were free to continue the requirement. The impact of NCATE's action on institutional requirements was not clear when this book was published. See NCATE, "A Statement from NCATE on Professional Dispositions, June 16, 2006, at www.ncate.org/public/0616_MessageAWise.asp?ch=150, accessed March 26, 2007.

19. James M. Smith and Connie Ruhl-Smith, "Corporate Answers to Public School Problems: A Call for Counteraction," *Education Leadership Review* (Winter 2004), 1–7.

20. Smith and Ruhl-Smith, "Corporate Answers," 1–7. See also Rita Kramer, *Ed School Follies* (New York: Free Press, 1991) for several examples of education courses that are blatant propaganda.

21. *Equity and Excellent Education*, brochure distributed by Routledge, a member of the Taylor & Francis Group, www.taylorfrancis.com.

22. Stanley Rothman, S. Robert Lichter, and Neil Nevitte, "Politics and Professional Advancement among College Faculty," *The Forum*, 3, no. 2 (2005), 1–16.

23. Sean P. Corcoran, William N. Evans, and Robert M. Schwab, "Women, the Labor Market, and the Declining Relative Quality of Teachers." *Journal of Policy Analysis and Management*, 23 (3). March 7, 2004, 449–470.

24. See *Kenmore Education Association v. Kenmore Public School District*, No. 28, 2006 ND36, 717N 2d, 603, 2006.

# 5

## The Real Cost of Public Education

$A$ great deal of attention is paid to the academic outcomes of public education—what they are, what they should be, how the outcomes in the United States compare to the outcomes in other nations, the comparisons between the states and ethnic and income groups, and so on. Much less attention is paid to the costs of education, which are often a fatal weakness in reform proposals and education policy generally. This chapter intends to identify the major gaps in the estimates of the costs of public education and alert readers to the importance of costs in evaluating reforms proposals and education policies generally. Although discussion focuses on dollar costs, it is not intended to deny the importance of other costs that may outweigh the financial ones in various situations.

### THE IMPORTANCE OF ACCURATE COST DATA

Charter schools underscore the importance of accuracy regarding costs. Legislation on the subject sometimes provides that the charter schools shall be paid a certain percentage of the per-pupil cost in public schools. If the cost of public education has been underestimated, the charter schools do not receive the amounts intended by the legislatures, and their success or failure is likely to be mischaracterized. Similarly, ignoring or minimizing the real costs of a policy is often essential to its political success.[1] In short, cognizance of costs is a pervasive issue that has the potential to affect an extremely broad range of educational policies and decisions.

In practice, the reported costs of education vary widely, according to the assumptions made by the estimator. A striking illustration of this point emerged during the 2004 and 2006 election campaigns. Democrats asserted repeatedly that the Bush administration had failed to provide the funds needed to implement the NCLB Act. Republicans just as vehemently asserted that this was not true. In Ohio, state superintendent of education Susan T. Zelman solicited reviews of a study of the costs of implementing NCLB by consultants employed by the Department of Education at the request of the Ohio legislature. In a report to the legislature on what the consultants had to say, Zelman commented that

> two believed that the analysis substantially underestimates the costs of implementing NCLB. Three believe that the analysis substantially overstates the costs. Three believe that the assumptions and degree of speculation on which the report is based substantially undermine the accuracy of the cost estimates. Eight of the ten experts believe that the analysis was hampered by the assumption that current state and federal revenue will continue to be used as it has been used in the past. . . . The estimated cost of student intervention represents 93 percent of the total identified. . . . Eight of the ten experts raised concerns about the appropriateness of this cost in the light of the lack of research to support the efficacy of the identified intervention strategies.[2]

Subsequently, Vanderbilt professor James W. Guthrie, one of the ten consultants, sought to explain the divergence in the estimates. Some analysts assumed that none of the current costs could be redirected to compliance with NCLB and, also, that all current costs were inviolate. Some analysts assumed that the annual salary increments for teachers could be used to some extent to cover the NCLB costs; other analysts made no assumption of this kind.[3] Guthrie urged development of a nonpartisan cost model that would enable observers to ascertain the costs of implementing NCLB, but such a model would be "nonpartisan" only among a small group of academics. Interest groups would quickly ascertain whether they would be better or worse off under the model, and the ultimate outcome would be the end of the nonpartisan model.

In 1987, Eric A. Hanushek published a study that concludes that there is no consistent relationship between expenditures and student achievement.[4] Hanushek's study was challenged on both technical and policy grounds, but it led to a more critical attitude toward arguments that more money would lead to higher levels of student achievement.[5] However, the fact that there is no consistent relationship between expenditures and student achievement does not justify negative conclusions about specific increases, which should be assessed on their merits.

## COST COMPARISONS

Most comparisons of the per-pupil costs in public and private schools are flawed because they leave out costs that would affect the results. For instance, comparisons of the average per-pupil cost in public and private schools may fail to take account of the fact that most special education students, whose costs are much higher than those of regular students, are in the public schools. At the same time, proponents of public education ignore the fact that many private schools specialize in educating handicapped children under contract with public school systems. Grade level differences are frequently ignored. Inasmuch as it usually costs a great deal more to educate secondary than elementary pupils, comparisons that ignore this factor are tilted in favor of the school systems that have a higher proportion of elementary students.

The variations in estimating the costs of education come to a head when the issue is the cost of achieving improved outcomes. For example, how much would it cost to reduce the achievement gap? Twenty states do not collect district-level data in ways that would make it possible to answer the question.[6] Without such a breakdown, it is extremely difficult to say how much districts would have to pay for a certain level of improvement.

In practice, educational finance experts have utilized four different ways of estimating the cost of providing an "adequate" education:

- The "professional judgment" model. Add up what the experts say is required for various activities needed for "adequacy."
- The "successful school" model. Ascertain what successful (based on test scores) schools spend and assume that other districts should be able

to achieve similar results. However, even when adjusted for differences among the student populations, this approach is not very reliable.

- The "evidence-based" model. In this model, experts ascertain the costs of successful practices and estimate the costs if the practices are utilized in all schools.
- The "cost function" model. This model is based upon the relationships between spending and achievement. After taking account of differences in pupil and district characteristics, an estimate is made of the costs of bringing pupils to specified levels of achievement.[7]

Hanushek, an educational economist, has shown that all of these approaches to the cost of an "adequate education" are flawed beyond repair. The reasons cited by Hanushek include the following:

- The absence of agreement on the meaning of an "adequate education."
- The lack of knowledge on how school funds are actually spent.
- The assumption that current spending patterns are the most efficient.
- The failure to take account of external factors that affect achievement; changes in the economy, labor markets, student populations, demographic factors, and efficiency-enhancing innovations are not factored into the estimates of the cost of an adequate education.
- The fact that the estimates are shaped to meet client objectives and, in some cases, the interests of the "experts" on school finance.

Although he does not mention the fact, Hanushek's analysis is a strong argument for a for-profit sector in education. In such a sector, there would be much more concern about tracking how funds for education are actually spent, a point applicable to most situations in which private investors are responsible for providing services for profit.

The upshot is that experts on school finance cannot legitimately say, "If you spend d dollars more on remedial instruction (for example), there will be improvement by a factor of y in subject z." And since the experts cannot say, "If you spend x more, you will get y more improvement in reading (for example)," the controversies over how much should be spent for K–12 education are really resolved by the balance of power among the interest groups active on the issue, not the persuasive force of their arguments.

The lesson to be learned here is fundamental. What public education costs, and what system changes would cost, is based upon untested assumptions that may differ a great deal.

## COSTS AND POLLS

Both liberals and conservatives rely heavily on polls to shape their strategy and tactics. In practice, most polls imply that government policies are cost free. For example, polls frequently ask respondents whether class size should be reduced; not surprisingly, the answers are overwhelmingly favorable. A 1997 NBC News/*Wall Street Journal* national poll found that 70 percent of adults believe reductions in class size would lead to big improvements in education.[8] When the cost figures are cited in the question, the support for class size reduction dissipates. Robert Weissberg asked 550 respondents, "How much would you be willing to pay for reducing class size to 15?" Thirty-one percent refused to pay anything, and only about one in four were willing to pay the official but underestimated cost of such a reduction.[9] Even this response overestimates the support for reducing class size to fifteen because it assumes no change in other demands for tax support. For instance, how much taxpayers are willing to pay for an educational reform is likely to be affected by their views on spending for national defense or health care, both of which will require substantially more tax support in the future.

At one time or another, most school boards must decide whether to provide a service by its own employees or employ a contractor to provide the service. Transportation and food service are the most frequent examples of contracting out, but the issue arises in security, legal advice, forecasting enrollment, board representation in collective bargaining, maintenance, custodial service, after-school instruction, and special education — even regular classroom instruction in some cases. Cost is always a potential issue in these situations; although not the only issue, it is frequently decisive, especially when the quality of service does not clearly distinguish the alternatives. Consequently, if the cost of providing the service by district employees is substantially over- or underestimated, the decisions will probably be the wrong ones.

In 2002, Florida voters approved an initiative that reduced class size in kindergarten and grades one through three. The initiative said nothing about the cost. The fact that the Democratic nominee for governor who supported the initiative could not give an estimate of the cost during a televised debate was a factor in his defeat, but the initiative carried by a 52–48 percent margin. Had the cost been shown, it is highly doubtful that the initiative would have carried. As it turned out, the initiative cost almost $1 billion of the state's $15.2 billion education budget in the first two years it went into effect. Needless to say, other groups paid from the education budget were not thrilled by this outcome.[10]

The cost data on public education are compiled by the National Center for Education Statistics (NCES), a unit in the U.S. Department of Education (USED). Using forms that have been refined over the years, NCES and the Bureau of the Census in the Department of Commerce elicit cost information, especially from the state departments of education. The latter get most of their information from school districts. Two examples illustrate the dubious accuracy of information provided this way.

The states provide funds to local school districts based upon the number of students who attend school in the districts; the more students, the more state aid. For this reason, the states usually audit the attendance figures submitted by school districts. An audit by the state controller in California revealed that the attendance figures submitted by the Los Angeles Unified School District (LAUSD) had erroneously increased its state aid by $30 million a year from 1996–1997 to 2001. In August 2001, the district was required to return $120 million to the state.[11] The Los Angeles overcount resulted in inaccurate cost figures at the local, state, and federal levels for four years.

In its reports to the media, NCES does not factor in the costs of capital outlay, debt service, and interest in computing costs per pupil. The rationale for the omissions is that the citizenry wants to know how school districts vary in their operating costs. Capital outlay, debt service, and interest vary widely and are allegedly not a good basis for cost comparisons. For example, a rapidly growing suburban district may incur heavy per-pupil expenditures for capital outlay compared to an urban district that is closing down schools; the fact that the former has much higher costs for capital outlay does not tell us anything about its operating efficiency. NCES has the information on the omitted items; it just does not include them with the operating costs in the estimates released to the public. The rationale is that the citizenry can get the omitted figures from NCES and add them to the operating costs if the total cost is their objective.

Although well understood by professionals in school finance, the references to the per-pupil cost of public education are interpreted by the citizenry as the total cost of it. Lay citizens have no way of knowing what is omitted, especially when it could easily be included with safeguards against improper use or interpretation. The absence of attention to the complete cost is understandable. Such attention would result in substantial cost escalations and would render it more difficult to argue that education is underfunded.

In any event, what is the amount of the omissions? At one extreme, districts have all the schools they need and have paid for all of the borrowing costs needed to pay for them. Their only infrastructure costs are for deferred maintenance, an item that is frequently omitted from district budgets. At the other extreme, there are districts in which the costs of capital outlay, debt service, and interest exceed the operating costs. Obviously, most districts fall somewhere between these two extremes, and some of the differences are completely justified. This chapter, however, focuses on underestimates that are present in a large number of school districts.

## UNFUNDED PENSION COSTS

Except for school districts utilizing defined contribution plans, school districts use defined benefit plans for their employee retirement systems. These plans work as follows: The teachers and the school districts, or the legislatures as the case may be, each contribute an amount that will ensure the funds required to meet the state's obligations to retiring teachers. The pension plans promise to pay retired teachers according to certain formulas, such as 75 percent of the teacher's average salary in the last three years before retirement. The states usually match or exceed the teacher contributions; also, the states set the minimum number of years before the pensions are vested. The states must also estimate how much they will be required to pay teachers who will retire in the future. The contributions of the teacher and the state are invested, and the returns on the investments plus the current contributions are expected to be sufficient to meet the states' obligations as teachers retire. To summarize, the retirement systems have three components: (1) the contributions from previous years' earnings and from employers, (2) the gains from the investment of the contributions, and (3) forfeitures from teachers who withdraw from the system before their retirement benefits are vested.

The critical discretionary element in this system is the expected return on the investments. Suppose a state anticipates a return of 7 percent, but the state revenues have declined precipitously, rendering it difficult for the state to make its contribution to the retirement fund. In these situations, the shortfall is sometimes solved by increasing the expected rate of return on the investments, whether or not the increase is justified. This exacerbates the long-range economic problem, but by forcing future legislators and government officials to take the unpopular measures to solve the problem, legislators achieve the short-range solution that meets their political needs.

The implications for cost issues are profound. Teachers are paid partly in cash and partly in promises by the state to pay retirement benefits according to an agreed-upon formula. When the retirement fund is underfunded, the state's financial obligations increase; there is a difference between paying someone $50,000 a year and paying someone $50,000 plus a commitment to pay the shortfall in state contributions to the teacher retirement fund. In practice, the commitment to pay the shortfall is not counted as part of the teacher's compensation. The amount of the shortfall is not counted, but the taxpayers have to pay it eventually. When they do, it is really a current expenditure for services in previous years.

## REMEDIAL EDUCATION IN INSTITUTIONS OF HIGHER EDUCATION

"Remedial education" in higher education refers to education in basic skills that are supposed to be taught and learned in K–12 education. Except for immigrants who may be literate in a language other than English, students in remedial education are mainly young adults getting another chance to learn to read and write and to learn simple arithmetical computations. In effect, remedial education is elementary and secondary education provided by institutions of higher education.

Many institutions of higher education try to avoid the stigma associated with remedial education by utilizing course titles that are not associated with it. Furthermore, it is extremely difficult to estimate the overhead costs of remedial education, such as more classrooms, more faculty, and more admissions personnel. Also, a significant amount of remedial education is provided by the private sector from government funds. The upshot is that there are several ways to estimate the costs of remedial education but none that is comprehensive or authoritative.[12]

NCES conducted an extensive survey of remedial education in 1995. The survey focused on courses in reading, writing, and arithmetic, courses that are widely accepted as remedial. The results of the survey include the following:

- Seventy-eight percent of the institutions of higher education that enrolled freshmen offered at least one remedial course in reading, writing, or mathematics.
- Ninety-nine percent of public two-year institutions offered remedial courses in three subject areas.
- Twenty-nine percent of incoming freshmen enrolled in at least one remedial course.
- About half of the public two-year institutions provided remedial services to local businesses and industries, whereas only 5 percent of the other institutions offered such services.
- Only about one in four institutions reported any limits on the length of time students could take remedial courses.
- Twenty-five percent of all institutions offered remedial courses in subjects other than reading, writing, and mathematics.[13]

The NCES survey did not inquire into the costs, which were obviously considerable. In a study of the costs of remedial education, David W. Breneman concludes that 2.25 percent of the state funds for higher education in Maryland and 1.5 percent of the costs in Texas were for remedial education. Utilizing these percentages, the costs nationally would have ranged from $900 million to $1 billion.[14]

Note that although remedial education in higher education is intended to help students who attended K–12 schools in the past, it is a cost of

K–12 education in the year in which it is made; the date is based upon the time of instruction, not the grade level of the students. In any case, estimates of the costs will vary according to whatever assumptions are made on the following issues:

- The costs of remedial education in courses not explicitly labeled as such.
- The costs of technology to compensate for employees' lack of basic skills.
- The costs of remedying work habits and attitudes that should have been learned in precollege education.
- The extent to which college-level work includes courses normally taken by high school students.
- Expenditures by vocational schools due to inability to distinguish expenditure for teaching basic skills from expenditures for job-specific skills.
- The capital costs of providing remedial education.
- The incidence of the failure of remedial education.[15]

A study of remedial education in Michigan on the basis of different assumptions on the above matters resulted in estimates from $311 million to $1.148 billion annually with an average of $601 million, not counting private costs.[16]

There is a trend to shift remedial education to junior colleges and branch campuses to reduce their costs. Consequently, even if there is no major change in the number of college students taking remedial courses, the costs should be less in the future, but remedial education in higher education will continue to be a significant cost of elementary and secondary education that is not included in government estimates of the cost of public education.

## EDUCATIONAL RESEARCH

School districts rarely spend for educational research that has the potential for improving education elsewhere. This is understandable; school districts are not for profit, and taxpayers are not likely to approve research expenditures if other school districts would be the main beneficiaries. This is why the educational community recommends federal support for educational research that is intended to have wide applicability. As chapter 3 points out, this recommendation is basically flawed, but at this point, let us try to estimate the costs of research on public education that are not counted in government statistics on the subject.

As pointed out on page 60, a 1998 NCES study indicated that approximately 27,000 full-time professors of education in the United States devoted 11.1 percent of their time to educational research. When one considers the cost of their time, support personnel, facilities, supplies, and equipment, the total costs of their educational research probably reaches billions annually.[17] Although the overwhelming share of their work is devoted to public education, the costs are categorized as costs of higher education.

Similarly, the costs of teacher education are not identified or estimated in government statistics on the cost of public education. This is contrary to the practice in other occupations. When a private employer provides entry-level training for future employees, the costs are routinely categorized as costs of the employer. Similarly, when our armed forces provide basic and specialized training for military personnel, the costs are included in the budget of the Department of Defense. This is not the case in public education; the costs of training future teachers and providing in-service education are carried on the budgets of institutions of higher education. Some of these costs are recouped by tuition from future teachers and teachers in service, and some are absorbed by private institutions of higher education, but the taxpayer costs are nevertheless very substantial on any reasonable basis for resolving the accounting issues.

## OVERHEAD COSTS

In private schools, the costs of fund-raising are included in the costs of school officials and support personnel. Decisions must be made about how much must be raised and by what means—tuition, philanthropy, government assistance, fund-raisers, denominational support, and so on. Public education faces a similar problem. Legislatures and school boards must decide how to fund public education. School district officials must plan their activities in the light of budgets that receive funds from a variety of sources. Nevertheless, there is a fundamental difference in the two situations.

Suppose a state legislature adopts a program of state aid that allocates 40 percent of $10 billion in state revenues to public education. The legislature has debated the mix of state sales and income taxes to raise the funds for public education. If public education did not exist, neither would the legislative costs of raising funds for it. Whereas the state legislative costs are not included as a cost of education, the fund-raising costs of private schools are included as part of their cost. Even if the local school board has the power to impose taxes to pay for the local share of the total costs, the costs of raising the state and federal share of school revenues are not counted as a cost of public education.

The same point applies to other state government overhead services. The state treasurers receive and disburse revenues for school districts. The state auditors audit school district financial statements. State labor relations agencies resolve disputes in school districts according to regulations governing collective bargaining in public education. Generally speaking, every state agency that serves or regulates two or more state services, one of which is public education, will devote a substantial share of its resources to public education.

How are the overhead costs to be estimated? The simplest way is to multiply the overhead cost of state government by the percentage derived from direct cost of public education. If the cost of state services amounts to $10 billion, and public education is one-half of the costs of state services, then one-half of the overhead costs should be attributed to education. This is the way a business would allocate the overhead costs of functions that apply to two or more divisions of the company.

For instance, in FY 1998–1999 the states spent $144 billion for "government administration"—a category that includes financial administration, judicial and legal expenditures, general public buildings, and other costs of government administration.[18] The National Association of State Budget Officers estimated that K–12 spending was 22.2 percent of all state spending.[19] Utilizing these figures, the conclusion is that $32 billion should be added to the cost of K–12 education for 1998–1999. The $32 billion could be reduced by 10 percent because the base includes the cost of regulating private education.

One objection to the preceding suggestion runs as follows: If there were no system of public education, there would still be a state legislature and a state judicial system. Therefore it is illogical to allocate a percentage of their costs to education. However, this way of looking at the matter leads to the untenable conclusion that the overhead costs should be zero. Each state service could argue that the state cost would be the same even if the service did not exist. Except for most denominational schools, the costs of decision making in private schools are included in the time that school officials devote to them. In other words, the costs of overhead services in private schools are included in the salaries and fringe benefits of private school personnel.

Not so in the public sector. For example, whereas the officials of a private school decide its graduation requirements, the requirements in public schools are often resolved by the state legislatures. Whereas teacher rights, such as the right to bargain collectively, are set by the state legislatures, private schools generally resolve the employment issues on their own time and resources.

The costs of all such legislative decisions about education are included and paid from legislative, not educational, budgets. Therefore, if we wish to know the real cost of public education, we should include its legislative costs. These include not only legislators and staff time, but also the costs of hearings, printing, communications, and other embedded legislative costs. The same principle applies to Congress when it deals with federal legislation on public education.

In private education, prices play a critically important role that affects school–parent relations. In public education, however, the consumers pay for education through a myriad of local, state, and federal taxes; nobody, not even specialists in educational finance, can say with any confidence who pays how much for public education. This is a huge strategic advantage for proponents of public education. If taxpayers don't know how much they are paying for something, it is difficult for them to argue that they are paying too much for it.

## DISINCENTIVE COSTS

Experts on public finance agree that taxes should not affect either the production or consumption of goods and services, but this principle is frequently violated.[20] A dramatic example of the disincentive cost of taxes occurred in 1990, when Congress imposed steep taxes on yachts.

As a result, the sale of yachts dropped precipitously. The yacht-building industry went into a steep decline, and workers in the industry had to apply for unemployment compensation as well as other welfare programs. The yacht tax was repealed in 1993; the total benefits were worth far less than the total costs.

James Payne suggests an interesting comparison to illustrate the importance of disincentive costs. Suppose every family has one child and pays $5,000 to have the child educated in a private school. Now consider an identical community except that each family pays $5,000 in taxes to support a system of public schools. Our first reaction might be that the two communities are alike economically, but Payne points out that there is an important difference. In the first community, shoemaker Jones has to earn enough income to pay for his child's education. This gives Jones an additional incentive to work. If there is any doubt about affordability, Jones will work harder, perhaps making ten extra pairs of shoes a month, to ensure enrollment of his child in the school of Jones's choice.

Now consider what happens in the tax-funded system. Smith doesn't have any motive to work harder to ensure his ability to send his child to his school of choice. Furthermore, Smith will be paying a tax to send all children to school—a tax that is not levied in the community in which private schooling holds sway. If the tax is based on Smith's production of shoes, the effect is to reduce Smith's incentives to work while reducing his after-tax income. Liberals tend to ignore these disincentive effects, but their presence among many taxpayers is undeniable.

Disincentive costs are the negative effects of taxes on work and investment. Studies of the disincentive costs of taxes are relatively new, but there is broad agreement that the disincentive effects vary according to worker attitudes and the work being done. For example, the disincentive effects of taxes on labor income was 28.7 percent; it was 21.8 percent for low-wage married men, and 58.1 percent for low-wage married women, who are more likely to quit work as taxes take an increasing share of their income.[21]

The disincentive effects on capital, such as the capital gains tax, are higher because capital is such a mobile factor of production; capital can leave when highly taxed, but labor usually cannot. Recent studies tend to show larger disincentive effects than earlier ones, but the topic seems to be pursued mainly by conservative economists.

# PHILANTHROPIC CONTRIBUTIONS
## AS A COST OF EDUCATION

In 2003, philanthropic contributions to K–12 education exceeded contributions to higher education for the first time, $1.23 billion to $1.12 billion. These totals reflected a reversal in the pattern of philanthropic contributions, which had been twice as much for higher education as for K–12 education.[22]

At a common sense level, gifts are not considered to be "costs"; if someone gives you two tickets to the Super Bowl, you would not ordinarily say that they cost you whatever the donor paid for them. Nevertheless, if the donor gave them to you to strengthen a business relationship, the donor could claim the cost of the tickets as a business expense. From an economic point of view, the cost of something consists of the resources used to make or buy the item, and the cost of education consists of the resources used to provide education.

This important point is often overlooked in education. Looking at the amounts appropriated for educational research, one might conclude that the problem is inadequate government funding; however, philanthropic contributions for educational research may rule out this explanation. Similarly, the contributions of PTAs and PTOs, as well as companies and company foundations, must be considered to be "costs" for certain purposes.[23]

## THE ECONOMICS OF "GOOD SCHOOLS"

The public school establishment constantly asserts that good schools are uppermost when parents must relocate. This may be true when individual families move, but the quality of schools is seldom a factor in plant location. Consider recent decisions on where to locate new car manufacturing companies:

- Spring Hill, TN (only unionized plant on the list)*: Saturn
- Georgetown, KY: Toyota
- Decherd, TN: Nissan
- Canton, MS: Nissan
- Greer, SC: BMW

- Smyrna, TN: Nissan
- Lincoln, AL: Honda
- Montgomery, AL: Hyundai
- Vance, AL: Mercedes-Benz

An article in the *Wall Street Journal* shows the wishful thinking associated with the idea that plant location accords a high priority to good schools. In 1993, Mercedes-Benz built its first U.S. plant in Alabama, a state that ranked second lowest in the number of adults that finish high school. The state offered incentives worth $169,000 per job that Mercedes agreed to provide. Honda (2001), Toyota (2003), and Hyundai (2005) also built plants in Alabama after Mercedes and also received substantial tax breaks for doing so.

Alabama outspent twenty states in the concessions it made to Mercedes. These concessions included paying only $100 for a plant site purchased by Tuscaloosa County, a tax concession that allowed Mercedes to pay for plant construction with funds that would otherwise have gone to taxes, and building a $35 million training center. In 2000, Mississippi outbid Alabama for a Nissan plant with $295 million in incentives for the company. In a lengthy article that described how Alabama became a major car-producing state, there was no mention of good schools being one of the attractions.[24] In short, good schools are a result more than a cause of plant location.

Disincentive costs, especially the cost of collecting taxes for education, are costs that are typically absent from government statistics on the cost of education. Public school partisans have ignored the issue, thereby leading them to exaggerate the net benefits of funding public education.[25]

We can see the importance of disincentive costs by comparing income taxes to property taxes. Property can be defined precisely, ownership can be identified easily, and opportunities for tax evasion can be kept to a minimum. In contrast, income taxes are problematic at every step of the process. The costs of compliance with income taxes is much greater than the costs of compliance with property taxes; on this issue, property taxes are clearly preferable.

Property taxes raise almost half of all local revenues for public education. Of course, the percentages vary from state to state and within states, but the cost factors for property taxes are quite similar from state to state.

First, there is an assessment of the property with a right to appeal to an equalization board, by whatever its title. In addition to the costs of assessments, there are costs associated with notifying property owners of the assessments and dealing with their complaints. In a few cases, the assessments are appealed to a state board of equalization or to the courts.

There must also be an agency that sends out notices of taxes due, records payments, and follows up on delinquencies. Typically, these are functions of the county treasurer's office, which usually carries out other functions that cannot be charged to education. However, taxpayers pay some of the costs of fund-raising for education. These compliance costs are incurred at four points when taxpayers question or challenge the taxes that they are required to pay:

- The taxpayer may discuss the tax with friends or with the assessor's office.
- The taxpayer appeals to the board of equalization. This requires preparation; appeals based on a generalized complaint that the claimant's taxes are too high do not bring about remedial action. Taxpayers frequently employ legal or accounting help at this stage. Depending upon the amounts involved, the taxpayer's time and costs of professional assistance may be a significant amount.
- The taxpayer's normal response to the notice of taxes due is paying the taxes. This may require only the time required to write and mail the amount due—less than one hour, in most cases.
- Finally, the pursuit of delinquencies involves significant costs, not in every case, but in enough cases to push the average cost well over $1,000. When taxpayers are not successful in efforts to reduce their property taxes, they may be able to arrange special payment plans with the appropriate county office.

Payne's study of the costs of tax collection in Spokane County, Washington, and Bonner County, Idaho, found the costs of compliance with property taxes in Spokane County were 2.96 percent of the revenues collected; in Bonner County, Idaho, the compliance costs were 6.31 percent of the amounts collected.[26] Payne's estimates are not necessarily typical, but they present the kinds of costs that must be included in studies of the disincentive effects of property taxes for public education. Note also that the costs of raising money for public education are, for the most part, not included in its costs but are included in the costs of private schools.

## LOTTERY REVENUES

Although lotteries were utilized early in our history, every state prohibited lotteries from 1900 to 1964, when New Hampshire adopted a lottery as the way to finance public education. Since 1964, thirty-seven states and the District of Columbia have adopted lotteries. In 1997, gross state lottery revenues exceeded $35 billion, and net lottery revenues exceeded $12 billion; however, only about half the states allocate some or all of their lottery revenues to public education.

Lottery revenues highlight the importance of the fund-raising costs of public education. In addition to the extremely low net return from lotteries, they are subject to the following criticisms:

- Lottery revenues are unstable.
- Lottery revenues often have a negative impact on economic growth, hence on revenues from other sources of public funds.
- When lottery funds are earmarked for education, they replace, not supplement, other revenues for education.
- Noneducation services benefit more than education from lottery revenues. The reason is that lotteries for education tend to give other services a higher priority in the distribution of general funds.
- Low-income citizens provide a disproportionate share of the resources from lotteries; hence the lotteries are not consistent with a progressive tax system.
- Lotteries require extensive administrative and advertising costs, all of which may lead to a larger state bureaucracy.

In short, no other way of collecting revenues for public education costs as much per dollar of net revenue. In Florida, the legislature requires that 50 percent of gross lottery revenues be awarded as prizes and not over 12 percent be used for administration. Not surprisingly, only about $11 billion out of gross lottery revenues of $32.1 billion became available to fund public services. Inasmuch as lotteries are a minor source of revenue for public education, there is considerable sentiment in education for scrapping them altogether.

## THE ECONOMICS OF EMPTY SCHOOLS

The public school establishment argues that schools for profit can flourish only by cutting back on teacher salaries, supplies, transportation, lunch programs, and courses and services that students need. A factual situation that arose recently in the District of Columbia provides a different perspective on the issue.

In 2000, the District of Columbia took control of thirty-eight school buildings previously owned by the D.C. Board of Education. Several buildings had been vacant or underutilized for years. The schools were not mentioned in the D.C. school system's financial report, although charter schools and various companies wanted to rent or purchase the buildings. Only two of seven charter schools that applied for space in empty schools were allowed such use.[27]

Note the contrast with a for-profit company in this situation. A company would not operate year after year without selling or leasing empty buildings if it had no plans to utilize the buildings. The vacant schools had materialized as a result of middle-class families moving to the suburbs, and there was virtually no likelihood of their returning with school children any time soon. School districts can get by with their failure to generate any revenue from their empty buildings; a private company would promptly convert the empty buildings into sources of revenue. Washington is not the only school district to ignore the financial implications of empty schools; many large school districts with dwindling pupil enrollments have also failed to generate any revenues from their empty schools.

## THE IMPLICATIONS OF TAX CREDITS AND TAX DEDUCTIONS

Direct expenditures for the education of pupils from low-income or no-income families is the political establishment's response to the low achievement levels of children from low-income families. Title I of the Elementary and Secondary Act of 1965 has received the largest federal appropriation for the education of pupils from low-income families, reaching $12.7 billion in FY 2005. Supposedly, this demonstrates the federal government's resolve to help pupils living in poverty.

The fact is, however, that if we take into account tax deductibility and tax credits, it is apparent that our tax policies for K–12 education provide greater dollar benefits to the upper-income strata than to pupils from low-income families. For instance, property taxes are deductible from federal income taxes and most, if not all, state taxes as well. A taxpayer in the 28 percent category who has a $1,000 property tax credit saves about $380. This benefit and others like it go mainly to upper-income taxpayers. The benefits of tax deductions and tax credits are probably greater than the direct federal subsidies for education.[28]

Tax deductions and tax credits for K–12 schooling complicate issues relating to who pays for it. Actually, we can distinguish four taxpayer categories relating to taxpayer support for schooling:

1. Taxpayers who have no children pay for public schooling only. (This is debatable because taxpayers pay for some of the costs of private schooling, like food stamps and Internet services, paid for all schools from general tax revenues.) Some analysts would add property tax exemptions to the list of taxpayer subsidies to private schools.
2. Taxpayers who have no children receive tax credits or tax deductions for contribution to private schooling.
3. Taxpayers with one or more children in private schools receive no tax deductions or tax credits for their private schooling.
4. Taxpayers with one or more children in private schools receive tax credits or tax deductions for the expenses of, or contributions to, the education of their own or other people's children. Tax rates and amounts exempt from taxation vary from state to state.

The complexity of the data on these variations and changing tax rates render it difficult to say how much taxpayers with children in private schools actually pay for their children's education or for the education of pupils in public schools.[29] Both liberals and conservatives are caught in severe conflicts of interest over the indirect but real costs. The public school establishment cannot raise the equity issue because it would shock virtually everyone to discover the real government cost of K–12 education. If public schools are criticized because they cannot educate pupils at

$10,000 per pupil, imagine the outcry if citizens discovered the real cost per pupil to government is much more than the government figures. For all of its rhetoric about "equity" and the "equality of educational opportunity," the public school lobby has more to lose than gain by raising the cost implications of tax deductions and tax credits; without tax credits or deductibility, taxpayer resistance to taxes for public education might well become too difficult to overcome. Consequently, the public school establishment does not raise the issue except when assistance for private schooling is involved.

Conservatives are similarly conflicted, but for different reasons. Any criticism of the tax credits and tax deductions for education expenses would be politically disastrous in conservative communities. Conservative legislators are trying to add to tax credits and deductions; a conservative could hardly risk asserting that fewer tax credits and tax deductions are desirable.

## THE UNCOUNTED COSTS OF POLITICAL, SOCIAL, CULTURAL, AND PROFESSIONAL CONFLICT

The costs of public education are greatly understated by the failure to take account of the huge private and public expenditures necessitated by majoritarian determinations of education policy. Consider a state or school district that includes the following organizations and interest groups:

- Democrats, Republicans, Libertarians, Greens
- Whites, blacks, Hispanics, Asians, Native Americans, Middle Easterners
- Christians, Jews, Muslims, Buddhists, secularists, atheists
- Business, taxpayer, and labor organizations
- PTAs
- Social issues organizations such as Focus on the Family; Concerned Women for America; Eagle Forum; People for the American Way; Planned Parenthood; Gay, Lesbian, and Straight Education Network; National Organization for Women
- NEA, AFT, unions of support personnel
- Organizations of school administrators, school boards, subject matter fields

- Labor unions and companies
- Environmental and senior organizations

These organizations and interest groups are active on scores of issues, such as

- School drug and safety measures
- Grading policy
- Graduation requirements
- Testing policy
- ROTC in the schools
- Policies on in-service courses
- State and national standards

- Bilingual education
- Sex education
- Social promotion
- Student dress codes
- Athletic eligibility
- Bus service
- Parent visits

How much or how many of these controversies would there be if parents could choose the schools, public or private, that educate their children? To be sure, some conflict would remain, but most of it would lose its raison d'être in a full-fledged school choice plan. Many parents claim the right to direct the education of their children; very few claim the right to direct the education of other parents' children. Nobody has added up the costs of these conflicts, but they involve private as well as government expenditures at the state and federal as well as the local levels. They include

- Political activity at the local, state, and federal levels
- Litigation at the local, state, and federal levels, often with intermediate levels as well
- Support of or opposition to political candidates due to their positions on educational issues
- Publications (articles, books, magazines, other print media)
- Radio and television programs on the conflicts
- The costs of academic and legislative and judicial resources devoted to school choice issues that would not exist under universal vouchers
- The costs of support and facilities for academics whose teaching fields include avoidable conflict under school choice
- The costs of promoting the views of individuals and organizations on educational issues, for example, People for the American Way,

Americans United for Separation of Church and State, Focus on the Family, Heritage Foundation, and liberal and conservative foundations that spend huge amounts annually opposing each other's agendas

- Legislative and judicial costs at all levels of government
- The share of dues and contributions paid to organizations active on educational issues (NEA, AFT, NCEA, ADL, AJC, NCEA)

Additional cost streams could be cited, but the ones listed may be sufficient to illustrate the huge costs of conflict in public education. Most of these costs are wasted in the sense that they do not bring about any improvement in education. Of course, the antagonists usually claim that educational improvement will occur, or education will not deteriorate, if their views are adopted, and a group may occasionally be justified in making this claim. Nonetheless, public education is an extremely inefficient system because it relies on lobbying instead of research and development to achieve improvement in results or costs. Unfortunately, funds spent for or against legislative changes are not likely to result in higher achievement levels or lower costs.

## NOTES

1. For example, legislative approval of excessive public employee pensions is often due to underestimates of their costs. Similarly, school boards have sometimes approved severance payments for unused sick leave. As a result, teacher utilization of sick leave declined precipitously, and the payouts were akin to golden parachutes.

2. Chester E. Finn Jr., "Is NCLB an Unfunded Mandate?" *The Education Gadfly*, February 12, 2004, 2–3; Alan Richard, "Rising Costs Predated Federal Law, Some Experts Argue," *Education Week*, February 4, 2004, 1, 22.

3. James W. Guthrie, "'No Child' Price Tag," *Education Week*, February 11, 2004, 30.

4. Eric A. Hanushek, "The Impact of Differential Expenditures on School Performance," *Educational Researcher*, 23 (1994), 5–14.

5. Faith Crampton and Terry Whitney, "*The Relationship between Educational Expenditure and Student Achievement: When Does Money Matter?*" (Denver, CO: National Conference of State Legislatures, 1996).

6. "Quality Counts 2005: No Small Change, Targeting Money Toward Student Performance." Special Issue, *Education Week* 24, no. 17, 18

7. "Quality Counts 2005," 32.

8. Hart & Teeter Research Companies, NBC News/*Wall Street Journal* poll, March 1997, question 108.

9. Robert Weissberg, "The Problem with Polling," *Public Interest* (Summer 2002), 37–48.

10. *St. Petersburg Times*, August 19, 2003, B5 www.sptimes.com/2003/08/19/state/Two_years_of_class_si.shtml, accessed October 11, 2005.

11. Beth Barrett, "LAUSD Says State Audit Flawed," *Los Angeles Daily News*, August 7, 2001, www.dailynewslosangeles.com/news/articles/0701/31/newo1.asp, accessed August 7, 2001.

12. Myron Lieberman and Charlene K. Haar, *Public Education as a Business: Real Costs and Accountability* (Lanham, MD: ScarecrowEduction, 2003), 138–140.

13. U.S. Department of Education, National Center for Education Statistics, *Higher Education Institutions in Fall, 1995*, NCES 97-584 (Washington, DC: Government Printing Office, 1996), iii.

14. David W. Breneman, "Remediation in Higher Education: Its Extent and Cost," in *Brookings Papers on Educational Policy*, Diane Ravitch, ed. (Washington, DC: Brookings, 1998), 359–383.

15. Jay P. Greene, *The Cost of Remedial Education: How Much Michigan Pays When Students Fail to Learn Basic Skills* (Midland, MI: Mackinac Center for Public Policy, 2000), 9–16. See also David W. Breneman and William Daarlow, *Remediation in Higher Education* (Washington, DC: Thomas B. Fordham Foundation, 1998); Ronald Phipps, *College Remediation: What It Is, What It Costs, What's at Stake* (Washington, DC: Institute for Higher Education Policy, 1998). The last two studies do not take the private costs of remediation into account in contending that remediation is a wise expenditure of government funds.

16. Greene, *The Cost of Remedial Education*, 9–16.

17. Linda J. Zimbler, U.S. Department of Education, National Center for Education Statistics, *Background Characteristics, Work Activities, and Compensation of Faculty and Instructional Staff in Postsecondary Institutions: Fall 1998* U.S. Census Bureau (Washington, DC: U.S. Department of Education, 2001), 40.

18. U.S. Census Bureau, *United States State and Local Government Finances by Level of Government: 1998–99* (Washington, DC: U.S. Census Bureau, 2002), 3, www.census.gov/govs/www/estimate99.html, accessed March 27, 2007.

19. National Association of State Budget Officers, *State Expenditures Report 2001* (Washington, DC: National Association of State Budget Officers, 2002), 2, www.nasbo.org/Publications/PDFs/nasbo2001exrep.pdf, accessed November 16, 2002.

20. David H. Monk, *Educational Finance: An Economic Approach* (New York: McGraw Hill, 1990), 135.

21. Jerry A. Hausman, "Labor Supply," in *How Taxes Affect Economic Behavior*, ed. Henry J. Aaron and Joseph A. Pechman (Washington, DC: Brookings Institution, 1981), 61.

22. Tamar Lewin, "Young Students Become the New Cause for Big Donors," *New York Times,* August 21, 2005, 21.

23. For a discussion of PTA fund-raising and distribution, see Charlene K. Haar, *The Politics of the PTA* (New Brunswick, NJ: Transaction, 2002). Strictly speaking, volunteer and parental time are costs.

24. "Big Incentives Won Alabama a Piece of the Auto Industry," *Wall Street Journal*, April 3, 2002, 1, A24.

25. This point is more fully elaborated in Lieberman and Haar, *Public Education as a Business*, 165–181.

26. See the discussion of Payne's experience in Lieberman and Haar, *Public Education as a Business*, 168–175.

27. V. Dion Haynes and Lori Montgomery, "Imbalance in School Funding Asserted," *Washington Post*, August 24, 2005, B17.

28. Susanna Loeb and Miguel Socias, "Federal Contributions to High-Income School Districts: The Use of Tax Deductions for Funding K–2 Education," *Economics of Education Review*, 23 (2004), 85–94.

29. Per-pupil costs based on data from 2001–2002 school year. U.S. Department of Education, National Center for Education Statistics, *Digest of Education Statistics* (Washington, DC: U.S. Department of Education, 2003).

# Part 2

## TEACHER REPRESENTATION: PAST, PRESENT, AND FUTURE

Chapters 6 through 8 show how teacher unionization emerged and how it has affected virtually every dimension of education and of U.S. politics generally. For this reason, it is essential to inquire into the causes and consequences of teacher unionization and whether there are better ways to provide representation for the nation's three million teachers. Obviously, those who benefit from the existing system of representation are likely to be opposed to any change that would weaken their benefits.

The practical and policy issues arising from teacher unionization often differ dramatically from the popular and professional views on these matters. In the nonfarm private sector, union membership has declined from 36 percent of the labor force in 1956 to 7.8 percent in 2006. During this period, membership in teacher unions has increased from less than 1 percent in 1956 to 75 to 80 percent in 2006.[1] Inasmuch as private sector unionization provided the model and the resources that launched teacher unionization, why hasn't the decline in private sector unionization led to a similar decline in teacher unionization? The answer to this question explains a great deal about how we got into the educational morass and how we can get out of it.

### NOTE

1. Bureau of Labor Statistics, "Union Members in 2006," January 25, 2007, ftp://ftp.bls.gov/pub/news.release/History/union2.01252007.news, accessed April 7, 2007.

# 6

## The Impact of Collective Bargaining in Public Education

With the exception of the decline of government-imposed racial segregation, the emergence of collective bargaining and teacher unionization is the most significant development in K–12 education in the past fifty years. To understand why, we begin with its impact on teachers.

In the prebargaining era, teachers worked under individual contracts drafted by the school boards and usually presented to teachers individually on a take-it-or-leave-it basis. There was no legal obligation on the part of school boards to consult with teachers or their representatives or to negotiate over the terms and conditions of teacher employment. Of course, many school boards considered teacher proposals and grievances conscientiously, but enough did not to constitute a problem, or the appearance of one.

Prior to collective bargaining, most school administrators were NEA members. Where and when administrators were members of the teacher associations, their mere presence had served as a brake on teacher association demands; however, administrator membership was eliminated or greatly diminished under collective bargaining. The process provides the unions with equal procedural rights on where and when to negotiate, setting the negotiation agenda, and the conduct of negotiations. Management was legally obligated to "bargain in good faith," meaning that it had to come to the table with an open mind and a sincere desire to reach agreement with the union. These obligations may seem to be vague, but practitioners know fairly well what they mean legally and in practice.

Collective bargaining in education is often justified because management supposedly gets the kind of employee relations that it deserves. Prior to bargaining, school management allegedly did not seek input from teachers in formulating and implementing policies. Teachers were not treated as "professionals." Finally, the teachers refused to be treated as mere "hired hands" who clocked in and out and were expected to do what they were told. Consequently, the teachers turned to collective bargaining. Such is the folklore of collective bargaining in education.

Although the details differ, collective bargaining in public education was launched in the states in which teachers enjoyed the highest salaries and benefits, and it has yet to be established, legally or practically, in the states with the lowest salaries and fringe benefits. For example, California's collective bargaining law for teachers, the Rodda Act, was enacted in 1976, a time when California had enacted more statutory benefits for teachers than any other state. Actually, unions are typically organized by skilled workers, not unskilled workers who can be easily replaced.

## TEACHER TENURE

The most frequent complaint about the teacher unions is that they have made it too difficult to fire incompetent teachers. The criticism of the teacher unions on this issue is often justified, but there is little understanding that the problem often arises in the contractual provisions on teacher evaluations and teacher files. In tenure cases, the adequacy of the teacher evaluations is often a decisive issue. In bargaining, the unions try to include the following items in the contract:

- The narrowest possible criteria of incompetence
- The smallest number of observations and the shortest duration of them
- Prior notice to teachers of observations
- A prompt meeting after observations to discuss the observation report
- A teacher right to union representation at postobservation conferences
- A teacher right to grieve an evaluation deemed unfair

- A teacher right to assistance if given an unfavorable evaluation and an opportunity to achieve a favorable evaluation by a different evaluator
- A teacher right to review his or her personnel file with a union representative
- Negative material in the teacher files to be discarded after two years if the negative conduct is not repeated within the two-year period
- No material to be placed in a teacher's file without prior notification to the teacher and a teacher right to respond to the material
- Teacher rights to make copies of materials in their files at district expense
- Information from anonymous persons not to be used as the basis for disciplinary action against the teacher under any circumstances

Consider the above items from the standpoint of a principal with a large number of responsibilities that can't be delegated. A negative evaluation will make it more difficult for the teacher to get a teaching position somewhere else; hence it will also stiffen teacher resolve to fight the dismissal. A negative evaluation will also lead to an early meeting with the teacher and his or her union representative, who will scrutinize everything about the process in the hope of finding flaws in it. If the dismissal goes to arbitration or a statutory hearing, the stakes for the principal escalate. Previous evaluations may have given the teacher favorable evaluations, and perhaps the teacher is only a few years away from having his or her pension vested. Considerations such as these frequently come into play in tenure cases.

If the alleged basis of dismissal is racial, religious, or sexual discrimination, the teacher may have a choice of local, state, or federal agencies and courts in which to pursue his or her remedies. One or more of these forums maybe have a justified reputation for excessive proplaintiff zeal in discrimination cases. Furthermore, the teachers who prevail must be reimbursed for any lost salary with interest and attorney's fees; if a case is dragged out for a year or two and the dismissal is not upheld (which sometimes happens), the district administration takes a big hit in public opinion.

Before bargaining, the school district could observe the teacher for as long and as frequently as it wished. With bargaining, the restrictions on management previously mentioned emerged. As matters stand, the U.S. teacher unions have too much power to block disciplinary action against teachers—not in every state and school district but in enough of them to be a serious problem. Nevertheless, the position that teachers are not entitled to any tenure protection, no matter how long they have worked for the district and how favorable their evaluations, is not reasonable. Instead of point-less arguments for or against extremist positions on tenure, more thought needs to be given to what protections are fair to teachers while allowing school districts to function effectively. In the meantime, calls to abolish tenure without any qualification are very helpful to the teacher unions. They would otherwise have to manufacture a credible threat to job security, which is not easy to do in view of its multilayered protections.[1]

## PROFESSIONALISM

The argument that unionization is antithetical to professionalism was and is the source of a great deal of confusion regarding unionization. Teachers pay union dues for protection, not for instigating charges of incompe-tence. After a teacher has paid union dues for several years, it is hardly ap-propriate for the union to assume the prosecutorial role, a consideration blithely ignored by union critics.

Historically, the union position has been that its function is to ensure due process for teachers charged with incompetence or conduct calling for disciplinary action. Nevertheless, disturbed by criticism over its role in dismissal cases, and confused by misguided notions of professionalism, a few teacher unions have become actively involved in identifying and dis-missing teachers charged with incompetence. This practice has led to se-vere conflicts of interest; the unions have even paid third parties to repre-sent teachers charged with incompetence because the union was actively supporting the dismissal proceedings.

Pundits, liberal and conservative, typically applaud the progress toward professionalism when teacher unions take an active role in identifying and terminating teachers charged with incompetence. Supposedly, this is what people in "true professions," such as doctors and lawyers, do. This line of thought confuses the position of fee takers with the position of salaried em-ployees who work for the same employer on a regular basis. In the fee-taking situation, it is practically impossible for employers (clients, patients) to evaluate professional competence; the interactions with the professional are very brief, and the patient or client usually lacks the expertise to evaluate professional performance. In education, however, teachers work in groups on annual contracts with the same employer. In this situation, there is ordinarily no need for school employers to depend on the unions to initiate or support charges of incompetence; dismissal is primarily a managerial, not a union, responsibility. It should be emphasized, however, that unions are not legally obligated to contest every dismissal.

The criticism of excessive union protection for incompetent teachers is often justified, but it has been justified for over forty years while matters have only gotten worse. This suggests a continuing failure of the critics to come to grips with the realities; the situation is symptomatic of their failure as well as the union's. Parenthetically, the incidence of excessive union protection of incompetent teachers is likely to drop precipitously in a competitive system. School management would have to take a much firmer stand in terminating incompetent teachers who are responsible for pupil withdrawals, and teachers will be much less inclined to protect anyone who is endangering their livelihood.

## GRIEVANCE PROCEDURES

After an agreement is reached, one of the parties may violate it. The most common way for the union to remedy alleged school board violations is through a grievance procedure that includes

- Who can grieve
- What can be grieved
- The steps in the grievance procedure
- The time limits for responding to each level of the grievance procedure
- Released time, usually with pay, for grievants, witnesses
- The terminal point, for example, school board, superintendent, advisory arbitration, binding arbitration
- Group grievances
- Required information to the parties

- Separate grievance files
- No-reprisals clause[2]

Each item in the grievance procedure can be highly contentious, with one or both parties repeatedly seeking changes in the procedure. The outcomes vary widely, but the trend lines favor the union. For instance, the first contract may read, "A grievance is a claim where there has been a violation of the contract, personally affecting the grievant." After several contracts, the definition may be, "A grievance is a claim by a teacher or the Association based upon the interpretation, application, or violation of this Agreement, board policies, or administrative decisions and practices affecting a teacher or a group of teachers." Obviously, the broader definition is likely to lead to more grievances, more time lost preparing for and participating in grievance hearings, more expenses for arbitrators and legal counsel, and a much more cautious school staff, concerned that whatever they do might be cause for grievance.

Grievance procedures vary widely, but most contracts covering teachers require an informal conference with the principal to resolve the grievance. In most contracts, if the informal conference fails to bring about a resolution, the union and the teacher who wishes to pursue the matter must submit a written grievance to the principal within a certain number of days after the act or condition giving rise to the grievance, and the principal must respond to the grievance within a specified number of days. If there is still no resolution, the teacher can appeal to the superintendent or central office labor relations officer and ultimately to an arbitrator if the school district fails to satisfy the grievant.

These procedures created strong pressures on school administrators to be sure that their actions did not violate the contract; many administrators conceded the legitimacy of the grievance rather than open up their own conduct to scrutiny.

## THE IMPACT OF TEACHER UNIONIZATION
## ON TEACHER ORGANIZATIONS

Teacher unionization had an enormous impact on the NEA. Prior to unionization, the NEA was the home of thirty national organizations that served specialized groups of teachers and administrators: mathematics teachers, science teachers, elementary principals, secondary principals, and so on. With the advent of collective bargaining, these organizations left the NEA and became free-standing organizations, while NEA staff, publications, and services changed to support for collective bargaining and political action.

Unionization led to huge increases in NEA staff and staff salaries. I estimate that the NEA and AFT employ over 8,000 staff and officers at the local, state, and national levels combined. Well over half of this group is paid more than $100,000 per year in salary and benefits. In 2005, the average salary in the NEA was $96,995 and $91,000 in the AFT. Neither union has provided data on the dollar value of its fringe benefits per employee, but in 2000, the Education Policy Institute (EPI) sought to ascertain the average amount paid for fringe benefits per NEA employee. After pursuing this matter with the NEA's accounting department, it appeared that the average cost of fringe benefits for 552 NEA employees was $27,333;[3] the costs of benefits for the three NEA executive officers were not included in this estimate. In fact, neither were the costs of the following benefits, which were treated as organizational expenses, not benefits:

- Replacing employees on paid leaves of absence
- Moving allowances
- Physical examinations
- NEA 401(k) contributions
- Sale of home expenses if transferred
- Low-cost loans
- Tuition reimbursement
- Travel amenities, such as first-class instead of coach fare and generous meal allowances
- Recreation and exercise facilities at the NEA building in Washington, DC
- Liberal car expense allowance

In view of the substantial increases in the cost of health insurance since 1999, the average cost of benefits for NEA employees in 2005–2006 is probably over $35,000. On this basis, it appears that the average compensation per employee in the NEA, excluding officers, was approximately $131,995 and $126,000 in the AFT in 2005.[4] Whatever may be the exact figures, the two unions clearly employ thousands of officers and employees with a huge economic stake in union growth and financial security. Rank-and-file union members are not aware of the total compensation of union officers and staff, but obviously, union leadership is under constant pressure to oppose any school district action or policy that might foster dissatisfaction with union membership.

Most teachers represented by NEA affiliates do not know how much their union representatives, known as "UniServ representatives," are paid. The NEA sends each state affiliate a lump sum to cover the NEA's share of the costs of the UniServ program. The state associations bargain with the union representing the UniServ directors, who are assigned by the state associations to the districts that they will represent. Consequently, the UniServ directors are not usually employed by the local teachers they represent, and the latter are not knowledgeable about UniServ terms and conditions of employment.

## THE IMPACT OF UNIONIZATION
## ON TEACHER COMPENSATION

The NEA and AFT face a difficult problem regarding teacher compensation. On the one hand, they must convince school boards, states, and the federal government that teachers are underpaid. On the other hand, they must avoid raising doubts about whether union dues are worth the benefits. If teachers are underpaid, whose responsibility is it when they are paying over $2 billion annually in local, state, and national dues?[5] And if teachers are being paid well, how effective can the unions be in efforts to negotiate sizable raises for them?

Up to the present time, the position that teachers are underpaid resonates with union membership; few teachers do not share this belief. Nevertheless, such a belief can easily lead to the belief that the union has not been effective. When this happens, there is an upheaval in the leadership ranks.

Understandably, the union impact on teacher salaries and fringe benefits is a matter of considerable dispute. This is due partly to the fact that most of the data on teacher compensation is provided by the NEA and the AFT, which have a compelling interest in persuading policymakers and the public that teachers are underpaid. Even the federal Bureau of Labor Statistics has relied on the data on teacher salaries provided by the NEA. These data typically overlook the following factors:

- Most teachers work less than 190 days per year. This is 40 to 50 days less than the average of other professionals.
- The teacher workday is shorter than the workday of other professionals. For example, the teacher workday in Chicago is six hours and forty-five minutes, including a duty-free lunch period. In New York City, the workday was six hours and twenty minutes including duty-free lunch until the agreement reached in September 2005 raised it by fifty minutes per week, or six and one-half hours per day.
- Teachers can generally retire earlier than private sector workers covered by Social Security or private company pension plans. In a 1994–1995 survey, the average age of teachers upon retirement was fifty-nine years. Generally speaking, teacher pensions are not affected by postretirement work.
- Over 99 percent of teachers have health insurance. Whereas only 20 percent of company plans pay the full amount for professional and managerial employees, 51 percent of teacher plans do. For family plans, only 10 percent of medium and large companies pay the full amount, but 51 percent of family plans for teachers are fully paid by the school districts.[6]
- Even in the absence of a contract, teachers with an "expectancy" of continued employment are constitutionally entitled to due process protections.
- Teachers generally enjoy more liberal leave time than private sector professional and managerial employees. Few teachers cannot take at least one or two days of leave for personal business without a loss of pay. Because substitute teachers are commonplace, teachers can usually take time off with pay for personal emergencies, such as a sick child. This feature of teacher employment makes teaching very attractive to individuals who want both a career and a family.
- Teaching seldom involves work in the evening or on weekends or holidays or out of town, an important consideration to individuals with heavy family responsibilities.
- Public school teachers are paid substantially more than private school teachers. Private school teachers start at salaries that are about 76 percent of public school teacher salaries.
- Teachers rarely have to be concerned about being laid off.[7] The fact that teachers often drop their union membership when accorded

tenure illustrates the fact that this benefit has a significant economic value. As one reads about the layoffs and probable loss of some retirement benefits in the automobile and airline industries, the economic value of secure employment is obvious.

- Judgments that teachers are underpaid are based primarily on comparisons of teacher salaries to salaries in other occupations requiring a comparable period of education. Such comparisons are usually made to lower-paid occupations with comparable education, such as journalists.[8]

The NEA and AFT argue that teacher compensation is higher in unionized than in nonunion states. This is true, but the teacher unions are not the reason why. In Connecticut, a unionized state, the estimated average teacher salary for 2003–2004 was $57,337, the highest in the nation. In South Dakota, a nonunion state, the average was $32,416, the lowest in the nation.[9] If South Dakota had been unionized and Connecticut had not been, their rankings would have been essentially the same.

A number of studies have challenged union claims to have increased teacher compensation higher than it would be in the absence of unionization. The factors underlying these challenges include the following:

- Unionization emerged during a period of rapidly rising inflation. Consequently, much of the increase in teacher compensation attributed to unionization was due to inflation.
- In the absence of unionization, employee compensation is increased in annual or semiannual increments. Because the increases are usually less than the increases at the beginning of a multiyear contract and there is no publicity when raises are awarded in nonunion employment, there is a tendency to believe that unions are more influential in raising wages than they really are.
- The large number of teachers renders it prohibitively expensive to provide substantial across-the-board increases in teacher compensation.
- The research that shows that teacher unions have significantly improved teacher compensation have erroneously drawn causal implications from correlations.

Nevertheless, other factors support the union argument:

- Unions often prefer increases in fringe benefits like health insurance, which are not taxed, to salary increases, which are taxed. Teachers undoubtedly enjoy more liberal fringe benefits than most private sector workers, especially with the rapidly increasing costs of health care.
- In some situations, teacher unions have accepted preparation periods or reductions in class size in lieu of salary increases. The benefits are not categorized as increases in compensation, but that is what they are, at least in part.
- Increases in state teacher retirement payments are funded mainly by the states, at least partly as a result of state teacher union lobbying. These increases are not categorized as salary increases, but they are an extremely important component of teacher compensation.

Yet even on these issues, there are counterbalancing factors. Higher teacher compensation conflicts with lower class size. Also, the cost of union dues and time devoted to union activities must be considered. Furthermore, the NEA and AFT are supporters of "social investing," that is, investment policies that advance union social objectives. Thus the AFT supports divestment of stocks in companies regarded as antiunion. In 1994, the NEA adopted a resolution that urged state retirement systems to avoid purchase or retention of stock in companies that supported privatization of educational services.

Virtually any policy that restricts investment options results in a lower rate of return, and NEA and AFT investment policies undoubtedly have had a tendency to do so. Again, however, there is a measurement problem. In general, social investing results in a lower return on investment, but how much in the case of teacher retirement funds has not been established.[10] Note, however, that the NEA and AFT are seeking to replace gubernatorially appointed with teacher-elected members of the state teacher retirement boards. Due to the tendency of union representatives on public employee retirement boards to support social investing, this objective conflicts with maximizing retirement fund assets.

A widely used textbook on labor economics argues that the union impact on wages is minimal because they do not have the right to strike, high wages run the risk of antagonizing the public, and the unions have had a significant upward impact on benefits because benefits are not so visible. Public officials often find it politically advantageous to grant benefit increases that are small at the outset but become much larger after the officials leave office. The real cost of benefits may not be known at the outset. These conclusions clearly apply to teachers, who are a major component of state and local public employees.[11]

## THE UNION IMPACT ON SENIORITY

Seniority often becomes a major issue in unionized employment.[12] The union case for seniority is based partly on the idea that the duration of service deserves priority when there is no clear basis for making a personnel decision. Stated this way, many would agree, but problems arise in deciding when there is no clear basis for administrative discretion. Management wants the right to decide which decisions should be based on seniority; its view of the matter is that very few decisions, if any, should be based solely on seniority.

The union view of seniority is based on union dynamics. For example, suppose the issue is the basis for deciding which teachers will be assigned to extracurricular activities for stipends. Whenever a less senior teacher is selected, the more senior teachers will complain to the union: "I have worked here for a longer time and am just as good (or better) than the teacher who got the job. The union should insist on seniority in the next contract."

Justified or not, the situation is a lose-lose one for the union, which is required to take sides in a controversy between union members. Seniority minimizes these controversies; there is a single, objective, easily applied standard, known to all from the first day of employment. The union tendency will be to minimize the differences between candidates for assignments, transfers, and promotions, arguing that they should be offered in order of seniority to qualified teachers. The school administration wants the freedom to appoint "the most qualified teachers."

The importance of seniority to teachers is often underestimated. In running a school, principals are often required to make decisions that affect teacher preferences. Who gets the highest-paid extracurricular assignment? The least-wanted? The gifted class? The slow-learner class? Whose free period comes first in the morning, which means that it is likely to be preempted by the need to replace a suddenly absent teacher? When the free period is last, the teacher rarely loses a free period because the district has gotten a substitute by then.

The number of these situations underlies the strong union preference for seniority. The union rationale for seniority also asserts that allowing managerial discretion would lead to favoritism, bias, and divisiveness, whereas seniority arguably places all teachers on an equal footing. Unfortunately, under union rules, fairness for teachers results in less than fairness for pupils in the inner cities, who are taught year after year by more than their fair share of new teachers, substitute teachers, and teachers not well prepared in the subjects they teach. Furthermore, less is spent per inner-city pupil than per upper-middle-class pupil; the higher salaries paid for teachers in the more affluent areas in the same school district constitute an inequity that is not eliminated by special appropriations for students from poor families or by increasing school district revenues. The teacher unions, which regard themselves as the leaders in the struggle for equity, are fierce defenders of the major inequity in school district expenditures.

## THE IMPACT OF TEACHER UNIONIZATION ON STUDENTS AND THE CURRICULUM

As we might expect, there is sharp disagreement over the impact of teacher unionization on students. Union leaders claim several student benefits: Higher teacher salaries attract better teachers; smaller classes enable teachers to give students more individual attention; preparation periods and sabbatical leaves result in better-prepared teachers—it is as if whatever is good for teachers is also good for students.

These serendipitous outcomes appear to be too good to be true—which is what they are. No student impact is as clear-cut as the negative impact of union seniority on inner-city schools. Union pressure to reduce the number of workdays and the hours of the school day has resulted in less instructional time. Excessive union protection of poor teachers is a disservice to students. Generous leave policies result in discontinuities in instruction and greater resort to substitute teachers. In short, a common sense assessment of the consequences of contractual provisions, plus the wealth of experience on the impact of similar clauses in the private sector, leaves little doubt that unionization is having negative effects on student achievement.

Most teacher union contracts provide that the school administration shall consult with the union on professional matters that are not subject to bargaining. The administration does so in many districts in which there is no such clause in the contract. Textbooks are one such matter, so the union appoints its representatives to the textbook committee—usually, but not necessarily, the teachers of the subjects for which the textbooks are to be purchased. If the subject is sex education, the NEA supports

> appropriately established sex education programs. Such programs should include information on sexual abstinence, birth control and family planning, diversity of culture, diversity of sexual orientation/gender identification, parenting skills, prenatal care, sexually transmitted diseases, incest, sexual abuse, sexual harassment, homophobia, the effects of substance abuse during pregnancy, and problems associated with and resulting from pre-teen and teenage pregnancies.[13]

We would not expect less from an organization that hands out condoms next to the registration tables at its annual meeting.[14]

On HIV/AIDS education, the NEA makes the following recommendation:

> The National Education Association believes that educational institutions should establish comprehensive aquired immunodeficiency syndrome (AIDS) education programs as an integral part of the school curriculum. HIV/AIDS education must include education about all means of transmission, including unprotected sex and unsanitary methods of tattooing, body piercing, and intravenous drug use. Information on prevention options must include abstinence and medically accepted protective devices. Instruction in decision-making skills to assist students in correlating health information and personal behavior is essential.
>
> The Association also believes that proper implementation of these programs requires education, employee training, and input. These programs should be presented by properly licensed/trained personnel and should be planned with the input of parents/guardians and other community representatives.[15]

The term *feminism* does not appear in the NEA's governance documents, but with a membership that is two-thirds female, it is not surprising that the NEA has a radical feminist ideology. For years after the defeat of the Equal Rights Amendment (ERA), the NEA refused to hold its convention in any state that had voted against it. The organization supports all efforts "to raise the pay of those jobs that are presently undervalued. The market value means of establishing pay cannot be the final determinant of pay scales since it too frequently reflects the race and sex bias in our society."[16] If the market cannot be "the final determinant of pay scales," what would be? "Government officials" comes to mind.

Several years ago, I was the negotiator for a California school district when the union sought to change the sick-leave clause in the contract from allowing teachers to use sick leave for the illness of spouse, children, uncle, aunt, nephew, and niece, to sick leave "for anyone residing in the same household as the teacher."[17] Upon inquiry, I learned that the change was intended to provide sick leave for the partners of unmarried and gay and lesbian couples who were living together. When I sought to estimate the potential cost of the change, I discovered that about a fifth of the teachers in the district were cohabiting. (Welcome to the sexual revolution!) The proposed change would also have allowed sick leave to care for the ailing partners of gay and lesbian teachers. In fact, the model contracts disseminated to local negotiators by the state teacher unions include language that prohibits discrimination "on the basis of sexual orientation," which covers gays, lesbians, bisexuals, and transgendered teachers (teachers who have undergone a sex change, either by operation or declaration).

As previously pointed out, the teacher unions are leading supporters of multicultural and bilingual education; nobody could rise to a leadership position in the teacher unions who advocated English immersion. Consultation with a local union on textbooks does not lead automatically to support for union-approved textbooks, but a substantial union effect on the curriculum is indisputable.

## THE ANTIMARKET CULTURE OF PUBLIC EDUCATION

The antimarket orientation of public education is evident from NEA policy statements, convention programs, political alliances, and the complete absence of any action supportive of a market system over a long period of time. In *Contracting Out: Strategies for Fighting Back*, the NEA lists "Points against Subcontracting." The first point is "Subcontractors are motivated by profit."[18] There was no attempt to spell out why being "motivated by profit" is disreputable. It is in these ways, large and small, the NEA reveals its anti-capitalist orientation. In recent years, the NEA has adopted over three hundred resolutions a year. The resolutions do not include a single policy supportive of our economic system. They do, however, include the following:

> The National Education Association believes that the struggles of working men and women to establish unions and the influence of the labor movement on the growth of the United States should be an integral part of the curriculum in our schools.
>
> The Association urges teachers, curriculum committees, and authors to include material that accurately presents the important contributions to our country's history and growth that have been provided by the unions involved in the labor movement and the individuals who led that movement.[19]

Although there is little doubt that majority refusal to become affiliated with the AFL-CIO was the decisive reason why the NEA voted against a merger with the AFT in 2002, the NEA overwhelmingly supports AFL-CIO positions. New Business Item (NBI) 2 adopted at the NEA's 2001 convention illustrates this point:

> NEA affirms and supports the decision of the Executive Committee to participate in the national Wal-Mart Consumer Education Campaign initiated by the United Food and Commercial Workers International Union. Further, NEA strongly encourages state and local affiliates and individual NEA members to participate in this campaign.[20]

## THE IMPACT OF BARGAINING ON PARENTS AND THE PTA

The union approach to parents in collective bargaining contracts is drastically different from its rhetoric about parent involvement. In bargaining, the union's position is that parental complaints might lead to disciplinary action, perhaps teacher dismissals. For this reason, parental complaints are treated as if they were threats to teacher tenure, and the teacher unions seek the protections of tenure in dealing with parental complaints. Therefore, the complaints must be in writing and signed by the parent. They must be very specific, and the teacher must have time off with pay and the right to respond and have it attached to the complaint. Complaints must be made within a few days after the teacher conduct that is subject of the complaint. The teacher has the right to have a union representative present at any meeting with the administration that might result in disciplinary action against the teacher. And so on.

Note the difference between public school and commercial practices on customer complaints. In the latter, companies encourage customers to express their complaints because the companies are sensitive to the fact that customers can take their business elsewhere. Public education, being a monopoly that is not concerned about customers taking their business elsewhere, can afford to encourage the expression of customer dissatisfaction, but this is not the union attitude. In teacher union contracts, parents are treated as adversaries, not colleagues. For immigrant parents and parents without much experience in dealing with social institutions, the obstacles to parental complaints are daunting indeed. In practice, the operative meaning of "parent involvement" in public education is parental action that makes the teacher's work easier. On any common sense view, parents who complain about teachers or textbooks or irreligious practices are involved in their children's education, but one looks in vain for any recognition of the fact in school district contracts.

Educational literature is replete with praise for parent involvement. Nevertheless, the National PTA requires local PTAs not to become involved in collective bargaining between local school boards and teacher unions. This policy is binding on all state and local PTAs. To understand its significance, consider some of the issues ordinarily resolved in collective bargaining:

- How much time before class must teachers be present?
- How long after the end of the student workday must teachers remain to help students?
- How many evening meetings must teachers devote to meeting parents who cannot be present during the regular workday?

- What are the teachers' obligations to respond to parent letters and telephone calls?
- What procedures are in place to resolve the parent and student grievances against teachers?
- How should districts respond to union proposals that parental complaints must be in writing, signed by the complainant? That teachers are entitled to have a union representative present when a parent appears to complain about an action by teachers?

A parent organization that cannot be active on these issues has lost its raison d'être. Nevertheless, PTA neutrality is easily explained. In the takeoff phase of teacher bargaining, teacher strikes occurred frequently, and in several cases, local PTAs supported the school board. Naturally, this did not please the NEA, which eventually notified the PTA that it would no longer tolerate PTA opposition in collective bargaining. If the PTA continued to allow this to happen, the NEA threatened to pull its teachers out of the PTA and establish its own parent organization. These developments took place at a time when the PTA occupied rent-free space in the NEA building in Washington, DC. The PTA adopted a neutralist position on bargaining issues in 1967, but the defining showdown materialized in Ohio nine years later.

In 1976, the Ohio PTA successfully opposed several legislative proposals by the Ohio Education Association (OEA). At its 1976 convention, the OEA adopted a resolution urging its members to drop their membership in the PTA, boycott its activities, and encourage parents to establish new organizations not affiliated with the PTA. Nationally, approximately 217,000 PTA members dropped their membership in 1976; of these, more than 50,000 were from Ohio. The message was not lost on PTA leaders, and the PTA's neutralist position has been in effect with only editorial changes since its initial adoption.[21]

Interestingly enough, the PTA's legal position is that it is not an educational organization, despite the fact that the names of the overwhelming majority of PTAs include the name of a school. The issue arose when the Government Accounting Standards Board (GASB) proposed new standards for government accounting that would have required school boards to include the financial activities of affiliated organizations controlled by the school districts. The PTA's legal position is that it is not such an organization; instead, it is a child welfare organization that just happens to use the schools as a place to meet.[22] To the PTA, "parent involvement" means lobbying for PTA causes and candidates, most of which are liberal causes not directly related to school operations.

One might suppose that a parent organization would support parental choice of school, but the PTA is adamantly opposed to any school choice legislation that includes private schools. Its president has twice been the nominal chairman of a coalition of public school organizations opposed to school choice (1978, 1998). Again, it must be emphasized that the National PTA's opposition to school choice, like all National PTA policies, is binding on its state and local affiliates.

The PTA's main legislative achievement in the 1990s was the addition of a parent involvement goal to Goals 2000 (the Democratic equivalent of NCLB under President Clinton). As Charlene K. Haar points out, "there is no evidence that this addition has had any positive effect on schools or, for that matter, on parent involvement."[23] The 2003 hiring of Warlene D. Early, the director of the NEA's Human and Civil Rights Program, as the PTA's executive director, strongly suggests a continuation of the PTA's subordination to the NEA and pursuit of a hardcore left agenda. PTA membership is roughly one in ten families with children in school; however, more parents are active in parent–teacher organizations (PTOs), which are parent organizations not affiliated with the PTA. Haar's study of the PTA estimates that PTOs enroll about half of the parents with children in public schools.[24]

The union treatment of parental complaints as tantamount to criminal indictments is a union overreaction, but conservatives sometimes help the unions make a persuasive case for protection against parents. Consider the "tips for parents" by the Center for Education Reform (CER), a conservative think tank founded by Jeanne Allen, a former education analyst for the Heritage Foundation and the U.S. Department of Education. After advising parents to become "informal evaluators" of teachers, the advice continues:

- Keep written records of all your observations. Your role as an "informal evaluator" is not useful unless you have written documents to show officials.
- If you see no change after addressing the teacher, go to the principal. Collect objective evidence. Save notes you have received with numerous

grammatical and spelling errors or incomprehensible homework assignments. . . .

- If the situation doesn't improve, send a letter to the principal, listing your
  concerns. Deliver copies to the superintendent and to school board members. Call to make sure your letters were received.
- Don't worry about retribution. . . . Remember that if a teacher singles out
  a child for unfair treatment, that's strong evidence against the teacher.
  Document the teacher's action and ask for an immediate transfer of your
  child.
- As a last resort, go public with your concerns. Speak out at school
  board meetings. . . . If the teacher is not tenured, you can prevent him
  or her from being granted tenure before it's too late. If the teacher has
  tenure, your actions will shine the spotlight on a system that may need
  rethinking.[25]

These "tips" would constitute adequate justification for the union
stance on parent involvement if others took them seriously. The fact that
an organization with this mentality has received millions from the U.S.
Department of Education and conservative philanthropies is not encouraging.

## THE IMPACT OF TEACHER UNIONIZATION ON POLITICS

In some respects, teacher unionization is having its most important impact
on persons holding or seeking public office, local, state, and national. The
rapid spread of public sector unionization and its decline in the private
sector highlights a critical difference between unions in the two sectors.
"Organizing" is not as critical in the public sector; most public sector
union revenues are used to influence government agencies at the local,
state, and federal levels.

In soliciting applicants for UniServ positions, NEA and its state and local affiliates post job descriptions and desired characteristics. Political responsibilities are typically listed as a part of the job description, and political experience is routinely included among the desired qualifications.
This makes sense because the UniServ directors are responsible for ar-
ranging interviews with candidates for office, chairing the interviews and

postinterview discussions, maintaining the records, and otherwise managing the political activities of the local associations. Such management calls for organizing Get Out the Vote (GOTV) campaigns, telephone banks, and demonstrations; distributing lawn signs and car stickers; and directing other activities of this nature.

The main responsibilities of UniServ directors are ostensibly to negotiate contracts and represent teachers in grievances; tenure cases in the courts are handled by union lawyers. School district labor contracts are usually two or three years in duration, but drastic changes in the contract are seldom necessary. Private sector companies seldom make drastic changes in the work rules from year to year; when drastic change is necessary, the cause is usually a technological development, but technological developments requiring changes in the work rules for teachers rarely occur.

How much of UniServ and field representative time is devoted to politics? In addition to heavy participation in state and federal elections, the local associations are very active in city and school board elections and state initiatives. Probably 10 to 20 percent of UniServ time is devoted to political activities, but assume that 10 percent is correct. Assume also that one-third of full-time AFT officers and staff devote 10 percent of their time to politics; however, both unions employ a substantial number of staff whose positions are completely political; for example, the NEA's Government Relations Department included forty-nine professional staff in 2003–2004. One must also take into account the backup staff required in accounting, facilities management, publications, travel, information technology, and other services. Furthermore, NEA and AFT state affiliates, especially the NEA's, also employ a number of staff members who function full-time as lobbyists and political specialists. A conservative estimate is that the NEA and AFT employ the equivalent of 250 full-time employees (FTEs) in their political operations—more FTEs than the Republican and Democratic parties combined.

The out-of-school political activities of teachers are often supplemented by in-school political activities as well. Legally, teachers are not entitled to use school facilities for political activities on terms that are not available to others. Although there is no comprehensive study of the matter, the research that has been done and an impressive amount of anecdotal evidence indicate widespread violation of this principle.[26] The violations include

- Use of district website, mail system, and e-mail system for political purposes
- Utilization of union bulletin boards for political messages when no other individuals or organizations are allowed to do this
- Utilization of pupils to carry home political messages, usually on forthcoming tax levies for education
- Classroom credit for attending political activities
- Exclusive union right to payroll deduction of the Political Action Committee (PAC) contributions
- Teacher political advocacy in the classroom
- Utilization of pupils in GOTV campaigns

The extent of these practices has not been studied, but it deserves serious scrutiny.

## THE NEA'S POLITICAL AGENDA

Since the mid-1800s, public education has been devoted to more government funding. "Build a school, close a prison," the mantra in the 1800s, is still with us today even though the U.S. has an enormous system of public education and by far the largest incarceration rates of any developed country.[27]

The NEA is opposed to any limits on taxes at any level of government. Understandably, its allies are the environmental, feminist, and gay and lesbian organizations, unions threatened by free trade, trial lawyers, and other interest groups whose ultimate success is based upon government appropriations or favorable statutory or regulatory treatment. Its need for allies explains why the NEA has adopted various policies that appear to have little or no relationship to education. Since 1976, when the NEA's first endorsement for president went to Jimmy Carter, the NEA has never supported a Republican candidate for president in a Republican primary general election or did support Arlen Specter for president, after which it supported his Democratic opponent in the general election.

## A CONCLUDING NOTE: NEA IN THE 2006 ELECTIONS[28]

In assessing the NEA's impact on politics, it is helpful to understand how the NEA visualizes its political potential and how it goes about achieving it. Its political program is based on the view that the NEA can affect 1 percent of the national electorate. Although the percentage will vary from state to state, 1 percent is a huge number that could affect the outcome of several local, state, and federal elections. Even changes of less than 2 percent could have resulted in Democratic instead of Republican administrations in 2000 and 2004, and in the absence of NEA and AFT support, Republicans would still have controlled the U.S. Senate after the 2006 elections.

Most NEA political activity is conducted under the guise of informing the association's members about forthcoming elections. Unions are allowed to utilize dues revenue for this purpose. In 2006, the NEA targeted twenty states that met its criteria for assistance:

- Alabama
- Arizona
- California
- Colorado
- Florida
- Iowa
- Maine
- Maryland
- Michigan
- Minnesota
- Nevada
- New Mexico
- Ohio
- Oregon
- Rhode Island
- Pennsylvania
- Tennessee
- Vermont
- Washington
- Wisconsin

For NEA assistance, the state affiliate must have

- A viable grassroots campaign
- Sufficient PAC Funds
- A detailed calendar for achieving the goals

The emphasis was on the gubernatorial campaigns, spurred by the conviction that NEA's presidential candidates would have won the elections in 2000 and 2004 if Democratic governors had been in office in Florida and Ohio.

Candidates for federal office, except incumbents who are safely in the fold, are asked to respond to an NEA questionnaire that asks for responses to NEA's wish list. The responses are graded with passing a cut score required for endorsement. In a previous year, the cut score had to be lowered so that the NEA could endorse a Republican and thereby lay claim to be "bipartisan" in its approach to endorsements. About sixteen NEA staff members worked full-time from May until the 2006 elections to implement the NEA's ambitious program of political activism. Obviously congressional Democrats are very unlikely to support policies opposed by the NEA and AFT.

## NOTES

1. Frederick M. Hess, resident scholar at the American Enterprise Institute, characterizes "employment at will" as a "common sense school reform." Few employers, even nonunion ones, would agree. Hess, *Common Sense School Reform* (New York: Palgrave MacMillan, 2004), 127.

2. For a discussion of the issues in negotiating grievance procedures, see Myron Lieberman, *Understanding the Teacher Union Contract: A Citizen's Handbook* (New Brunswick, NJ: Transaction, 2000), 161–177.

3. Study conducted by Charlene K. Haar for the Education Policy Institute, 2000.

4. Bess Keller and Vaishali Honawar, "Union Filings Give In-Depth Look at Spending Patterns," *Education Week*, January 11, 2006, 7; Form LM-2, submitted by the NEA and AFT to the U.S. Department of Labor, December 2005.

5. Author estimate.

6. The data and conclusions about teacher compensation are taken largely from Michael Podgursky, "Fringe Benefits," *Education Next* (Summer 2003), 71–78.

7. Podgursky, "Fringe Benefits, 71–78.

8. For an unpersuasive analysis that asserts that teachers are paid considerably less than comparable occupations, see Sylvia A. Allagretto, Sean P. Corcoran, and Lawrence Mishel, *How Does Teacher Pay Compare?* (Washington, DC: Economic Policy Institute, 2004). The Economic Policy Institute is supported largely by union contributions.

9. NEA Research, *Estimates of School Statistics 2003* (Washington, DC: National Education Association, 2004), cited in *NEA Today* (October 2005), 29.

10. Roberto Romano, *Politics and Public Pension Funds* (New York: Manhattan Institute, 1994).

11. Ronald G. Ehrenberg and Robert S. Smith, *Modern Labor Economics*, 5th ed. (New York: Harper Collins, 1994).

12. See Lieberman, *Understanding the Teacher Union Contract*.

13. Resolution B-42, Sex Education, *NEA Handbook* (Washington, DC: National Education Association, 2004–2005), 210.

14. The condoms were handed out by the National Education Association Health Information Network, an organization established to provide health information to 2.5 million education employees and over 40 million students. NEA HIN is based in the NEA building. It is funded by the Center for Disease Control and Prevention, Environmental Protection Agency, Robert Wood Johnson Foundation, NEA, Publicis, and American Cancer Society. *NEA Handbook*, 2004–2005, 46–47.

15. Resolution B-43, HIV/AIDS Education, *NEA Handbook*, 2004–2005, 210.

16. Resolution F-2, Pay Equity/Comparable Worth, *NEA Handbook*, 2004–2005, 248.

17. The language was and is union boilerplate in many union proposals and contracts.

18. NEA, *Contracting Out: Strategies for Fighting Back* (Washington: National Education Association, 1996).

19. Resolution B-47, *NEA Handbook 2005*, (Washington, DC: National Education Association, 2005), 212.

20. New Business Item (NBI) 2, supporting Wal-Mart Consumer Education Campaign, adopted at 2001 NEA convention in Los Angeles.

21. For a full account of these developments, see Charlene K. Haar, *The Politics of the PTA* (New Brunswick, NJ: Transaction, 2002), 78–84.

22. A detailed account of this surprising stance of the PTA can be found in Haar, *The Politics of the PTA*, 10–11. The PTA and other organizations were successful in changing the rule so that school district financial reports are not required to include PTA revenue even if the revenues are completely devoted to school activities.

23. Haar, *The Politics of the PTA*, 158.

24. Haar, *The Politics of the PTA*, 151.

25. Center for Education Reform, *The Center for Education Reform in the News* (Washington, DC: Center for Education Reform, 2000), 109.

26. See Cheri Pierson Yecke, *Kids, Schools and Politics: Protecting the Integrity of Classroom Resources* (Minneapolis: Center of the American Experiment, 2005); Myron Lieberman, *Collective Bargaining in Florida School Districts* (Tallahassee: James Madison Institute, 2001).

27.  International Centre for Prison Studies, World Prison Brief, "Entire World-Prison Population Rates per 100,000 of the National Population," www.prison studies.org, rates updated March 20, 2005, by Alastair Dunning based on 2004 data, accessed September 14, 2005.

28.  The information in this section is based upon confidential reports of NEA members present at the 2006 meeting of NEA-Retired and the Representative Assembly in Orlando.

# 7

# Union Power or School Board Weakness?

In 1971, I served as an expert witness for the NEA in two cases. In one case, the North Carolina state NEA affiliate was challenging a North Carolina statute that rendered public sector collective bargaining illegal in that state.[1] The other case involved an NEA effort to render Florida's sunshine laws inapplicable to collective bargaining in public education. In North Carolina, my side lost; in Florida, it won, and I received a congratulatory note saying that my testimony played a significant role in the victory. Today, however, I believe that my testimony in both cases was wrong on the issues; were I to testify again on these matters, I would testify that collective bargaining in Florida and as proposed in North Carolina should be struck down unless drastically revised. This chapter sets forth the reasons for my change of mind on the issues at stake in these cases.

Theoretically, the school board represents the interests of third parties: pupils, parents, vendors, taxpayers, and so on. This is impractical in the bargaining context. The school board cannot elicit the reactions of others to last-minute union offers and counteroffers and meld them into a coherent position at the table. Other parties have not been at the table and will not be knowledgeable of the data and reasons for and against the proposals; these can change at any time. Bringing new parties to the table up to date would be highly disruptive. And suppose, as is the usual practice, the union and the school board agree that neither will release any statement to the public on the progress of negotiations until agreement is reached on the entire contract or the parties have reached an impasse in bargaining. Obviously, such agreements minimize the time available to others to study and express their views on the proposed agreement before it becomes public policy.

When agreement is reached, the union holds a membership meeting to ratify the agreement as soon as possible to minimize the emergence of opposition. As soon as the union ratifies the tentative agreement, the board does also to avoid the emergence of opposition from the community. In some situations, the union ratifies the tentative agreement in the afternoon and the school board does so the same evening.

Normally, legislative bodies do not allow a large number of public policies to be placed on the agenda and approved the same day, with practically no time for public analysis and reactions. Note that the school board is usually committed to approve the agreement when it is placed on the board agenda for ratification. In the absence of a major mistake or fraud or sudden change in circumstance, a school board refusal to ratify could be an unfair labor practice. School board ratification is merely a formality in most cases because a competent board negotiator will be constantly in touch with the board through the superintendent or directly.

The policies established in teacher union bargaining are public policies, like speed limits, housing codes, and tax rates. To appreciate the incompatibility of teacher union bargaining with our normal procedure for establishing public policy, we need only cast teacher union bargaining in political terminology. Teacher bargaining then becomes a process in which public policy is made by negotiations between a legislative body and one interest group in a process from which other individuals and groups are excluded.

Under normal school board processes, proposed policies are submitted to the school board, which might refer them to a subcommittee for review. The proposals would go on school board agendas to be considered at scheduled meetings open to anyone. All interested parties would have time to submit their reactions before a vote on the proposal. If adopted, there is no legislative bar to changing the policy any time thereafter. There is no legal bar against any citizen attending a school board meeting and urging support or opposition to a proposal. Despite exceptions and qualifications, this is the common pattern. The bargaining process violates our basic norms for making public policy, but when the process is defined in bargaining terminology, the underlying conflict with our political norms is obscured.

Collective bargaining in school districts violates our political norms in other ways. Suppose A, B, C, D, and E are school board members in a state without a bargaining law. There is no union, but the board members believe an effort will be made to unionize the teachers. The board members agree to raise the salary schedule by 5 percent, but if the teachers vote to unionize, they will raise the schedule only 4 percent, to cover the additional costs of collective bargaining. This would be legal, whatever else one thinks about it.

Now suppose that in a school district in Florida, a bargaining-law state, 30 percent of the teachers have signed authorization cards designating an NEA affiliate as their exclusive representative. This action requires an election to determine whether a majority of the teachers voting wish to be represented by the NEA affiliate. At this point, if not before, the Florida labor law becomes applicable:

Notwithstanding the provisions of subsections (1) and (2), the parties' rights of free speech shall not be infringed, and the expression of any argument or opinions shall not constitute, or be evidence of, an unfair labor practice or of any other violation of this part, if such expression contains no promise of benefits or threat of reprisal or force.[2]

In short, the school board members in district Y have lost the right to say what they will do if the teachers reject unionization. This is true even though we routinely expect elected officials and candidates for public office to tell the electorate what they will do under certain circumstances.

*Abood v. Detroit Board of Education* was a case involving a union assessment of $5 per Detroit teacher for union political activity. Michigan law allowed unions to use union dues for political purposes, and because agency fees equal to dues were allowed at the time, teachers could not avoid the assessment by nonmembership in the union. A group of Detroit teachers filed suit to avoid the assessment, arguing that it forced them to contribute to political causes to which they were opposed—allegedly "a deprivation of the plaintiffs' freedom of association rights protected by their 1st and 14th Amendments rights."[3]

In its decision, the U.S. Supreme Court held that agency fees per se did not violate the constitutional rights of objecting teachers. It also held that the agency fees were chargeable only to the extent that the fees supported collective bargaining, grievance processing, and contract administration (hereinafter, "collective bargaining"). Everything else, including union political activities, was not chargeable to the dissident teachers.

The point of interest here is Justice Powell's comment in his separate concurring opinion:

> An individual can no more be required to affiliate with a candidate by making a contribution than he can be prohibited from such affiliation. The only question is whether a union in the public sector is sufficiently distinguishable from a political candidate or committee to remove the withholding of financial contributions from First Amendment protection. In my view no principled distinction exists.
>
> The ultimate objective of a union in the public sector, like that of a political party, is to influence public decision making in accordance with the views and perceived interests of its membership. Whether a teacher union is concerned with salaries and fringe benefits, teacher qualifications and in-service training, pupil–teacher ratios, length of the school day, student discipline, or the content of the high school curriculum, its objective is to bring school board policy and decisions into harmony with its own views. Similarly, to the extent that school board expenditures and policy are guided by decisions made by the municipal, state, and federal governments, the union's objective is to obtain favorable decisions—and to replace persons in positions of power who will be receptive to the union's viewpoint. In these respects, the public-sector union is indistinguishable from the traditional political party in this country.
>
> What distinguishes the public-sector union from the political party—and the distinction is a limited one—is that most of its members are employees who share similar economic interests and who may have a common professional perspective on some issues of public policy.[4]

Do the similarities between collective bargaining and conventional school district policymaking demonstrate that school board bargaining is a political action—or do the differences demonstrate that school board bargaining is not a form of political action? To answer these questions, consider the similarities between these two ways of making public policy:

- The same parties are involved: the public, the teachers, the teacher union, parents, students, and the school board.
- The strategy and tactics are very similar, if not identical. In bargaining, the teacher union uses picketing, telephone banks, demonstra-

tions, advertisements—all prominent tactics in political campaigns. The main difference is that a teacher strike or threat of strike does not play a role in political campaigns.

- The objectives of the parties in bargaining and political action are the same.

The differences are important, but as Justice Powell points out, "no principled distinction" can be made between public sector unions and political parties. Nevertheless, as a result of the *Abood* decision, twenty-two states require or allow agency fees. This does not make sense if it is unconstitutional to force citizens to contribute to causes to which they are opposed.[5] Teachers who pay agency fees are generally opposed to union policies including the agency fees. Justice Powell did not apply his insight to the case in which he expressed it.

Regardless of whether teacher union bargaining is a form of political action, it gives the teacher unions enormous advantages in the school board policy process. Can collective bargaining be salvaged without violating democratic political norms? Probably not, but a state could require meetings with stringent guidelines until agreement is reached between the parties. The agreement would go on the school board calendar for public hearings, perhaps for fifteen working days after the agreement is reached and published on the district website. At this time, the school board could exercise the right to modify the agreement unilaterally, and unfair labor practice charges would not be applicable. This would pose the danger of board bad faith at the table, knowing that it could unilaterally change a tentative agreement without any penalties. Of course, any such change would generate intense opposition from school district unions, but some form of the idea might be worth a try. The founding rationale for collective bargaining in public education was that it would ensure that school boards would sincerely consider teacher views on terms and conditions of employment. Convoluted as it is, this suggestion would satisfy that concern.

## THE INFLUENCE OF POLITICAL FACTORS ON BARGAINING

The influence of political factors on bargaining is an important difference between public and private sector bargaining that is clearly advantageous to teacher unions. Politics affects not only what is proposed, accepted, rejected, and modified, but also the timing of concessions, the management stance on grievances, and the extent of management support services for bargaining. Even the choice of management negotiator may be subjected to an unofficial but real union veto.

Teacher union political influence is often underestimated because it is not always obvious. The influence is often more veto power than "do" power. One should not be misled, however, by the fact that the union-backed candidates do not always support the teachers or may even oppose them on occasion. Such situations notwithstanding, the political dimension is advantageous to public employees. Governors and state legislators are rarely in a position to affect the substance of private sector bargaining, but the governor is typically the most important single individual in the annual aid to education controversies in the state legislatures. Governors frequently have a decisive role to play in whether there is to be public sector bargaining at all and, if there is, in the composition of the state labor boards that regulate the process.

The in-kind services provided by teachers adds considerably to NEA and AFT political influence. For several years, the teacher unions have urged their members to vote by absentee ballot so as to be free for campaign activities on election day. The unions sometimes urge their members to take "personal necessity leave" on election day to be available for election day support activities. This tactic is especially convenient where the union contract allows one or more days of "personal necessity leave" at no loss in pay and no questions asked.

In short, the prebargaining scenario in which the teacher organizations could not provide grassroots support for candidates for public office disappeared when collective bargaining emerged; the NEA and AFT probably provide more in-kind support for political candidates than any other organization active in American politics. Teachers work 180 to 190 days a year and have less than an eight-hour day when they are working. More than the average voter, they work in telephone banks, put up signs on homes and cars, provide accurate mailing lists of probable voters, vote more often and for union-endorsed candidates and positions, distribute literature, show up for rallies, write letters to the editor, and go door to door when that is called for. Understandably, there is virtually unanimous agreement that the NEA and AFT are among the most powerful interest groups in the nation.[6] According to the *Economist*, "it is only a small exaggeration to describe the Democratic Party as a wholly-owned subsidiary of the teachers unions."[7] It was not surprising that Hillary Clinton announced her candidacy for the U.S. Senate at a 2000 United Federation of Teachers function in New York City. Among large mainstream organizations, voters were more likely to vote for a candidate because of an NEA endorsement and less likely to oppose candidates for this reason.[8]

Table 7.1 is from an NEA manual to encourage teachers to become active politically.[9] It reflects a drastic difference between teacher and private sector unions on the importance of politics. When you add the greater importance of politics to the unparalleled opportunities teachers have to meet voters (parents) on a regular basis, it is understandable why the teacher unions have extraordinary influence in political affairs.

**Table 7.1.**

**Who are the decision makers who actually make the following decisions for you?**

| | |
|---|---|
| Your salary | |
| Amount of federal school aid | |
| School budget | |
| Certification standards | |
| Class size | |
| Length of school year | |
| Social Security participation | |
| Course content | |
| Your fringe benefits | |
| Employee rights and due process | |
| Retirement benefits | |
| Mandatory classes | |
| Tuition tax credits | |
| Corporal punishment policies | |
| School system insurance carrier | |
| Chapter I (Title I) funding | |
| Duty-free lunch | |
| Length of workday | |
| Health and safety standards | |
| Hiring practices | |
| Worker's compensation | |
| Unemployment compensation | |

**Now that you've completed the above list, go on to see how many decisions you can identify that have the same direct bearing on your personal or professional life that are *not* political.**

*Source: NEA Series in Practical Politics* (Washington, DC: National Education Association, n.d.), 3.

Teacher union political power is a paradoxical outcome of unionization. When the NEA enrolled school administrators, local associations were not ordinarily significant political actors. School administrators had no interest in building a strong local association that could effectively oppose school boards and school officials. Many teachers had no interest in joining administrator-dominated associations, but superintendents often made joining them a condition of employment. However, in order to justify teacher membership in teacher associations, it was essential to demonstrate that the associations were promoting teacher welfare. The solution was to have local associations work with their state affiliates to enact legislation, such as state aid to education, that benefited both administrators and teachers.

Under this strategy, there were no benefits for any teachers unless all teachers and administrators in the state could benefit. Situations in which a strong local association could achieve benefits were lost by this strategy. Collective bargaining enabled teachers to take advantage of opportunities at the local level, and as the NEA unionized, it adopted the union practice of unified membership. Teachers could no longer join only the local, state, or national organization; they had to join at all three levels. Thus bargaining led to the huge NEA membership increases at all levels, and its political influence at all levels was greatly enhanced by its membership growth. Collective bargaining, which emerged as a reaction to the ineffectiveness of legislative approaches to teacher welfare, greatly enhanced teacher union ability to enact teacher welfare legislation.

## THE NEA POSITION: "EVERY EDUCATION DECISION IS A POLITICAL ONE"

Ironically, an NEA press release asserts that "Every education decision is a political one."[10] This NEA statement is very close to if not the truth of the matter. However, our political system assumes that the teacher unions can and should be regulated like private sector unions whose activities can be distinguished as either political or nonpolitical. Thus we have the teacher unions telling their members to become active politically because "every education decision is a political decision," while officially reporting until 2006 that no union general revenue funds are spent for politics.[11]

In adopting these contradictory stances, the teacher unions are simply taking advantage of flawed legislation that assumes a clear-cut distinction between collective bargaining (allegedly a nonpolitical activity) and political activity in the public sector. Instead of trying to narrow the scope of teacher union political activity, perhaps the conservative position should have been precisely the opposite — to agree that "every education decision is a political decision determined by elected or appointed officials"[12] and try to get all teacher union activity declared political activity.

In such a framework, union dues would have to be treated as political contributions. School board policies on terms and conditions of employment would be subject to the same framework as school board policies on other issues; no longer would they be negotiated with one interest group. Teachers could still choose collective representation, but the representative would not have any statutorily privileged access to the school board.

## THE DUAL SYSTEM OF BENEFITS

Prior to collective bargaining, teachers relied heavily on state legislation for benefits. As it turned out, the existence of statutory benefits did not preclude the unions from bargaining for additional benefits. If a statute provided ten days of sick leave, the teacher unions bargained for twelve or fifteen. Usually, the unions tried to incorporate the statutory benefits in the contracts; for example, if a statute provided a thirty-minute duty-free lunch, the union negotiator would say, "We already have this benefit by law, so you wouldn't be giving us anything, but it would make the contract (or me) look better if we included it in the contract." Using such rhetoric, the unions were frequently successful in incorporating statutory benefits in the contract; by incorporating the statutory benefits in the contract, school management gave the union a contractual remedy. Teachers would not sue the school board because they received only twenty-nine minutes of their thirty-minute duty-free lunch, but filing a grievance over the issue was a different matter. The grievance might be a convenient way for the union officers to demonstrate their commitment to teacher rights, or a way to harass a principal who had aroused union antagonism, or serve as a warning against future encroachment on the duty-free lunch. Furthermore,

having the benefit in the contract ensured that the teachers would have it
if the statute were repealed.

The upshot was and is a dual system of benefits that has no counterpart
in the private sector. Private sector employees have statutory benefits but
not on the scale of statutory benefits for teachers. Repeal of the statutory
benefits or taking them out of the scope of bargaining should have been
included in the state bargaining laws, but this did not happen. As a result,
teacher bargaining often started from a high benefit level.

California is the bargaining-law state with the most extensive dual system of teacher rights and benefits. In 1992, there were over four hundred
statutes on matters subject to bargaining. As might be expected, the statutory terms and conditions of employment in addition to a bargaining
statute have been a management disaster. I served as a labor negotiator for
twelve California school boards from 1977 to the mid-1980s. On several
occasions, conflict over dual benefits and remedies was the most contentious issue in the negotiations. The unions frequently sought to add
statutory rights to contracts; the board position was one or the other, but
it was not going to agree to forum shopping.

To illustrate the problem, in addition to local antidiscrimination statutes
in most California communities, there are state and federal antidiscrimination statutes. Nevertheless, the teacher unions always proposed a contractual antidiscrimination clause. Board reaction might have been, "We
will accept such a clause if you are willing to waive other remedies," but
the California bargaining statute provided that contracts could not deprive
teachers of their statutory rights and benefits. Thus, even if the union
agreed to the board proposal, it would not bind the teachers; even losing
a discrimination case in arbitration would not necessarily preclude a
teacher from filing and winning a lawsuit under the state or federal antidiscrimination statutes.

A counterargument is that teachers should not be deprived of their
statutory benefits merely because they had been accorded bargaining
rights; however, legislators could have met this objection by sunsetting
the statutory benefits in three to five years. This would have given the
unions opportunities to include the statutory benefits in their contracts before they were phased out. In any event, the continuing practice of adding
statutory to contractual benefits on the same issue is undermining school
board viability in the states that allow it to happen.

# UNION ADVANTAGES IN SCHOOL
# DISTRICT COLLECTIVE BARGAINING

The supporters of collective bargaining had argued that it would increase productivity; employees who were treated fairly would be a happier, more productive labor force. The problem with this argument is that experience is overwhelmingly to the contrary; nonunion companies have been more productive in one industry after another. This would not happen if unionized companies were more productive.[13] Indeed, if that were the case, management should be promoting unionization, but this is obviously not happening.

Furthermore, the argument that unionization fosters productivity is contrary to the dynamics of unionization. The union negotiator's typical argument is that the employees are not being paid what they deserve, especially compared to others in the same field working for nearby employers. Union negotiators know that dissatisfied employees put more pressure on employers than satisfied ones, so generating dissatisfaction is a common union tactic in bargaining.

Collective bargaining gravely weakened school boards in several ways. School boards accustomed to policymaking on their own schedule found it difficult to operate on a schedule that they could no longer control. Not only did teacher unions have the right to bargain on the schedule itself, but some of the deadlines were established by statute or labor board regulations. Many school board members could not cope with the pressure to consider and make decisions on dozens of school board policies within a relatively brief time.

School board members and administrators often fear union retaliation at the polls for opposing union demands in bargaining. This is especially true when school board elections are held separately from general elections; it is commonplace for the teacher unions to be the only interest group active in school board elections, which often elicit only 3 to 5 percent of the eligible voters. School administrators worry about their future, even their present, position, as the teacher unions conduct campaigns against candidates for school board and administrators deemed "antiunion" or "antieducation" for opposing union demands.

Here again, the differences between school district and private sector bargaining are critical. In the private sector, the management bargaining team is composed of company officials with huge career and company stakes in the outcome. In public education, the school board usually consists of five, seven, or nine citizens with no expertise in bargaining or career stake in the outcome or in getting the best possible contract. In many cases, the private interests of school board members, especially in getting reelected, are highly conducive to excessive concessions, especially if their costs are delayed for several years. Of course many board members and school administrators contribute outstanding services, but school board incentives differ drastically from private sector incentives and constitute a huge union advantage. The private sector competence advantage is often reduced but not entirely eliminated by the employment of outside labor negotiators, a common practice in public education also.

In the private sector, the market responds immediately to the contract; company shares rise or fall, depending on perceptions of the contract by stock analysts and shareholders. In public education, few, if any, individuals in or out of the school district read the contract and can interpret its provisions in conjunction with district resources and educational plans.

Consider the weakness of school boards in strike situations. The number of strikes isn't very informative because it doesn't tell us how many strikes were averted by unjustified concessions. Also, strikes encompass a much broader range of concerted actions than teachers not showing up for work en masse. For instance, in many states, teachers cannot be required to supervise extracurricular activities for pay. A mass refusal to coach athletic teams would be legal and involve minimal economic loss but generate huge pressure on the school board to accept union demands. A strike need affect only a small number of classes to be effective, and teachers often utilize their children to disrupt school operations or carry proteacher signs—activities sure to be publicized in newspapers and on television. Furthermore, there is no economic risk in a mass effort to shut the schools down because the days that schools are shut down must be made up to obtain the state aid essential to pay everyone. Thus the teachers get the tactical benefit of the disruption without the economic losses inherent in most private sector strikes.

Note also that the school districts have difficult problems relating to support personnel. If a strike is threatened, should school bus drivers and cafeteria employees be directed to go to work, stay home, or await directives until the last possible second? And through all of these scenarios, the unions have an array of staff experienced in strike situations, whereas school districts usually have none. And if the situations described above are not serious enough, what happens to the illegality of strikes when state judges are elected?

School boards find it extremely difficult to discipline teachers for strikes or similar disruptive actions. First of all, replacements are not available, except in very small districts. Second, meeting the legal requirements for dismissal can sometimes be very difficult. Unions sometimes threaten to strike and pull back at the last second; after the district hires replacements, the teachers show up on the same days as the replacements. If the school administration closes the schools, their phones ring continuously with calls from parents who want to go to work but don't want to leave their young children alone in the house all day. The parents naturally put pressure on the administration, not the union; the superintendent and school board determined to resist excessive concessions often see their public support dwindle rapidly as more and more parents are inconvenienced by the strike. Anticipating this development, some school board members and school superintendents make the concessions and spare themselves the trouble of resisting.

In the private sector, the employers can lock out the employees, subcontract some operations out, shift operations to another plant, stock up in anticipation of a strike, and replace striking employees. In short, private sector employers have a broad range of defensive measures not available to school boards. Because the costs of the concessions to the union can be shifted to future generations, it is not surprising that the concessions are often made.

## UNION SURVIVAL: A CRUCIAL PUBLIC–PRIVATE SECTOR DIFFERENCE

In the private sector, unionized companies may

- Go out of business
- Produce more with fewer employees due to technological progress
- Contract out work to nonunion companies
- Establish nonunion plants in states hostile to unions
- Transfer operations to other countries with much lower labor costs

The cumulative upshot of these factors is that private sector unions must continually organize new bargaining units just to maintain their membership, revenues, staff, and political clout. Obviously, this is not the case in public education or in the public sector generally. The dissident unions that withdrew from the AFL-CIO in July 2005 were mainly private sector unions that wanted the AFL-CIO to devote more of its resources to organizing. Most of the government sector unions, like the NEA and AFT, do not face the daunting problems of staying alive; their focus is on expanding unionization in the government sector.

Nevertheless, it is remarkable that less than 8 percent of private sector nonfarm workers eligible to join a union are actually union members. Most citizens assume that the percentage is much higher, but labor historian Leo Troy expects the decline to continue, albeit not to the point of extinction. Troy refers to the nonunion workers as preferring "individual representation" instead of "no representation," the phrase used in National Labor Relations Board elections.[14]

Why is there so little public understanding that individual representation far exceeds union representation in the private sector? One reason is that labor conflict is news. When unions strike, the media take note as they do not when adjustments in compensation are made routinely in nonunion companies. Salary adjustments made annually are not news; salary increases at the expiration of a three-year contract, allegedly to prevent a strike, call for news conferences and self-congratulatory comments about what the union has won for members. Naturally, the attention accorded individual representation did not increase as collective bargaining declined in the private sector, where it was never the majority practice to begin with.

## THE DUTY OF LOYALTY

In the private sector, employees are limited in what they can say publicly about their employer. A private sector union can urge a boycott to help the union get a "fair" contract, but it cannot urge a boycott because the employer makes the worst widgets in the country. This duty of loyalty is completely absent in public education. For constitutional reasons, teacher unions and teachers can allege that the district has the worst education system in the country without fear of violating the duty of loyalty because legally, there is none in public education. Limitations on teacher rights to criticize school operations or policies would be unconstitutional; the point is that their representational rights should have taken this into account. The absence of any restrictions on teacher criticism in conjunction with the lengthy impasse procedures exacerbated school board–teacher union conflict, contrary to union claims that collective bargaining would result in harmonious relations between teachers and administrators.

## JOINT BARGAINING

Still another difference relates to the ability of employers to protect their interests by joint bargaining. Consider the hotel industry. If some hotels are open during a strike against other hotels in the area, the open hotels can earn huge profits while the hotels that are not open are experiencing huge losses. The hotel unions try to get a contract with the weaker hotels, none of which can hold out individually against the union. To counteract this union strategy, the hotels form a united front to bargain on area-wide terms and conditions of employment. This is intended to avoid union ability to force the weakest hotel to be the first to agree to a contract and then use the first contract as the minimum that will be accepted in the contracts with the other hotels. In addition, joint bargaining avoids the possibility that any particular hotel would be devastated by the costs of protracted bargaining. Any hotel that breaks ranks and reaches agreement with the union must pay huge liquidated damages to the other hotels to ensure that defections do not materialize.

School boards cannot adopt joint bargaining for two reasons. First, school boards cannot delegate their powers as private employers are free to do. More explicitly, school boards cannot delegate their powers to a coalition that bargains through a single representative, with the costs of bargaining shared among the coalition members. Even if such an arrangement were clearly legal, the political problems are usually too difficult to overcome. Suppose a union official or union supporter is elected to a school board in the coalition. It would be extremely difficult, if not impossible, to avoid devastating leaks to the union bargaining team. Meanwhile, because full-time union staff usually negotiate for all of the local unions in the area, the union negotiators usually know which districts can be pressured to settle first on terms favorable to the union.

The interaction between political power and teacher union power is evident in recent legislation that provides public sector unions with protections that are not available to private sector unions. For example, several municipalities have enacted legislation that increases the minimum wage for local public employees. This illustrates how public sector union political power can reinforce their bargaining power.

## FUTURE COSTS: THE PUBLIC–PRIVATE SECTOR DIFFERENCE

In the private sector, the erosion of managerial authority and the additional costs imposed by union contracts are limited by competition and shareholder interests. In 1983, the Kaiser Steel Company had to declare bankruptcy because its contractual obligations to pay for the health benefits of retirees and their dependents were greater than the worth of the company. Private sector opposition to absorbing all of the rising costs of health care reflects imperative company needs to avoid another debacle of this kind.[15] As matters stand, these employer incentives are not operative, or as fully operative, in public education; escalating costs are a problem for future taxpayers but do not threaten to end the enterprise. In short, the runaway cost problem is much more serious in the public sector because public agencies do not face the threat of competition and costs can be deferred to future taxpayers.

## CAN SCHOOL BOARD WEAKNESS BE FIXED?

If the preceding analysis is valid, why is the focus of reform overwhelmingly on teacher union power? There are thousands of public intellectuals, professors of educational administration, educational policy, public administration, public policy, and political science whose broad field includes school board structure and operations, but very few have been professionally interested in bargaining issues. School administrators are painfully aware of the dysfunctional nature of school boards, but expressing that opinion would endanger their prospects for continued appointment or promotion. For various reasons, no major interest or scholarly group is concerned with pursuing school board issues, and politicians have nothing to gain by addressing them. Professors of educational administration ignore the issues; their subject matter is how to get along with school boards, not how to get rid of them or their structural weaknesses.

Three strategies to cope with teacher union power come to mind:

- Replace school boards by placing education under the control of mayors or other public officials responsible for most public services. The National School Boards Association (NSBA) adopted a resolution criticizing this policy at its 2006 convention.
- Weaken the teacher union power to block reform.
- Elect school board members to office who are not beholden to the unions.

There are positive and negative factors in each option, and situational factors will often dictate the choice of option, which are not exclusive; however, the discussion is limited to a brief comment on the third option.

At first glance, electing more school board candidates equipped to deal with union issues seems to be a hopeless endeavor. Most school board candidates or potential candidates lack knowledge of union vulnerabilities and the campaign resources to exploit them. Of course, union issues cannot be the focus of every school board campaign, but they would be much more prominent if more candidates were better informed on union issues.

Arguably, the advantages resulting from the political orientation of school board members are neutralized by the fact that school employers are not as free to commit funds as private sector employers. State statutes may limit the amounts that school boards can commit and the duration of agreements, to cite two frequent limitations on school boards as employers. Although the limitations occasionally hamper bargaining, or are used as excuses by school board negotiators, they are seldom an operative factor at the table. School boards cannot purchase supplies at a discount because they are poor; neither can they employ teachers at much less than the going rate. Furthermore, there are several ways to compensate for inadequate district funds, such as fewer workdays or a shorter school day.

The upshot of the foregoing discussion is that teacher union power has been mischaracterized to some extent. The teacher unions are powerful because school boards lack the options available to private employers when their operations are threatened by a union. Furthermore, no group or organization has been able to remedy the situation created by school board weaknesses as employers. Having mayors responsible for education would be an improvement but would be of limited applicability outside of large urban school districts.

Ironically, just as hardly anyone paid any attention to the weakness of teacher organizations before collective bargaining, hardly anyone pays any attention to the weakness of school boards during and after the establishment of collective bargaining in education. Its negative consequences are enormous but under the radar screen.

It is doubtful whether an effort to change the school board structure would be successful. The American people are accustomed to school boards; their very weakness has shielded them from criticism. It is astonishing how often the teacher unions are criticized for certain contractual provisions while no one criticizes the school boards for agreeing to them. There is no consensus on what should replace the school board structure, and the controversies over the issue would drag out for decades. For many successful politicians, school boards were the first step up the political ladder, and for many others, they have been welcome opportunities to serve their communities.

Note that the teacher unions usually oppose the abolition of school boards. In Los Angeles, the United Teachers of Los Angeles (UTLA), a joint NEA–AFT local, fought Los Angeles mayor Antonio Villaraigosa's efforts to transfer the school board's authority to the mayor, even though Villaraigosa had been an AFT representative in Los Angeles before he entered politics. Similarly, the UFT in New York City opposed mayor Michael Bloomberg's efforts to govern the public schools in New York City. The unions are aware that they have a good thing going, and they will not give it up easily.

## UNION-INITIATED REFORMS

The NEA and AFT and their state and local affiliates are well aware of the criticism directed at them for blocking reform and sponsoring new policies that arguably exacerbate low achievement. To counter the criticisms and to raise achievement levels, twenty-one NEA and AFT locals formed the Teacher Union Reform Network (TURN) in 1996; the number increased to thirty locals by 2006.

Over time, TURN and its participating local affiliates received funding and in-kind support from the following sources:

- National Education Association (NEA)
- American Federation of Teachers (AFT)
- Broad Foundation
- MacArthur Foundation
- Pew Charitable Trusts
- U.S. Department of Education (USED)
- Center for Policy Research in Education (CPRE)
- National Commission on Teaching and America's Future
- Graduate School of Education, UCLA
- Educational Laboratory (LAB) at Brown University[16]

## RATIONALE

According to its mission statement, TURN is to seek consistently higher levels of student achievement by "seeking to expand the scope of bargaining to include instructional and professional issues."[17] This mission statement underscores the confusion that pervades union issues. Expanding the scope of bargaining is expanding the policies that are negotiated bilaterally by school boards and teacher unions. TURN does not define "instructional and professional issues," but if given their commonly understood meanings, not much is left for resolution either by democratic representative governments or individual teachers. We would not expect unions of doctors to negotiate the procedures for brain surgery, but our reform-minded teacher union leaders believe that collective bargaining over how to teach reading is the way to achieve educational reform.

According to Adam Urbanski, president of the Rochester (New York) Teachers Association and founding chairman of TURN,

> In addition to the traditional "bread and butter" issues such as salary and benefits, teacher unions should seek to negotiate class size, curricular matters, the content of professional development, the structure of instructional

time, the organization of teaching schedules, and all the other professional and instructional issues that are now, at best, elective items of bargaining. Because these are not mandatory items of bargaining, representatives of management can and often do refuse to address them at the negotiating table. One way to change that is to change the existing legislation that keeps these issues off the bargaining table.[18]

Urbanski's rationale is vague, factually inaccurate, and indefensible from almost any standpoint. Items such as class size and the content of professional development are subject to bargaining in most bargaining-law states. The fact that a matter is not subject to bargaining does not restrict the teacher unions from expressing their views to management about it. School management is typically required to consult the union on matters not subject to bargaining or agrees to do so regardless. Note also that Urbanski does not cite examples of his argument: Where did the unions propose and school management fail to consider union positions on "curricular matters" that would have enhanced student learning?

Urbanski's rationale would require school boards to bargain on scores of additional issues, including a host of items on which teachers disagree; the costs of bargaining would escalate dramatically, as would conflict within and between the union and the school board. To whom would the unions be accountable and for what if they insisted upon policies that turned out to be disastrous? Suppose the parties bargain for a "structure of instructional time," but after the contract is signed, overwhelming evidence emerges that the structure is ineffective. Would the union and the teachers feel bound to adhere to the contractual structure? If not, what is the point of including it in the contract? There is none, and there is no point to Urbanski's proposal to extend the scope of bargaining.

## CONCLUSIONS

As pointed out previously, the state teacher bargaining laws were more or less patterned after the National Labor Relations Act (NLRA). This pattern did not adequately take account of the differences between the public and private sectors. The differences were not completely ignored; for example, the prohibitions against teacher strikes (though often ineffective) usually differed sharply from the treatment of strikes under the NLRA; however, the different economic consequences of collective bargaining in the two sectors was also overlooked, to the detriment of public sector labor relations.

In the private sector, nonunion employers in the same industry are a major threat to unionization. The nonunion employers enjoy a competitive advantage over unionized employers; the latter are disadvantaged in product markets, and this is a major constraint on union bargaining power, as is amply illustrated by recent experience in the automobile industry; U.S. unions cannot extend their terms and conditions to carmakers in Japan, South Korea, and other countries, possibly excepting Canada. In short, producer competition severely limits the bargaining power of U.S. unions in the automobile industry. In order for unions to be effective in a competitive industry, they must "take wages out of competition," that is ensure that all producers face the same labor costs, hence are not disadvantaged in competition with other producers.

In contrast, the teacher unions function in what is essentially a noncompetitive industry in the market for teacher services. Union benefits in a particular school district do not disadvantage the school district vis-à-vis other school districts; on the contrary, the main effect of its higher labor costs is to spur teacher efforts in other districts to unionize in order to achieve the higher benefits due or thought to be due to unionization. School boards with higher labor costs do not fear being forced out of business as a result; on the contrary the school boards in low-wage districts are under strong pressure to raise teacher compensation, not to maintain it at a lower level than its neighboring school boards.[19]

## NOTES

1. *Bassett v. Braddock*, no. 71-1462, Circuit Court of 11th Judicial District, Dade County, Florida. Decided March 25, 1971.

2. Florida Statute 447.501 (3), Florida School Laws, 2003 edition.

3. *Abood v. Detroit Board of Education*, 431 U.S. 209 (1977), 212. Frequently, teacher union proposals are headed by a boilerplate sentence stating, "This agreement constitutes board policy for its duration and may not be amended or terminated, in whole or in part, by the school board without the express written agreement of the

union." Actually, the sentence is redundant; the agreement would be board policy for its duration even without it.

4. *Abood v. Detroit Board of Education*, 259.

5. In January 2007, the U.S. Supreme Court heard argument in *Davenport v. Washington Education Association*, a case involving the rights of agency fee payers to avoid payment of agency fees spent for political activities to which the fee payers object. A decision is expected some time after this book is published.

6. For summaries of teacher union political and bargaining power, see Terry M. Moe, "Political Control and the Future of School Accountability," in *No Child Left Behind*, ed. Paul E. Peterson and Martin R. West, (Washington, DC: Brookings, 2003), 80–106; Myron Lieberman, *The Teacher Unions* (New York: Free Press, 1997), 69–115.

7. "Lexington: Inching toward Reform," *Economist*, July 6, 2002, 14.

8. Terry M. Moe, "The Union Label on the Ballot Box," *Education Next* (Summer 2006), 59–66.

9. *NEA Series in Practical Politics* (Washington, DC: National Education Association, n.d.), 3.

10. "Political Activism Takes Center Stage at 2004 Annual Meeting," NEA Press Release (Washington, DC: National Education Association, July 2, 2004).

11. The Landmark Legal Foundation has launched Phase II of its NEA Accountability Project, a major effort to expose the various ways that the NEA and its state affiliates conduct political operations while claiming that they do not spend any union revenues for this purpose. *NEA Accountability Project Phase II* (Washington, DC: Landmark Legal Foundation, 2005). In 2005, the U.S. Department of Labor issued new regulations for union reporting on DOL form LM-2, which closed some of the loopholes by which labor unions avoided disclosure of their political expenditures.

12. "Political Activism Takes Center Stage," NEA Press Release.

13. The union argument that students in unionized school districts achieve at higher levels than in nonunionized districts illustrates this argument. Former Harvard dean and professor Susan Moore Johnson has opined that there is insufficient evidence on the issue while avoiding any explanation of why the effects of unionization on productivity elsewhere in the economy would not be applicable to education.

14. Leo Troy, *Beyond Unions and Collective Bargaining* (Armonk, NY: M. E. Sharpe, 1999).

15. As this was written, General Motors, which pays over $1 billion annually in health benefits for its new employees and retirees, had just avoided bankruptcy by a United Auto Workers (UAW) agreement to accept cash payments for early retirement and substantial savings in health benefits.

16. TURN Exchange, "Partners and Foundations," www.turnexchange.net/resources/partnersfoundations.html, accessed July 22, 2006.

17. TURN Exchange, "Mission Statement," www.turnexchange.net/about.html, accessed March 22, 2007.

18. Adam Urbanski, "Reform or Be Reformed," *Education Next* (Fall 2001), www.educationnext.org/20013/38urbanski.html, accessed July 22, 2006.

19. For a discussion of why and how private sector unions do not enjoy as much power to raise wages as is commonly ascribed to them, see Paul C. Weiler, *Governing the Workplace* (Cambridge, MA: Harvard University Press, 1990), 105–133.

# 8

## Individual Representation: Back to the Future?

The preceding chapters are critical of collective bargaining but do not suggested any alternative system of representation. To do this, let us review briefly the rise and decline of unions and collective bargaining in the private sector for any clues that would be helpful in public education. In the private sector, union density in nonagricultural employment has decreased from a high of 36 percent in 1953 to less than 8 percent in 2007. During this time, union density in public education increased from less than 1 percent to about 75 percent. Inasmuch as private sector experience paved the way for public sector bargaining, we should consider the possibility that changes in the private sector portend the emergence of new employment structures in public education.

Preliminarily, it should be emphasized that diminution of NEA and AFT influence on education policy would not necessarily be tantamount to improving it. The status of education in states without a bargaining law underscores the point that no upsurge in constructive change would automatically follow weaker or different or no teacher unions. The fact remains, however, that the teacher unions have blocked several desirable policies and are responsible for several dysfunctional ones. Inasmuch as their power to take these actions is based upon collective bargaining as a system of teacher representation, we should consider alternative systems that might provide adequate teacher representation without the negatives associated with collective bargaining.

Prior to the Wagner Act (1935), private sector employment was largely at will. This meant that, as one case famously put it,

> men must be left without interference to buy and sell where they please and to discharge or retain employees at will for good cause, or no cause, or even for bad cause, without thereby being guilty of an unlawful act per se. It is a right which an employee may exercise in the same way, to the same extent, for the same cause or want of cause as the employer.[1]

## COLLECTIVE BARGAINING: THE CONGRESSIONAL RESPONSE TO UNEQUAL BARGAINING POWER

The critics of employment at will emphasized the practical inequality that resulted from it. For example, to a company that employs 10,000 workers, it makes little difference who fills many of its positions; if one leaves or is dismissed, the company can easily find an adequate replacement. To the employee summarily dismissed, however, the consequences can be traumatic, involving change in residence, schooling, economic security, employability elsewhere, and other matters too numerous to mention. Furthermore, the employee had to absorb all the costs of any legal action to challenge his dismissal, a discouraging prospect in view of the resources usually available to the company. Just the costs of finding alternative employment can burden employees heavily.

To be sure, the "unfairness" of employment at will could, and sometimes did, run in the other direction, as when farm workers struck without warning when the crops they were hired to pick were perishable fruit that had to be picked within a few days or their entire value would be lost. In any event, collective bargaining was the congressional solution to the problem of unequal bargaining power, real or alleged, that existed between individual workers and employers. Under the National Labor Relations Act (NLRA), enacted in 1935, employers had to bargain with an exclusive representative for all of the employees in an appropriate bargaining unit. The idea was that a union representing all of the employees with the power to strike would equalize the bargaining power between employers and employees. Despite strong initial opposition, management accepted collective bargaining, mainly because it was the law, not because it was deemed to be a superior system of employment relations.

In public employment, *Perry v. Sindermann* is a landmark case on employment at will.[2] Sindermann had been an instructor at Odessa Junior College in Texas for ten years. Faculty did not receive tenure no matter how long they had been employed, but in 1968, Sindermann was fired without any statement of reasons. Therefore, he had no opportunity to rebut the reasons. Sindermann sued, alleging that his constitutional rights had been violated. His argument was that as a result of his ten years of service, he had acquired an "expectancy" of reemployment. This "expectancy of reemployment" was asserted to be a property interest that had been taken from him without due process of law. Eventually, the U.S. Supreme Court upheld his argument.

From a constitutional point of view, the college should have provided the following elements of due process to fire Sindermann so that he had no legal recourse:

- Reasonable prior notice of any proposed action that would deprive an employee of a property interest
- A written statement of the proposed action and reasons for it
- The right to be represented by counsel at a hearing on the merits
- The right to examine and cross-examine witnesses
- A written record of the proceedings
- A written decision on the merits
- Some type of court review

The upshot of *Sindermann* is that public employers who wish to fire employees are held to standards that do not apply to private sector employers. Even in the absence of a tenure law or a collective bargaining contract, public school teachers have a constitutional right not to be fired arbitrarily or capriciously. In effect, *Sindermann* limited dismissal at will for public school teachers, as do tenure statutes in most states. Employment at will as described in *Payne v. Western and Atlantic Railroad* has disappeared and will not return in the foreseeable future.

Actually, state and federal law had eroded employment at will prior to the *Sindermann* decision. For example, under the U.S. Supreme Court decision in *Brown v. Board of Education* and the Civil Rights Act of 1964, employers cannot dismiss employees on the basis of race, color, religion, national origin, or sex. It has been illegal for private sector employers to fire an employee for trying to organize a union since 1935. As is evident in the following sections, many other federal and state statutes limit employer discretion in a variety of ways relating to their employees.

## STATUTORY RIGHTS

As the deficiencies of collective bargaining became increasingly apparent, the unions began to focus on statutory rights to achieve their objectives. Statutory rights are rights like teacher tenure laws; employees are entitled to these rights as a matter of law. Congress has established statutory rights in the following legislation:

- Equal Pay Act, 1963
- Age Discrimination in Employment Act, 1968
- Mine Safety Act, 1969
- Occupational Safety and Health Act, 1970
- Rehabilitation Act, 1973
- Employee Retirement Income Security Act, 1974
- Age Discrimination in Employment and Worker Adjustment and Retraining Notification Act, 1988
- Americans with Disabilities Act, 1990
- Family and Medical Leave Act, 1993

In addition to the rights that were enacted, there have been unsuccessful efforts to enact federal legislation that would prohibit unjust dismissals, require health benefits, or provide additional worker rights.[3]

Although some of this legislation has been helpful to employees, in no case has it led to all of the benefits envisaged by its sponsors. Generally speaking, the statutory rights movement has been unsuccessful in adding significantly to worker rights, but the unions have managed to defeat legislation that would weaken or eliminate the rights that they have. Their successes, such as the Family and Medical Leave Act of 1993, have come on issues on which they can build support from other organizations because the legislation is not viewed as "prounion" but as supportive of a much broader constituency.

There are several reasons statutory rights have not fulfilled the hopes of their union supporters:

- The complexity of legislation that tries to cover tens of thousands of companies of varying sizes, resources, and financial status. In some cases, such as the Employee Retirement Income Security Act (ERISA), the legislation spawned a mini-industry of consultants to inform the parties affected how the legislation related to them.
- The statutes were sometimes easily evaded with negligible penalties for violations.
- The statutes overlooked the incentives to violate their intent. For example, ERISA provided tax-free funds for employers while the government absorbed the cost of failures; this encouraged excessive risk taking by the companies.
- The statutes included vague standards that were interpreted differently by different political appointees.
- Enforcement staff was inadequate.[4]

The foregoing reasons are frequently applicable to the statutory rights of teachers, but they do not imply that the statutory approach to worker rights has always failed to remedy a weakness of collective bargaining.

## ENTERPRISE RIGHTS AND EMPLOYEE HANDBOOKS

Enterprise rights are rights that employees have been granted by employers in the absence of a union or have been awarded judicially. They emerged in situations when nonunion employees were egregiously fired and sued their employers, claiming they were entitled to the rights set forth in the company handbooks distributed to employees. The companies may have adopted a fair dismissal policy but never envisaged that it would become a legal obligation superseding employment at will, but state courts began to rule otherwise. In *Toussaint v. Blue Cross and Blue Shield*, the Michigan court treated the rights in the employee handbook as an offer and the employee's accepting employment as the acceptance of the offer.[5]

Some employers discontinued their handbooks; others included explicit statements that the employee rights in the handbook could be abrogated by the employer at any time, but this was an awkward position for the employer. It was hardly conducive to employee morale to spell out employee rights and then tell employees that their employment could be terminated at any time for any reason. At any rate, forty-one states adopted the reasoning in *Toussaint* in the 1980s. A few did so even when the handbook included explicit language to the effect that it was not part of a contract; however, most state courts held that the handbooks were not contractual statements when they included explicit statements to this effect. Judicial intervention often involved veteran employees who were fired for morally indefensible reasons, such as refusal to testify falsely at the employer's request.

## ARE ENTERPRISE RIGHTS RIGHT FOR EDUCATION?

With the decline of employment at will, statutory rights, and collective bargaining, enterprise rights have become the predominant mode of employment relations in the private sector. This means that individual or self-representation is the most common system of representation in the private sector. The question naturally arises whether enterprise rights and individual representation will or should replace collective bargaining in public education as it has in the private sector.

In some ways, individual representation is much more feasible in public education than in the private sector. School board regulations serve several functions of employer handbooks, especially because school districts sometimes distribute handbooks as a management policy. In the private sector, a company without an exclusive representative can modify its enterprise rights unilaterally without bargaining over the changes. It may suffer in the market for employees, but aside from the statutory restrictions such as minimum wage laws and antidiscrimination statutes, it is free to change the terms and conditions of employment as it deems appropriate.

Theoretically, school boards can do the same, but there are major differences in the two situations. If a school board wishes to change its sick leave policy, the change has to survive all the procedures for adoption of school board policy generally. Minimally, this provides teachers with time to bring pressure to bear against any diminution of benefits and can force the board to explain and defend its actions. In contrast, there is no such pressure, or there is much less pressure, on private sector employers to defend their actions, and the changes are not ordinarily matters of public interest. Consequently, teachers appear to enjoy greater security under enterprise rights than private sector employees who have opted for it instead of collective bargaining.

Any suggestion that it might be desirable to revert to enterprise rights and individual representation in public education, with school board handbooks replacing collective bargaining contracts, will inevitably evoke a flood of horror stories about what happened to teachers before the advent of collective bargaining. Nevertheless, it is possible logically to accept the truth of the horror stories (as I do) and take seriously the suggestion that individual representation could be the system in the best interests of most teachers.

One evidentiary basis for this conclusion bears close examination. All of the evils of individual representation in the private sector were present after union density in the private sector began its steady decline in 1954. Nevertheless, union representation in the private sector has declined drastically since then in formerly unionized industries despite employee freedom to be represented by unions. One reason is that federal, state, and local antidiscrimination legislation has largely eliminated protection against invidious discrimination as a reason to join unions—which were sometimes the discriminators, not the good faith representative of the victims of discrimination. Union corruption was another factor, as were higher dues despite union inability to protect workers from declining markets.

A major reason for the decline of union representation in the private sector is that unionization led to costs that could not be maintained in the face of competition from nonunion producers. This is widely recognized, but another reason is highly controversial. The unions assert that collective bargaining legislation favors employers who are determined to resist unionization; employers and employer-oriented organizations assert that the decline is due to widespread rejection of unionization by private sector employees. This controversy is at the center of union efforts to amend the NLRA by requiring employers to recognize and bargain with a union when a majority of eligible employees sign cards authorizing a specific union to represent them. Currently, the union must win a majority of the votes in an employee election on the issue; the unions allege that employers intimidate and deceive employees in the run-up to the elections. The rebuttal is that employees often sign authorization cards as a result of union misrepresentations that can be exposed preceding the election. It is also alleged that employees often sign authorization cards to avoid union pressure on the issue, but a secret ballot election elicits the uncoerced views of employees on union representation.

Basic changes in management philosophy and practice have also been a major contributor to the decline in union representation.[6] These changes are reflected in the emergence of "human resource managers," that is, staff persons whose job description includes fostering a company culture that emphasizes cooperation and recognizes that company and employee interests are better served by fair treatment of employees, respect for their interests and opinions, and cooperation than by adversarial postures.

The human resource approach does not regard labor unions as tantamount to communism, as many employers did in the 1930s. If employees choose to be represented by a union, the human resource approach is to treat it pragmatically, just as it would any other problem in its jurisdiction. Leo Troy, the nation's leading labor historian, firmly rejects the idea that the main objective of human resource managers is to keep the company union free; were that the case, human resource managers would be unable even to accomplish that objective. From recruitment to retirement, the human resource managers meet with employees to make sure that their grievances, opinions, and views about company practices are respected. The HR staff monitors company practices, fairness in treatment, attitudes toward the company—everything that bears on employee welfare and effectiveness. Note that there is nothing the unions can do to prevent employers from adopting proactive policies that have a negative effect on union membership.

The main argument against individual representation is that it is rigged against the employee from its inception to the conclusion. The process is funded and controlled by employers, who are not likely to fund a system that operates against their interests. Whether funded or not, many employers have adopted employer-promulgated arbitration agreements (EPAAs) to counter this criticism. These agreements are partly an effort to overcome the assumption that grievance procedures culminating in employer decision makers will inevitably support employer positions. The employer usually pays the costs of arbitration although some allow the employee paying half as an option. Sometimes the grievant has to pay a small amount that is returned if the grievant prevails in arbitration. The usual practice, which applies only in nonunionized companies, is for the employer to require new employees to waive their statutory rights to redress and to sign a statement that they will accept arbitration awards as final and binding; in effect the employee agrees not to appeal to the courts for redress of grievances.

In 1994, the American Arbitration Association (AAA) and the National Academy of Arbitrators (NAA), a prestigious organization, changed their policies to allow their members to participate in employer-promulgated arbitration agreements. Prior to the change, AAA and NAA rules prohibited participation by their members in EPAAs. Needless to say, the AFL-CIO and its affiliated unions vehemently criticized AAA and NAA for the change and urged unions not to employ any arbitrator who accepted EPAAs. The unions asserted that AAA and NAA had abandoned impartiality and their change of policy was due to the shrinking market for labor arbitrators. The unions object to employer-promulgated arbitration for the following reasons:

- The acceptance of EPAAs is really a return to employment at will even though it is characterized as expanding workplace justice.
- Employers are turning to EPAAs to avoid large jury awards in unjust discharge cases.
- Employees ordinarily can't afford the costs of a civil action for unjust dismissal.
- EPAAs are less expensive than cases under the rules of labor arbitration, a big gain for employers.
- State statutes on wrongful dismissal do not provide awards sufficient to pay the costs to employees and their lawyers.
- There are serious procedural problems in EPAAs. For instance, an arbitrator who insisted upon reviewing the employer's records on an altercation between a grievant and supervisor would be unlikely to be asked to serve by other employers.
- Employees are subject to longer delays in EPAAs.

- Although some companies pay for specialized help or witnesses for the grievant, grievants are usually unable to pay for witnesses and specialized help.
- Decisions in EPAAs are made from the bench, and the arbitrator's rationale is not in writing.[7]

Some of these criticisms have merit, but whether they justify avoidance of employer-promulgated arbitration is a different matter. Arbitration in the absence of unions is a relatively new development, and we can expect changes in it as experience with it grows. Also, the criticisms portray employees as helpless and hopeless victims. Perhaps some are, but many are not. The criticism that arbitrators put their own interests ahead of employee interests is just as applicable to the unions as it is to arbitrators.

From the employer's point of view, the danger is buyer's remorse because arbitrators are more likely than judges to agree with grievants. This caveat is challenged by Richard Edwards, one of the country's leading scholars on employment issues. Edwards identifies the following reasons for the growth of EPAAs in the private sector:

- The huge increase in litigation and the erosion of employment at will
- Excessive damages and litigation expenses in contesting statutory rights
- The decline in union-represented employees
- Statutory and judicial encouragement of arbitration

Interestingly enough, Edwards explicitly argues that union avoidance was not always a factor in the increase in EPAAs. As evidence, he points to the fact that companies often required managerial and supervisory personnel as well as employees represented by unions to sign EPAAs. The crux of his argument is that a growing number of employers believe that an arbitral, not a judicial, forum is in their best interests.[8] A critical factor is the number and content of federal and state statutes giving rise to employee claims. The more such statutes, the more desirable EPAAs are to employers.

Whether or not employer-promulgated arbitration is intended to weaken union attractiveness, it undoubtedly has that effect. Nevertheless, to my knowledge, not one nonunion school district has adopted or even considered it. In fact, most school boards oppose binding arbitration of grievances even if they have agreed to it. Obviously, the unions oppose EPAAs, regardless of the employer's rationale for it.

## TEACHER UNION REFORM: A DISSENTING VIEW

Individual representation is not likely to result from legislation that diminishes the state bargaining laws; the state teacher unions are too powerful, at least in most states. Consequently, several analysts have asserted or taken for granted that challenging NEA power directly is a hopeless endeavor.[9] The conclusion to be drawn is that the possibilities for reform are limited to persuading union leaders to adopt constructive policies through long-range efforts to change the "environment" of collective bargaining. The analysis here takes a very different view.

The NEA asserts that teachers are well satisfied with the services they are getting from the NEA and its affiliates. Its argument is that teachers have freedom of choice in representational matters; they would have chosen a different union or no union if they were dissatisfied with NEA services. As a practical matter, however, meaningful choice of representation rarely exists. Defending the union monopoly is the NEA with revenues of more than $1.5 billion annually from unified membership dues, over 5,000 full-time staff (including state and local affiliate staff), the capacity to reach all teachers repeatedly in school or at home, and strong incentives to avoid competition.[10] In contrast, teachers who wish to decertify an NEA local must finance their campaign from their personal resources, while most of the benefits go to teachers who have spent nothing to decertify the incumbent NEA affiliate. Furthermore, rank-and-file NEA members have very little information about the association that its leadership does not wish to see widely disseminated. Notwithstanding isolated victories by independent (nonaffiliated) unions, or districts in which the teachers have opted for no representation, the financial obstacles alone preclude a serious challenge to NEA and AFT representation in most school districts in the bargaining-law states. In any case, the argument that NEA and AFT affiliates must be doing a good job because teachers have not exercised their right to decertify them is a useful fiction and nothing more.

Theoretically, teachers can choose to vote for either the incumbent union, a different exclusive representative, or for no representation. The first two choices accept collective bargaining; the third choice rejects it. For the sake of discussion, assume that the choice is between a local-only teacher union (LOTU) and an NEA affiliate. To some extent, the constituencies for LOTUs and no union overlap, but an LOTU would usually be longer lasting. A vote for no union can be challenged one year after the vote for it. In contrast, LOTUs can negotiate multiyear contracts that shield the LOTUs from challenge until thirty to ninety days before the expiration of the contract. Also, an LOTU could utilize LOTU funds to compete against challenges to its status as exclusive representative; in the no representation situation, individual teachers would have to contribute from personal funds every time there is a challenge to no representation. The advantages of payroll deduction of dues would ordinarily enable LOTUs to build a defense fund, albeit less than what the NEA would spend to regain exclusive representation rights.

## THE CONSTITUENCY FOR LOCAL-ONLY UNIONS

What would happen if adequate resources were available to the supporters of no representation or a local-only union? We cannot be sure because several factors would affect the outcomes, but several facts support the conclusion that both choices would win a significant number of elections.

Prior to unified membership, NEA membership could be local, state, and federal. While these choices existed, membership in the state associations greatly exceeded membership in the NEA. Reliable statistics on membership in local associations are not available, but many had only nominal dues and were largely social organizations. Nevertheless, teachers were clearly far more interested in their local and state associations than the national affiliate. In the three years after the NEA adopted unified dues, 518,706 new members joined the NEA.[11] These figures are strong evidence that many teachers would drop their national membership if it was not tied to state or local membership. Of course, it can be argued that the services of teacher unions are much more valuable to teachers than the services of their prebargaining associations.

A much neglected fact is that a sizable number of teachers join the NEA as the lesser of two evils. If they do not join, they must pay agency fees roughly equal to 70 percent of unified dues, do not have any voice in contract negotiations and ratification, and are often harassed over their non-membership status. Estimates of the percentage of unwilling members vary widely, but it probably is at least 10 percent in some of the largest states that require teachers to pay agency fees.

A large group of NEA members are strongly opposed to affiliation with the AFL-CIO. If convinced that the NEA is moving in this direction, which it is, many of these teachers are likely to vote against their incumbent NEA local as the exclusive representative.

There is no serious controversy over the statement that most NEA members are opposed to affiliation with the AFL-CIO. This became clear when the effort to merge the NEA and AFT was defeated at the 1997 Representative Assembly by a 58–42 margin. The AFT overwhelmingly approved the merger.

The debate at the Representative Assembly and the literature distributed by the activists on both sides clearly showed that affiliation with the AFL-CIO was the key issue. Significantly, the Buffalo Teachers Federation, the NEA's local in Buffalo, refused to support the 2006 merger agreement in that state; the federation's action was led by Philip Rumore, its president and leader of the antimerger forces at the 1997 NEA Representative Assembly that rejected the NEA-AFT merger. Although it can be taken for granted that the reasons for opposition to merger vary in both content and intensity, they could be important in competition between local-only unions and NEA affiliates.

Another constituency for a local-only union consists of teachers who are deeply concerned about the NEA's positions on political and social issues and its contributions to several organizations shown in table 8.1. The list of recipients in table 8.1 arises as much out of political necessity as from conviction. If an organization's platform calls for substantial increases in government employment, higher taxes at all levels of government, and increased protection for the education establishment and does not show any support for military defense or for policies that would maintain U.S. global competitiveness, where will it find allies? The answer is in the list of recipients in table 8.1: feminist, ethnic, environmental, and gay and lesbian advocacy groups, interests opposed to free trade,

**Table 8.1. NEA Contributions, Gifts, and Grants to Nonaffiliated Organizations**

| Receiving Organization | Description/Category | Amount |
| --- | --- | --- |
| AIDS Walk Washington | Gay/lesbian/bisexual rights | $5,000 |
| American Federation of State, County, Municipal Employees | Labor union support | $5,000 |
| Amnesty International | Human rights, no death penalty | $5,000 |
| Asian Pacific American Institute for Congressional Studies | Ethnic organization support | $5,000 |
| Aspira Association | Ethnic organization support | $5,000 |
| Center for Law and Education | Education, liberal orientation | $45,000 |
| Center for Women Policy Studies | Feminist agenda | $5,000 |
| Central Intercollegiate Athletic Association | Twelve black colleges | $30,000 |
| Congressional Black Caucus Foundation | Ethnic organization support | $39,940 |
| Congressional Hispanic Caucus Institute | Ethnic organization support | $35,000 |
| Democratic Leadership Council | Democratic party support | $25,750 |
| Economic Policy Institute | Labor union support | $45,000 |
| Educational International | International teacher organizations | $11,254 |
| Everybody Wins DC | Reading/mentoring program in DC | $7,903 |
| Frederick D. Patterson Research Institute | Black education | $20,000 |
| Gay, Lesbian, and Straight Education Network | Gay/lesbian/bisexual rights | $5,000 |
| Gephardt Legacy Fund | Children's charities | $10,000 |
| Gay and Lesbian Alliance against Defamation Media Awards | Gay/lesbian/bisexual rights | $5,000 |
| Health and Education Research Operative Services, Inc. | Health and family policies | $20,000 |
| Human Rights Campaign | Gay/lesbian/bisexual rights | $15,000 |
| Joint Center for Political and Economic Studies | Assistance to black elected officials | $10,000 |
| The King Center | Martin Luther King Jr. Memorial Center | $10,000 |
| Leadership Conference on Civil Rights | Civil rights | $10,000 |

*(continued)*

**Table 8.1.** *(continued)*

| Receiving Organization | Description/Category | Amount |
|---|---|---|
| League of United Latin American Citizens | Ethnic organization support | $5,000 |
| Learning First Alliance | Eleven public school organizations | $51,350 |
| Mexican American Legal Defense and Education Fund | Ethnic organization support | $5,000 |
| National Association for the Education and Advancement of Cambodian, Laotian, and Vietnamese Americans | Ethnic organization support | $5,000 |
| National Association for Asian and Pacific American Education | Ethnic organization support | $5,000 |
| National Association for Bilingual Education | Ethnic organization support | $5,000 |
| National Council of La Raza | Ethnic organization support | $5,000 |
| National Indian Education Association | Ethnic organization support | $5,000 |
| National Women's Law Center | Feminist agenda | $5,000 |
| National Alliance of Black School Educators | Ethnic organization support | $30,000 |
| Organization of Chinese Americans | Ethnic organization support | $5,000 |
| Rainbow Push Coalition | Jesse Jackson's base | $5,000 |
| Rebuild America's Schools | Educational facilities | $20,000 |
| The Ripon Society* | Support for liberal Republicans | $10,000 |
| United South and Eastern Tribes | Ethnic organization support | $5,000 |
| Valis Associates | Government relations, lobbying | $200,000 |
| Volusia Teachers Organization | Union assistance, AFT oriented | $8,000 |

*Notes:*
- Nineteen ethnic organizations are included, more than any other category.
- Organizations listed have or may claim broader agendas than the agendas specified.
- The organizations listed do not include the NEA's state and local affiliates who received approximately $63 million, mainly for political activities, or a small number of nonaffiliates whose activities do not appear to be controversial.

*Contribution enables the NEA to say that it is bipartisan.
*Source:* National Education Association LM-2, 2005 Annual Report, Schedule 17.

and private and public sector unions. The Ripon Society is the only business or Republican-oriented recipient in table 8.1, but it has minimal traction in the Republican Party.

The point here is simple but fundamental. The NEA cannot get the support of other groups for NEA objectives unless the NEA supports their objectives. However, the recipients in table 8.1 are considerably left of the NEA's political center. The information in table 8.1 would undoubtedly hurt the NEA among its rank-and-file members; the fact that the NEA severely restricted access to the list of recipients when DOL regulations did not require posting the contributions on the Internet is evidence for this.

Here we come to a basic NEA vulnerability that has been noted but not fully understood by NEA critics. The NEA's political needs require it to support causes and organizations that are often opposed by large numbers of NEA members. The NEA has avoided internal conflict by restricting member awareness of its support for causes that would be internally controversial if its membership were fully informed about the situation. NEA leadership has taken advantage of the fact that most NEA members, like most people generally, are not political activists. Nevertheless, if made aware of the full range of NEA contributions to organizations and causes that are contrary to their beliefs, rank-and-file members might be much more receptive to change.

Currently, conservatives in the NEA react only to highly visible instances of NEA action, or proposed action, that conflicts with their beliefs and values. At the national level, there is no umbrella caucus to take advantage of scale in opposing liberal control of the union. Note, however, that representation elections would often provide a much more favorable forum for the opposition to NEA's agenda—again, if the resources are available and spent sensibly. The NEA can easily handle occasional brush fires that do not threaten the basic structure.

Another potentially significant constituency for no union consists of teachers who believe that NEA and AFT dues are excessive. Note that in three non-bargaining-law states (Georgia, Missouri, and Texas), independent teacher organizations enroll more members than NEA or AFT affiliates.[12] The implication is clear: The state teacher bargaining laws have resulted in an NEA and AFT monopoly in teacher representation services. As is evident, this monopoly has had the same outcomes as monopolies have generally: excessive costs for services geared to the welfare of the producers.

The excessive dues argument was dramatically confirmed by the 2002 revelations of union corruption leading to jail terms for the presidents of the Washington Teachers Union and the Miami-Dade County Teachers Association. The cases revealed the fact that union members did not notice any diminution of union services while millions in union dues were diverted to the private use of union officers without any oversight by the national AFT.

The NEA does not bargain for local associations. Its legal position is that members pay national NEA dues to support a capability that can come to the aid of local associations in unusual circumstances; the NEA allegedly functions like an insurance company that provides help when it is needed unexpectedly. Although the U.S. Supreme Court accepted this argument, it makes no sense when one looks at the numbers. Consider a local association with 1,000 members and total dues (local, state, and national) of $600 ($135 NEA, $300 state association, and $165 local dues). Consequently the 1,000 teachers pay $600,000 (1,000 x $600) in NEA dues during the year. The vast majority of NEA locals rarely need help from the NEA; ordinarily, when the locals need external help, they get it from their state associations. When a local does need help that is not available from its state association, it could buy the help needed for a lot less than it pays in national and state dues every year. In short, the NEA is an immensely profitable but highly vulnerable organization, aided and abetted by opposition ignorance of union vulnerabilities. To assume NEA invulnerability to challenge in the absence of funding and member information on NEA vulnerabilities is not a realistic analysis.[13]

Another potentially sizable group of dissidents consists of teachers who resent the excessive benefits and perquisites of NEA officers and staff—or who would resent them if they knew about them. My view is that whatever teachers wish to pay their representatives is their business, but on the condition that the members know how much they are paying. As of now, they do not. Of course, other factors play a role from district to district, but the aforementioned ones might be part of what would lead to a majority for decertification in a significant number of NEA locals. The strategic problem is the absence of funding, campaign materials, and local leadership; leaving it up to each local group of teachers to fund a decertification campaign is seldom successful.

## TEACHER UNIONS OR NONUNION REPRESENTATION: A COMMENTARY

What system of representation is in the best interests of the teachers? Presumably, this is the system they would eventually support, but the question is not so easily answered. Indubitably, the availability of a union alternative has sometimes been essential to the success of nonunion systems of employee representation. If employers provide benefits to avoid unionization, it would be misleading to ignore this fact in comparing the benefits of union to nonunion systems of representation. However, it is a fallacy to assume that union avoidance is or always was the main motivation in either the employer or the employee preference for individual representation. Clearly, a substantial group of teachers prefers nonunion representation, but this preference faces virtually insuperable obstacles in the bargaining-law states.

The best system from the teacher standpoint is a framework in which it is relatively easy for teachers to change from individual to union representation and vice versa. Unfortunately, although it is easy for teachers to go from a nonunion to a union mode of teacher representation, it is extremely difficult if not practically impossible under collective bargaining for teachers to go from union to individual or local-only union representation.[14] The weaknesses of school boards as employers and the financial obstacles to decertification are the main reasons.

Section 8(a)(2) of the National Labor Relations Act (NLRA) makes it an unfair labor practice for an employer "to dominate or interfere with the formation or administration of any labor organization or contribute financial or other support to it." Section 2(5) defines a labor organization as "any organization of any kind or any agency or employee representation committee or plan in which employees participate and which exists for the purpose, in whole or in part, of dealing with employers concerning grievances, labor disputes, wages rate of pay, hours of employment, or conditions of work."

The unions feared that employer-supported entities would be used to weaken unionization, and they were able to achieve the sweeping prohibitions of such in 8(a)(2). Although the NLRA is not directly applicable to public school teachers, many state bargaining laws track the NLRA and the decisions of the National Labor Relations Board. The bias against employer support of organizations representing employees was simply folded into the state teacher bargaining statutes and state labor regulation.

Actually, several large U.S. companies had very successful systems of nonunion representation when the NLRA was enacted in 1935. These systems were not necessarily established to prevent unionization; the companies, at least in some cases, had adopted a nonunion system of employee representation because the companies believed that it was the right thing to do. Regardless, these systems had to be abandoned because of the NLRA's sweeping prohibition of employer support for any organization that represents employees on terms and conditions of employment. However, the prohibition amounted to overkill. The United States is the only developed nation that prohibits employer-established committees from discussing matters of mutual interest, including terms and conditions of employment.[15]

The changing nature of employment also suggests that employer-supported representation has an important role to play. A significant amount of work, especially in the knowledge economy, requires frequent consultation with management on a wide variety of problems that include or affect terms of employment. Prohibition of management-supported committees or councils to discuss these matters is a high price to pay for ensuring employee freedom from employer domination in collective bargaining. Unfortunately, there is virtually no discussion of these matters in the universities that train school administrators and the think tanks that are supposed to come up with new ideas occasionally.

At any rate, support for nonunion representation may be much broader in the United States than is widely assumed because of its absence. As previously noted, there is a great deal of support for amending the NLRA to limit the restriction in 8(a)(2) to employer domination instead of employer support. This change should be applicable to public education.[16]

Obviously, the mix of vulnerability factors will vary from district to district and time to time in the same district. Notwithstanding, my conviction is that in a substantial number of districts, a majority of teachers could be persuaded to vote for no union or a local-only union. Of course, funding would be essential to identify the target districts, prepare attractive materials on the key issues, establish a campaign organization with a media capability, identify leadership and supporters in the community, and perform all the other tasks essential in such campaigns. Note that when NEA and AFT affiliates were competing to become the exclusive representative, both sides took it for granted that external resources would be essential for victory.

In any event, large-scale ouster of NEA affiliates as exclusive representatives would not happen immediately, partly because only about one-third of the teacher union contracts expire in any given year, and it will take time to prepare to challenge NEA affiliates in representation elections. Nonetheless, even a relatively small number of defections might lead to significant changes in the NEA. To forestall large-scale defections, the NEA might have to lower its dues, move away from its close ties to the Democratic Party, moderate its hard-core liberal agenda, and reduce its contributions to organizations that promote it. These possibilities are admittedly speculative, but real competition to represent teachers might well have some of these effects.

The preceding argument is not that an adequately financed, competently led campaign to decertify NEA affiliates would always be successful. It is that until tried, there is no overwhelming reason to conclude that it would not be successful in a substantial number of school districts.

The overriding fact in this situation is that noncoercive methods of resolving conflicts of interest are potentially much more beneficial to the parties than coercive methods. An example may illustrate the importance of this point. Compare the resolution of disputes between North and South Korea (or India and Pakistan) to the resolution of disputes between the United States and Canada. In the first case, the two countries spend huge amounts on military forces for security from their neighboring country. The United States and Canada have no need for such expenditures. Economically, their mutual reliance on noncoercive methods to settle disputes results in huge savings that are available for the welfare of the populations in both countries.

As every economist knows, the same principles apply to settlement of disputes among conflicting economic interests such as between employers and their employees. There are coercive and noncoercive ways to settle such disputes; the latter are potentially much more efficient, but the culture of the parties must reflect their long-term interests.

Union advocates sometimes claim that if it were not for poor management, there would be no need for unions. Historically, however, unionization materialized in the states like California, in which teachers were treated the most generously prior to unionization. Furthermore, the unions do not go out of business when good management, even by union standards, emerges. The prounion argument has shifted; unions are allegedly now necessary to prevent management from backsliding to take advantage of employees. On this assumption, there is nothing employers can do to avoid the inefficiencies of union representation. The precipitous decline of unionization in the private sector shows that this argument for continued union representation has not been persuasive in the private sector, and there is even less reason to accept it in public education.

## NOTES

1. *Payne v. Western and Atlantic Railroad*, 81 Tenn. 507 (1884), 518–519.

2. *Perry v. Sindermann*, 408 U.S. 593 (1972).

3. In 2006, Maryland enacted legislation that required employers of over 10,000 employees to devote at least 8 percent of their payroll costs to employee health care. The legislation, introduced at the behest of labor unions, affected only Wal-Mart and was expected to trigger similar legislation in other states.

4. Richard Edwards, *Rights at Work* (Washington, DC: Brookings, 1993), 102–133.

5. *Toussaint v. Blue Cross and Blue Shield*, 292 N.W. 2d 880 (Mich. 1980). The other leading cases are *Pine River State Bank v. Mettile*, 333 N.W. 2d 622 (Minn. 1983); and *Woolley v. Hoffman-LaRoche, Inc.*, 491 At. 2d 451 (1985), modified 499 A. 2d 515 (N.J. Super. A.D. 1985). For an excellent discussion of these cases, see Edwards, *Rights at Work*, 163–187.

6. Leo Troy, *Beyond Unions and Collective Bargaining* (Armonk, NY: M. E. Sharpe), especially 47–99.

7. John L. Zalusky, "A Union View of Nonrepresented Employees' Grievance Systems," in *Labor Arbitration under Fire*, ed. James L. Stern and Joyce M. Najita (Ithaca, NY: ILR Press, 1997), 182–207.

8. Edwards, *Rights at Work*, 188–232.

9. For example, see articles by Linda Kaboolian, Frederick M. Hess, Martin R. West, and Terry M. Moe in *Education Next* (Summer 2006).

10. Myron Lieberman, *The Teacher Unions* (New York: Free Press, 1997).

11. *NEA Handbook, 2003–2004* (Washington, DC: National Education Association, 2003), 192.

12. Figures for NEA membership were taken from *NEA Handbook, 2004–2005*, 99. Figures for independent associations in Georgia, Missouri, and Texas were provided by Concerned Educators Against Forced Unionism, a project of the National Right to Work Committee. The organizations involved do not use the same categories of membership, but K–12 regular teachers are by far the largest component in both the NEA affiliates and the independent teacher organizations. Also see Mike Antonucci, *Education Intelligence Agency Report* (Elk Grove, CA: Education Intelligence Agency, June 27, 2001), 1–2.

13. Troy, who showed impressive prescience in predicting the decline of private sector unions, does not expect a similar development in the public sector.

14. Bruce Kaufman and Daphne Taras, *Nonunion Employee Representation: History, Contemporary Practice, and Policy* (Armonk, NY: M. E. Sharpe, 2000).

15. Samuel Estreicher, "Nonunion Employee Representation: A Legal/Policy Perspective," in Kaufman and Taras, *Nonunion Employee Representation*, 196–222.

16. See Leo Troy, *The Twilight of the Old Unionism* (Armonk, NY: M. E. Sharpe, 2004), and the comprehensive treatment of nonunion representation in Bruce E. Kaufman and Daphne G. Taras, *Nonunion Forms of Employee Representation: Proceedings at a Conference on Nonunion Forms of Employee Representation*, Banff Centre for Conferences, Banff, Alberta, Canada, September 3–5, 1997.

# Part 3

## SCHOOL CHOICE

Chapters 9 and 10 are intended to critique the substances as well as the strategy and tactics of enacting and implementing school choice legislation. A recurring analytical problem is that what appear to be differences over strategy and tactics often reflect substantive differences. For example, supporters of a free market in education sometimes regard means-tested vouchers as a step toward their objective, but many others see means-tested vouchers as itself the major objective of the school choice movement, to wit, providing opportunities for pupils from poor families to get a better education. This substantive conflict has been papered over in recent years, but it is implicit in much of the literature on school choice. The discussion here intends to present the issues objectively, and my views are clearly identified as an aid to evaluating my success in achieving this objective.

# 9

## The Triumph of the Equalitarians

The preceding chapters are devoted to reforms in our existing system of public education. School choice would allegedly constitute a different system. This chapter explains why this claim is not applicable to existing school choice plans. It also argues that the school choice plans in effect in 2006 were making it more difficult to enact school choice plans that would materially improve the quality and lower the costs of K–12 education.

### SUBSIDIES: TO PRODUCERS OR CONSUMERS?

Vouchers for K–12 education raise an interesting issue that has received one answer in K–12 education and a different answer in higher education, to wit, to achieve social objectives, is it better to subsidize producers or consumers? Should we subsidize food producers or provide food stamps? Should health care be provided by government employees or through private providers chosen by clients who are reimbursed by government? In K–12 education, government subsidizes the producers; in higher education, the subsidies go largely to consumers. Generally speaking, subsidizing consumers is the most effective way to ensure quality services for the poor. The reason is that it fosters competition, which subsidies to the producers are unlikely to do.

The parties to conflict over school choice are usually characterized as "pro-choice" or "anti-choice," but these characterizations are misleading. For example, the teacher unions are willing to tolerate public school choice, but they are adamantly opposed to choice of public or private schools subsidized by vouchers or tax credits. The parties who support school choice for denominational schools oppose any voucher plan that excludes denominational schools; the parties who support school choice for equity reasons are opposed to universal school choice plans. It is a fundamental mistake to regard such differences as "details" that are secondary to being pro– or anti–school choice.

Obviously, clarification of "school choice" is essential. According to the National Working Commission on School Choice in K–12 Education, "The basic definition is any arrangement that gives parents options among schools. The question of whether 'choice' is a good thing has no single answer. Since the response depends on how choice is designed, the answer can vary from one design to another."[1]

This book accepts both the definition and the implication drawn by the National Commission—whether school choice is a good thing depends on the features of the plan. Consequently, there is little, if any, point to controversy over school choice per se; what makes sense, or might make sense, is controversy over specific school choice plans. Otherwise, most controversy over school choice merely adds to confusion; it is like controversy over whether drugs are good for sick people, without any regard to the illness, specifications, symptoms, dosage, frequency, and contraindications.

School choice plans differ with respect to

1. Who authorizes choice.
2. Who is eligible to exercise school choice.
3. The schools that can accept choice students; for example, what grade levels are included, whether denominational and for-profit schools are eligible, the eligibility of schools with an "anti-American" orientation, and so on.
4. How much government support will be provided for students who exercise choice.
5. What regulations about school safety, location, and facilities should apply to systems of school choice.

6. What reporting requirements, if any, must be made to government officials, parents, and citizens generally.
7. How often choice can be exercised.
8. What the appeal procedure will be, if any, on choices that are rejected.

Inasmuch as there is a huge number of school choice plans, let us start with Milton Friedman's 1962 proposal that jumpstarted the contemporary school choice movement. Friedman's rationale for school choice was for a specific version of it—a free-market plan. Writing in 1955 and 1962, he relied upon a wealth of evidence from thousands of industries worldwide that showed that competitive market systems produced and distributed goods and services of higher quality and lower costs than government provision. Friedman did not see any plausible reason the outcome would be any different in the provision of educational services.

Friedman regarded school choice primarily as a freedom issue: the freedom of parents to have their children educated as the parents wish. This was an important freedom that should not be abridged in the absence of a strong reason for doing so. Friedman was also impressed by the studies of E. G. West, who had published a study showing a very high literacy rate in England before the advent of compulsory education financed by government.[2] The gist of Friedman's argument was that for-profit schools would have the same outcomes as private enterprise has in competitive industries generally. Because public education was a monopoly, it could not bring about the lower costs and higher quality that characterize competitive industries.

Friedman was well aware that certain conditions must prevail in order to have meaningful competition in education markets. These conditions include

- Providers should easily be able to enter the market, not be kept out of the market to protect other providers.
- There is no control of the market by any particular providers or consumers.
- Reasonably good information about offers and acceptances is available.
- Providers are free to sell to anyone, and consumers are free to buy from anyone at prices mutually agreed upon.
- A scale exists sufficient for the above conditions to prevail.

These conditions are matters of degree. There are very few, if any, markets in which the conditions are present without some qualification or deviation from the ideal. In fact, Joseph A. Schumpeter has argued that perfect competition is impossible and would be undesirable if it were possible.[3] In any case, "imperfect competition" characterizes the overwhelming majority of competitive goods and services. A "free market" in education does not mean a system free of all regulations and limitations on competition. Friedman has asserted that voucher plans that are less than ideal may be adequate to bring about the benefits of competition, or they may be an essential step toward a system that can achieve such benefits; however, the assumption that every plan labeled "school choice" constitutes progress is a huge mistake.

Several changes since the structure of K–12 education was established over a century ago have strengthened the case for a market system of education.

- Transportation has improved tremendously, weakening the importance of proximity to the schools, especially at the middle and secondary levels.
- Most parents are much better educated than parents were a century ago. This suggests that most are better able to evaluate education services than the parents when public education was being established.
- As government grows, the pressure for higher taxes becomes more and more difficult to resist. The demands for senior benefits and services are especially threatening since the number of seniors is expected to increase dramatically while the birth rate, except for immigrant families, is expected to decline, thereby weakening the political support for K–12 education.
- Increases in the urban population have made competition much more feasible than it was when our nation was largely a rural, agricultural society. Furthermore, the development of information technology has provided more alternatives to rural areas.
- American society has become much more diverse. This has led to increased conflict over education, and hence to the social and economic costs of such conflict at local, state, and national levels.[4] Praise for diversity cannot conceal the fact that it has led to a great deal of social conflict over several aspects of education.

It is hardly possible to overemphasize the importance of the requisite conditions for a market system. Nevertheless, analysts and pundits often cite the outcomes of voucher plans without these characteristics as evidence that free markets cannot be effective in education. For instance, Jeffrey R. Henig's book is explicitly devoted to demonstrating the limitations of the "market metaphor" in education. Referring to a voucher proposal by John E. Chubb and Terry M. Moe, Henig asserts,

> The Chubb and Moe proposal, for the most part, represents an elaboration of the Friedman model. . . .
>   The Chubb and Moe proposal is designed to accommodate a few redistributory and regulatory provisions that Friedman did not mention but that are not directly contrary to his basic design.[5]

This comment is egregiously erroneous. Moe was one of the small group of voucher proponents who declined to support Proposition 174, a 1993 California voucher initiative endorsed by Friedman, after Moe and others unsuccessfully tried to weaken its free-market features. Moe's later book on vouchers explicitly asserts that vouchers did not make any headway until voucher supporters concluded that the free-market approach to vouchers was wrong in principle and ineffective politically.[6] Furthermore, the Chubb and Moe book includes several restrictions on vouchers that Friedman opposed. For example, it advocates a prohibition against parental add-ons to the voucher amount, a policy to which Friedman objected strongly.[7]

In his book, Henig asserts that "in an initiative that comes closer than any other to approximating the voucher model that Friedman envisaged, Wisconsin in 1990 began a program to allow low-income Milwaukee residents to attend private schools with tuition assistance from the government."[8]

The main features of the Milwaukee plan when Henig wrote his commentary were as follows:

- Participation in the voucher plan was restricted to 1 percent of the enrollment in the Milwaukee public schools. Accordingly, maximum potential participation in 1990–1991 was 936 pupils in grades K–12.
- Pupils who participate must be from families whose income did not exceed 175 percent of the poverty level.

- Voucher students could not exceed 49 percent of the students in any school that accepted voucher students.
- Schools for profit and schools affiliated with religious denominations were ineligible to participate.
- Voucher schools were required to accept all voucher-carrying students as long as space was available.
- If voucher students exceeded the spaces available, applicants had to be selected by lot.
- The Milwaukee school district was required to provide transportation as it would for public school students.
- The amount of the voucher was set at 43 percent of the average amount spent per pupil in the Milwaukee public schools in 1990–1991 (approximately $2,500).
- Participating schools did not receive additional funds for learning-disabled or emotionally disturbed pupils, as did the public schools.
- Schools that redeem vouchers could not charge students more than the amount of the voucher.

Clearly, the Milwaukee voucher plan did not even remotely resemble a free-market plan.[9] Henig's analysis illustrates the inaccuracies and poor scholarship that characterize most criticism of free-market voucher plans. Granted, one book does not constitute a common practice, but the evidence that Henig typifies most of the critics of free-market voucher plans is overwhelming.[10]

Some of the most ardent proponents of competition share Henig's confusion about the Milwaukee school choice program. Frederick M. Hess, a resident scholar at the American Enterprise Institute (AEI), regards the choice program in Milwaukee as a test of the idea that competition can improve public schools.[11] Among his reactions, Hess opines that "making education competitive requires much more than just high hopes; the very culture and rules of public schooling must be overhauled."[12] This implies that the task ahead is to overhaul the culture and rules of a monopoly to a culture appropriate to a competitive industry, an utterly hopeless task. Competition in education will emerge, if it emerges at all, even if a majority of teachers and administrators are opposed to it. Their culture will change because survival in a competitive education industry requires it, not because somebody has persuaded public school teachers, administrators, and school boards to adopt the outlook of a competitive education industry.

The kind of competition that underlies tremendous increases in productivity and raises quality while lowering costs is competition based on research and development funded from profits. Improvement to avoid stigma is not to be denigrated but is not likely to lead to significant increases in achievement or lower the costs of education.

## EQUITY ISSUES FROM A FREE-MARKET PERSPECTIVE

The free-market position on equity is that the dynamics of the free enterprise system are especially advantageous to the poor because the system brings higher-quality and lower-priced goods and services to an ever-growing group of consumers. The evidence for this is overwhelming. Black-and-white (later color) television, automobiles, telephones, photocopiers, frozen foods, pharmaceuticals, travel, computers—the list of goods and services that have risen in quality and declined in cost is too large to require debate. The free-market position is that the poor have benefited the most from this system because they could not afford these things prior to the reductions in costs and improvements in quality that resulted from competition.

Clearly, this has been the outcome in widely different industries in countries around the world. Consequently, the question that should be asked is this: Why wouldn't the same outcome materialize in education if public, nonprofit, and for-profit schools were required to compete for students who received vouchers and were free to pay any additional amounts agreed upon by the students' families and the schools? Most analysts agree that the free market generally functions to improve quality and lower prices. However, they also cite instances wherein the market functions like a race to the bottom; the markets for pornography and illegal drugs are illustrative.

The basic objections to a free market in education are based upon "externalities," that is, the consequences of market behavior that fall upon third parties who are not involved in the market transactions that led to the consequences. A frequently cited example is air pollution resulting from factories that burn coal for energy. The residents who suffer from the pollution are not involved in the conduct that led to it. Similarly, the objections to a market system of education consist mainly of the negative externalities that allegedly would result from such a system. These externalities include greater inequality and the growth of schools that emphasize separatist or antidemocratic values instead of our common heritage.

Although Friedman's voucher proposals received some attention from economists, they were more ignored than rebutted in educational literature. This may have been due to the upheavals over school integration and the Great Society legislation of the 1960s; it is difficult to see how educational vouchers could have upstaged the controversies over racial discrimination and segregation in education; the launch of several federal programs, such as Head Start, that were expected to remedy the effects of racial discrimination; and teacher unionization; any one of these developments would have left little energy, political or intellectual, to cope with the idea of a competitive education industry. Furthermore, some Southern states and school districts adopted school choice plans as a way to avoid racial integration, and these actions led to black opposition to school choice that continues to be cited half a century later as a reason to oppose it. As it became clear in the 1970s and early 1980s that reforms were not leading to significant improvement, interest in educational vouchers emerged again as an idea to be reckoned with but with rationales that differed from Friedman's. School choice was advocated as a moral issue, a freedom of religion issue, an equity issue, and, in recent years, as a civil rights issue. The supporters of school choice continued to mention the benefits of competition, but it was pro forma; by 1991, "competition" was merely a rhetorical add-on to other arguments for school choice. While proponents mentioned the benefits of competition, they supported school choice plans that could not possibly bring about market competition in K–12 education.

The most highly publicized plan was the school choice plan in Milwaukee. As we have seen, however, the Milwaukee plan cannot by any stretch of the imagination be regarded as a free-market school choice plan. Furthermore, the Milwaukee plan was not viewed as a step toward a free market in education; on the contrary, its minority leaders explicitly stated that they would oppose expansion of the plan to middle-class students.[13] According to Moe,

Milwaukee was the dawning of a new era. . . . Since Milwaukee, the voucher movement has attracted a very different following: more equalitarian in outlook, less impressed with free markets, less concerned with religion. Many conservatives in its ranks continue to see vouchers in universalistic and market-oriented terms. But to many of the newer supporters, vouchers are not just about choice, competition, and performance incentives. Nor are they necessarily for all children. They are about bringing equal opportunity to the children in greatest need.[14]

Moe's comment underscores the division in the school choice movement between the "equalitarians" and "free marketeers." This division goes back to the late 1960s and 1970s. For instance, in 1978, John E. Coons and Stephen D. Sugarman published *Education by Choice*. In the preface to the 1996 edition, they comment about the changing rationale for school choice:

During the mid-1970s, however, the intellectual focus of school choice began to shift from social concern to economic efficiency. Reviewing the literature of the day, we were puzzled that many champions of school choice pictured the market as its own justification, often scorning to cite specific social benefits of choice, as if doing so might suggest reservations about the invisible hand. The market was not an instrument to be justified by its results; the results were to be justified by whether it was the market that achieved them. This curious idolatry of the market has provided enemies of choice with what is still their favorite target.[15]

Although historically inaccurate, the quotation illustrates the depth of the divisions in the school choice movement. These divisions came to a head in 1993 over a voucher initiative in California. The initiative ultimately went on the ballot as Proposition 174, but it had been preceded by basic disagreement between Friedman, who supported a free-market version, and Coons, Sugarman, and Moe, who supported critical anticompetitive provisions, such as a ban on family payments for tuition in addition to the voucher amount. For instance, Chubb and Moe stated in 1991,

While it is important to give parents and students as much flexibility as possible, we think it is unwise to allow them to supplement their scholarship amounts [voucher amounts] with personal funds. Such "add-ons" threaten to produce too many disparities and inequalities within the public system, and many citizens would regard them as unfair and burdensome.[16]

In contrast, Friedman pointed out the absurdity of allowing parents to spend for liquor, tobacco, and other harmful products while denying them the right to spend more on the education of their children.

Why did the parties seek to promote their voucher plans in California, the state with the strongest opposition to any voucher plan? The answer is that the activists and the main funders were in California. The fact that there was no search for a state with better prospects for success suggests the danger of generalizing from the California experience in 1993. The same point can be made about the 2000 initiatives in California and Michigan. In any event, Friedman's views prevailed; Proposition 174 was a free-market plan that did not include the restrictions to ensure equity supported by Moe, Coons, and Sugarman. These equalitarians declined to support Proposition 174, which was defeated by a 7–3 margin in November 1993.[17]

Actually, the Separation of School and State Alliance is a libertarian organization dedicated to separating government from the funding as well as the provision of schooling. This point of view lacks widespread support and may be more useful to the opponents than to the supporters of school choice. The public school establishment will characterize every step toward inclusive school choice as part of a plot to end government-paid schooling altogether; to the extent that this argument is taken seriously, parents and probable parents concerned about the costs will be more likely to oppose even minimal steps toward privatization.

The equalitarians see school choice as primarily an equity and equal educational opportunity issue. According to Moe,

- Means-tested vouchers are the most effective way to provide equality of educational opportunity, especially for low-income minorities in large urban school districts.
- The American people have consistently rejected a free-market version of vouchers by wide margins. A majority will not accept the kind of unregulated vouchers being promoted by the free marketeers.

- Americans like the public school system and will reject changes that weaken it.
- Government regulation is essential to ensure accountability, fairness, and equality.
- Although vouchers may eventually be available to all children, the American people will accept only vouchers targeted to needy children and incremental change at this time.
- Two-thirds of the American people have never heard about vouchers, according to their responses in polls.[18]

Moe's analysis is primarily devoted to ascertaining the basic features of public opinion on vouchers. By assuming that supporters of a free market in education would accept only health and safety measures in voucher legislation, he concludes that the American people have repeatedly and decisively rejected the free-market position on vouchers. Although Moe mentions the argument for universal vouchers, he clearly is not concerned about the possibility that universal vouchers would not emerge for perhaps as many as twenty years, if ever.

The same substantive issue arose in the 2000 "Draper Initiative" in California, named after Timothy Draper, a Silicon Valley entrepreneur. Draper spent over $20 million to promote what was essentially a free-market voucher initiative that also lost by a 7–3 margin. Writing in 2001, Moe interprets the defeat of voucher initiatives in California and Michigan in 2000 as additional confirmation that only means-tested voucher legislation would be acceptable to the American people, and then only if it were not seen as a stepping stone to a free-market version. Moe's view is that as the liberals recognize that more and more conservatives support means-tested vouchers on their merits, not as a strategic move to bring about a market system of education, support for vouchers will continue to grow. Clearly, however, Moe felt vindicated by the political decline of the free-market rationale for vouchers. Referring to Coons and Sugarman, Moe comments,

Soon thereafter, they published a major book, *Education by Choice*, that made a strong case for vouchers—focusing less on the wonders of the marketplace than on the value of vouchers in giving greater control to families and in helping to ameliorate the social inequities that, as they saw it, were profoundly rooted in the current system.[19]

One may ask about this sentence, why not "advantages" or "benefits" instead of "wonders?" "Wonders" is a putdown in this context, just as "idolatry" is in the quote from Coons and Sugarman. These putdowns reflect equalitarian hostility and an attitude of moral superiority toward free-market views and help to explain the absence of a unified coalition among the pro-choice groups.

Moe supports an incremental, means-tested approach to vouchers; his thought is that as citizens become familiar with public school choice, their opposition to means-tested vouchers will decline over the next ten to twenty years. Moe also emphasizes that the teacher unions are the most powerful political interest group in the United States, a consideration that suggests minimal progress on school choice for many years to come.[20]

What Moe failed to recognize is that many supporters of the free-market rationale for vouchers are much more skeptical than he is about the effects of regulation, even when they are adopted to ensure equity and fairness. Furthermore, in arguing that the American people will not accept a free market in education, Moe adopts an unduly restrictive view of "free markets":

> The vast majority of economists would argue that while markets have great potential for promoting efficiency and other valued outcomes, how well they actually do depends on the real world conditions under which they operate — and there are some conditions that can undermine their effectiveness and actually lead to social problems. . . . The solution among economists, however, is not to abandon markets but rather to address their imperfections through an appropriately designed framework of governmental rules and then to put markets in good use within this framework. This, in fact, is the way most nations in the Western world have structured their economies, which are not free markets in any meaningful sense but mixed systems in which governmental rules constrain and channel how markets work.[21]

Moe's statement that Western economies "are not free markets in any meaningful sense" is misleading. Most economists refer to "imperfect competition" to denote the fact that perfect competition rarely, if ever, exists in the real world. Nevertheless, "imperfect competition" includes a large number of industries characterized by fierce competition. For instance, cars, fast food, and pharmaceuticals, although closely regulated, are competitive industries in the United States, and so are a host of other

U.S. industries operating under various degrees of regulation. This is true even though a great deal of regulation of competitive industries has been enacted to protect the producers, not the consumers. The fact that industries often remain competitive despite such regulation does not justify treating such regulation as desirable; furthermore, as will be evident, the benefits of competition under the kind of regulation that Moe proposes is just wishful thinking.

Joseph Viteritti's *Choosing Equality* is an excellent statement of the equalitarian view that reflects a sincere effort to treat it fairly.[22] Nevertheless, even Vitteritti's analysis has crucial gaps, such as his failure to present the free-market position on equity. In any case, the equalitarians hold prestigious think tank and academic positions at Harvard, Stanford, the Heritage Foundation, Brookings Institution, Fordham Foundation, Hoover Institution, and the American Enterprise Institute.[23] Friedman was a senior scholar at the Hoover Institution, but he was not a member of Hoover's Koret Task Force on Education, which is preponderantly equalitarian.[24]

Like the Milwaukee plan previously discussed, none of the school choice plans that have been operative since 1990 are free-market plans. Unfortunately, as long as the media and most of the professional literature do not draw any distinctions between school choice plans, the acceptability of free-market plans will be dependent on the outcomes of plans that are basically contrary to free-market positions on school choice.[25]

## COMPETING PERSPECTIVES ON "COMPETITION"

In opposing competition, its critics often argue that competition leads to negative practices. Examples are legion, from a wide variety of industries. For-profit HMOs cut services to the patients who need expensive medical services. Athletic competition leads institutions of higher education to establish easy-to-pass courses and lower their admission requirement.[26] Competition to manage public schools for profit leads to replacement of good but high-salaried teachers by ineffective but low-salaried ones. The point is that the supporters of competition ignore these negative effects in their argument that competition will force schools to improve or go out of business.

Competition sometimes does have negative effects, but they are much less likely in an enterprise that relies on repeat customers, and they are not the reason the public school establishment opposes a competitive education industry. This is evident from the statements of leading critics of the free-market position. For example, consider the following question and answer at a debate on school choice: "What are the features of K–12 education that render producer competition inappropriate?" The answer by Gerald Bracey, one of the nation's leading critics of competition in education, was that education is a service, not a product.[27] This answer is patently absurd; competition is alive and well in hundreds of service industries, such as dry cleaning and air travel. Yet after decades of educational and political conflict over competition in education, this is the intellectual level of the debate.

To be fair, most proponents of school choice are as much responsible for this situation as the opponents of it. By enthusiastically embracing every school choice plan while continuing to claim that school choice fosters competition, they have fostered the idea that the conditions and regulations of school choice do not matter insofar as competition is concerned. The supporters of a free-market approach have occasionally objected to the practice, but they have lacked the numbers and the visibility to overcome the confusion over the issue.[28]

The supporters of school choice differ on the extent of government regulation they will accept. The libertarian wing wants to restrict government regulation of private schools to health and safety regulations applicable to schools generally; they prefer as little regulation as possible, but it is inaccurate to portray them as insistent upon the complete absence of regulation or upon limiting regulation to health and safety issues. Their main concern is that state education bureaucracies hostile to vouchers will try to regulate them out of existence. This issue underlies much of their opposition to regulation, and their experience provides ample justification for their concern.[29] The denominational supporters of school choice are worried about excessive regulation of denominational schools; on occasion, they have been more resistant to regulation than the free-market supporters of it.

The equalitarians propose a variety of measures intended to bring about equity. These measures include the prohibition of add-ons, the requirement that private schools that admit voucher-bearing students reserve a certain percentage of admissions for children from poor families, and the use of lotteries when there are more applications than vacancies. These and other measures favored by equalitarians drastically weaken competition.

Theoretically, virtually any choice fosters competition to some degree; however, the equalitarians have exaggerated the competition resulting from the school choice plans that have been adopted. In the three largest equalitarian voucher programs in the United States (Milwaukee, Cleveland, and Edgewood, Texas), the public school districts did not respond to vouchers by trying to become more efficient or productive. Instead, they responded by increasing public relations programs and relaxing some of the rules and regulations to gain public support.[30] In any event, the possibility that nonmarket school choice leads to "competition" can be true but highly misleading because the competition is marginal at most.[31] However, if and when vouchers are available under the requisite conditions for competition, they can be expected to lead to more effective educational services at lower costs. Therefore, restrictions that would virtually forestall competition and research and development leading to industry-wide improvement should be strongly opposed. This does not mean that school choice programs cannot or should not make any concessions to an equalitarian point of view. Even Adam Smith, the most revered proponent of free markets in over two hundred years, supported universal basic education at government expense—not as a political concession, but as the right thing to do for efficiency reasons.[32]

In school choice legislation, there will have to be trade-offs, and the trade-offs will have to be made in a specific context. For this reason, it is difficult to say what deviations from a free market would or would not be acceptable. Most free marketeers do not oppose school choice proposals that enable some students to attend different public schools, *but such proposals per se cannot generate significant market competition*. The damage is done when the equalitarians claim their proposals will bring the benefits of competition. Helping children from poor families attend a different, and hopefully, better school is not necessarily fostering competition; the claim that it does is naive and jeopardizes support for school choice plans that really would foster it.

In the equalitarian view of competition, it is an incremental process; equalitarians do not expect any fundamental change in the process except over a long period of incremental changes.[33] However, this is not the way that leading scholars think about the process. In his classic study of capitalism, Joseph A. Schumpeter points out that the most important advances occur by a process of "creative destruction" when an entire industry is revolutionized: from horse-drawn carriages to gasoline-fueled cars, ship to airplane travel, frozen food instead of canned food, and so on. In his words,

> The first thing to go is the traditional conception of the *modus operandi* of competition. Economists are at long last emerging from the stage in which price competition was all they saw. As soon as quality competition and sales effort are admitted in to the sacred precincts of theory, the price variable is ousted from its dominant position. However, it is still competition within a rigid pattern of invariant conditions, methods of production and forms of industrial organization in particular, that practically monopolizes attention. But in capitalist reality as distinguished from its textbook picture, it is not that kind of competition which counts but the competition from the new commodity, the new technology, the new source of supply, the new type of organization (the largest-scale unit of control for instance)—competition which commands a decisive cost or quality advantage and which strikes not at the margins of the profits and the outputs of the existing firms but at their foundations and their very lives.[34]

Realistically, there is virtually no chance of such a development under equalitarian plans. The investment in educational research and development in means-tested school choice plans, if any, has been miniscule and overwhelmingly devoted to comparisons of voucher to regular public school students. Such plans are not a threat to the established order; arguably, means-tested vouchers are propping up the system they are supposed to replace.

Albert O. Hirschmann's analysis of monopolies explains why equalitarian type voucher plans strengthen the status quo. Hirschmann distinguished two kinds of monopolies. One kind, "profit-making monopolies," fights aggressively "to prevent any deviation or exception." The other kind, labeled "lazy monopolies," seeks to avoid conflict with parties who are likely to challenge the monopoly unless they get what they want.[35] The lazy monopolies tolerate, and may even foster, alternatives that will satisfy the potential dissidents. Thus the public school establishment, which is a lazy monopoly, does not challenge parental rights to send their children to private schools at their own expense. If every child were required to attend public schools, the resulting conflict might jeopardize the lazy monopoly.

These considerations apply to means-tested vouchers. They satisfy minority leaders who would otherwise participate in efforts to effectuate more inclusive school choice plans. A solution that provides the activists with an acceptable alternative without jeopardizing the status quo meets the needs of the lazy monopoly; one of the coalition constituencies, having gotten a solution that satisfies it, is no longer a threat to the status quo. Thus we come to an unpleasant but unavoidable conclusion: The equalitarians, for all their good intentions, are pursuing a course of action that will not lead to basic changes in the status quo. The reasons can be summarized as follows:

- The overriding emphasis on equity has strengthened the erroneous assumption that no major changes are needed if we can improve educational achievement among disadvantaged minorities.
- The equalitarian voucher plans have not and cannot provide the benefits of competition; however, by claiming that their voucher plans foster competition, the equalitarians are jeopardizing the acceptability of voucher plans that would foster it.
- Equalitarian plans attract and satisfy activists who are essential to enact competitive school choice plans. These activists focus on implementing noncompetitive plans, not on expanding competitive plans.
- Whatever innovations of general applicability may emerge from equalitarian school choice programs—and none have to date—they will face an extremely difficult time getting accepted elsewhere. Middle- and upper-class school districts are not likely to accept the idea that innovations in economically disadvantaged areas have any relevance to their situations.
- Means-tested vouchers are not leading to investment in research and development or innovations that improve the efficacy of public education.

Nobel prize–winning economist Amartya Sen criticizes means-tested benefits for the following reasons, all of which are applicable to educational vouchers:

- *Information distortion*. Parties understate their income in order to get or retain eligibility for benefits. Monitoring eligibility renders it likely that some qualified parties will be held ineligible for the benefit.

- *Incentive distortion.* Some parties will work less in order to retain eligibility.
- *Disutility and stigma.* Being characterized as poor or unable to take care of your children damages the self-respect of both parents and children, outcomes seldom fully appreciated by parties who have never been poor.
- *Administrative costs, invasive loss, corruption,* and "social cost of asymmetric power that bureaucrats exercise over supplicants." Targeting benefits involves administrative costs, loss of privacy, and possibilities for corruption as beneficiaries try to influence decision makers regarding eligibility.
- *Political sustainability and quality.* Targeting is an *attempt*, not a *result.* "Since the case for means-testing and for heavy targeting has gained so much ground recently in public circles (based on rather elementary reasoning), the messiness and the disincentive effects of the proposed policy are also worth emphasizing."[36]

Education should foster equality of educational opportunity, but not by eviscerating the benefits of a free market in education.


## THE EQUALITARIANS: A HISTORICAL NOTE

Developments in school finance since the 1970s severely weaken equalitarian credibility on voucher issues. Taxable property per student varies enormously from state to state and within states. The result is that districts with substantial taxable property can raise more revenues than property-poor districts, even with lower tax rates in the former. In *Serrano v. Priest*, the leading case on the issue, the plaintiffs pointed out that Beverly Hills was able to raise more than twice as much per student from its property tax as Baldwin Park, even though the Baldwin Park tax rate was more than twice as high as the Beverly Hills rate. The plaintiffs argued that it is unfair to allow the wealth of parents or school districts to determine how much was spent per student in the California public schools.[37] Inasmuch as local school boards are legally agencies of the state governments, the argument was that the state of California was violating the U.S. constitutional requirement of equal treatment of its citizens, public school students in this case.

In 1973, the U.S. Supreme Court held that intrastate differences in per pupil spending did not violate the U.S. Constitution, but it left open the question of whether the differences violated the state constitutions in states that relied on property taxes to raise school revenues.[38] In 1976, the California Supreme Court agreed that the disparities in spending per student violated the equal treatment required by the California Constitution, and the case was eventually resolved under California law along the lines sought by the plaintiffs; approximately 95 percent of California students in public schools now attend schools whose per-pupil revenues from property and state taxes do not vary by more than 5 percent. By 1999, seventeen state courts had held that the inequalities in funding that resulted from reliance on property taxes violated their state constitutions.

Much of the legal support for the *Serrano* plaintiffs was provided by University of California, Berkeley, law professors John Coons and Stephen Sugarman, equalitarians whom Moe praises lavishly for their leadership on means-tested vouchers. Coons and Sugarman supported a system of school finance known as district power equalization (DPE). According to DPE supporters, the critical flaw in the existing system of school finance was the huge school district variations in the taxable wealth per pupil. Coons and Sugarman proposed to remedy this problem by treating every school district in the state as if its tax rate was uniform throughout the state. Districts were to be free to spend at a higher or lower tax rate, but if they wanted to spend more than the state average, they had to share the excess amount with property-poor districts. The rationale was that the affluent districts would continue to spend more per pupil, even if some of their money for this purpose had to be shared with property-poor districts.

District power equalization became the equity plan of choice among the equalitarians; however, although the tax rates are lower in property-rich districts, home owners in these districts pay more for their houses because of this fact. In other words, the taxes are capitalized. Low taxes increase the price of a home; high taxes result in lower prices for homes. Furthermore, district power equalization inexorably led to a shift from reliance on local property taxes to reliance on state taxes. Before district power equalization, property owners benefited from good schools because good schools increased the value of their property. Under district power equalization, the local incentives to spend more on education were no longer operative because so much of the increase went to property-poor districts.

Contrary to the expectations of supporters of district power equalization, it did not raise the level of spending for public education; in fact, it has had a depressive effect on public school revenues. Dartmouth professor William A. Fischel observes,

> As many observers have detailed, spending per pupil in California has slipped from its pre-Serrano position near the top of the 50 states to a persistent position in the lower quartile. In comparison with the resources available, California ranks at the bottom among the states, and even a 1988 initiative that required that 40 percent of the state's budget be devoted to education has been unable to budge it. . . . One seventh of the nation's children attend public schools that would be far better than they are but for the Serrano decision.[39]

In praising Coons and Sugarman as the architects of the equalitarian position, Moe appears to have been unaware of the actual results of their activism.

District power equalization also overlooked the fact that more poor families resided in high- than in low-wealth districts. In high-wealth districts many parents, especially affluent ones, reacted to Serrano legislation by establishing public school foundations devoted to the particular schools attended by their children. Thus by trying to achieve equity in government spending per pupil across school districts, equalitarian policies also exacerbated inequities within districts.

## INTRADISTRICT EQUALITY OF EDUCATIONAL OPPORTUNITY

As chapter 6 makes clear, intradistrict inequities are a more serious problem than the interdistrict ones in several school districts. The experienced teachers whose seniority enables them to exercise transfer rights are paid more than teachers with less seniority. The result is that teachers in the poorest neighborhoods are paid considerably less than teachers in middle- and upper-class schools in the same district.

As we might expect, the public school establishment has concealed the inequity as much as possible. Perhaps the most striking failure is on the part of the equalitarians. Their mantra is "equity" and concern for the underfunded minorities; however, by focusing on funding inequities between school districts, they brought about a lower level of funding than would exist were it not for their efforts. Meanwhile, they overlooked the large intradistrict inequities in the cost per pupil, which are remedial by school district action.[40] At the same time, conservatives have overlooked a valid, politically potent argument that might appeal strongly to minority communities, but they do not wish to risk defections from their middle-class supporters who benefit from the inequities.

As Paul Hill points out, there is a feasible way to achieve equity in the situation. That way is to show the actual cost of its teachers in school budgets. Equity could be achieved in a few years without displacing any teachers because the teachers in the affluent areas tend to have more seniority and retire at a higher rate than teachers elsewhere in the district, but there is more turnover in low-income areas. To illustrate, suppose the costs of salaries and benefits is $70,000 per teacher in school A and $40,000 in school B (benefits will also cost more per experienced teacher). The equity goal is an average cost of $55,000 per teacher. As a $70,000 teacher retires, school A would have to hire a $40,000 teacher; as a $40,000 teacher leaves school B, it would employ a $70,000 teacher. It would normally require only three to five years without displacing anyone for the average per-pupil cost to be the same in both schools; the time required could be shortened by requiring some transfers not based on seniority. In any case, the inequity could usually be removed within a reasonable time without forcing teachers to transfer out of a preferred assignment.[41]

## PUBLIC EDUCATION AND FREE MARKETS

The pervasive failure of the critics of a free market in education to understand it illustrates a much larger failure — that of the American people generally to understand how free markets function. As renowned economist Mancur Olson points out,

> the politics of the United States as of other countries is influenced, and influenced for the worse, by the fact that the use of markets are [*sic*] imperfectly understood by a majority of citizens. No doubt this popular ignorance of economics does on occasion lead to the gratuitous or even harmful use of

government to perform certain social functions for which the government does not have a comparative advantage. Though there are some valid arguments that point in the opposite direction, it is surely a reasonable hypothesis that the limited understanding of economics among the laity leads to a somewhat bigger public sector than would be optimal.[42]

Obviously, many professors and think tank gurus are among the laity that does not understand how markets function. For example, Michael J. Petrilli, vice president of the Fordham Foundation, concludes under the heading "What If Competition Doesn't Work?" that "it's hard to find much evidence, after 15 years with charters and vouchers, that competition has transformed dysfunctional school districts. . . . But is it time for those who support such reforms to stop claiming that competition will lift all boats?"[43] The answer is that it is not time to stop making the claim, but it is time for Petrilli and those of his ilk to stop asking questions based on fallacies.

## NOTES

1. Paul T. Hill, *School Choice: Doing It the Right Way Makes a Difference, A Report from the National Working Commission on Choice in K–12 Education* (Washington, DC: Brookings, 2002), 11.

2. E. G. West, *Education and the State*, 3rd ed. (Indianapolis: Liberty, 1994). Initially published in 1965.

3. Joseph A. Schumpeter, *Capitalism, Socialism and Democracy* (New York: Harper & Row, 1976), 77–78, 103–105.

4. See Neal P. McCluskey, *Feds in the Classroom: How Big Government Corrupts, Cripples, and Compromises American Education* (Lanham, MD: Rowman & Littlefield, 2007); Mark Harrison, *Education Matters: Government, Markets and New Zealand Schools* (Wellington, New Zealand: Education Forum, 2004), 364–369.

5. Jeffrey R. Henig: *Rethinking School Choice: Limits of the Market Metaphor* (Princeton, NJ: Princeton University Press, 1995). Henig's reference is to John E. Chubb and Terry M. Moe, *Politics, Markets, and America's Schools* (Washington, DC: Brookings, 1990). Henig's book was initially published in 1994; the 1995 edition includes a twenty-page afterword.

6. Terry M. Moe, *Schools, Vouchers, and the American Public* (Washington, DC: Brookings, 2001), 293–343.

7. Chubb and Moe, *Politics, Markets, and America's Schools*, 220.

8. Henig, *Rethinking School Choice*, 110.

9. Henig did not refer to my 1993 book, which includes a detailed explanation of why the Milwaukee project cannot be considered to be a free-market school choice plan. See Myron Lieberman, *Public Education: An Autopsy* (Cambridge, MA: Harvard University Press, 1993), 11–13.

10. My criticism in this paragraph takes into account the following books and too many articles to list: Henig, *Rethinking School Choice*; Moe, *Schools, Vouchers, and the American Public*; Chubb and Moe, *Politics, Markets and American Schools*; Richard D. Kahlenberg, ed., *Public School Choice vs. Private School Vouchers* (New York: Century, 2003); Edward B. Fiske and Helen F. Ladd, *When Schools Compete* (Washington, DC: Brookings, 2000); Bryan P. Gill, Michael Timpane, Karen E. Ross, and Dominic Brewer, *Rhetoric versus Reality* (Santa Monica, CA: Rand, 2001); David W. Kirkpatrick, *Choice in Schooling* (Chicago: Loyola University Press, 1990); Joseph P. Viteritti, *Choosing Equality* (Washington, DC: Brookings, 1999); and John Witte, *The Market Approach to Education: An Analysis of America's First Voucher Program* (Princeton, NJ: Princeton University Press, 2000). My criticisms are intended to apply only to the treatment or neglect of free-market school choice plans in these books. Of the seven books listed, three are pro-choice, three are anti-choice, and one asserts that there is as yet no clear-cut case for or against vouchers.

11. Frederick M. Hess, *Revolution at the Margins: The Impact of Competition on Urban School Systems* (Washington, DC: Brookings, 2002).

12. Frederick M. Hess, "The Work Ahead," *Education Next* (Winter 2001), 10.

13. Moe, *Schools, Vouchers, and the American Public*, 319, 389.

14. Moe, *Schools, Vouchers, and the American Public*, 35.

15. John E. Coons and Stephen D. Sugarman, *Education by Choice: The Case for Family Control* (Berkeley: University of California Press, 1978); Reprinted by Educator's International Press, Inc., Troy, NY, in 1999.

16. Chubb and Moe, *Politics, Markets, and America's Schools*, 220.

17. Moe, *Schools, Vouchers, and the American Public*, 359–365. The equalitarian refusal to support Proposition 174 was not the cause of its overwhelming defeat.

18. Moe, *Schools, Vouchers, and the American Public*, 341–342.

19. Moe, *Schools, Vouchers, and the American Public*, 22.

20. Terry M. Moe, "No Teacher Left Behind," *Wall Street Journal*, January, 13, 2005, A12.

21. Moe, *Schools, Vouchers, and the American Public*, 23.

22. Joseph Viteritti, *Choosing Equality* (Washington, DC: Brookings 1999).

23. Partisans on school choice in Harvard's Graduate School of Education are generally opposed to it, whereas the partisans of it in the political science department support various versions of school choice.

24. Herbert J. Walberg is the task force member most clearly committed to a free-market approach. See Herbert J. Walberg and Joseph L. Bast, *Education and Capitalism* (Stanford, CA: Hoover Institution, 2003).

25. For the best discussion of this point, see John Merrifield, *The School Choice Wars* (Lanham, MD: ScarecrowEducation, 2001), 20–43.

26. Many examples of the negative effects of competition are cited in Robert Kuttner, *Everything for Sale* (Chicago: University of Chicago Press, 1996).

27. I pursued it at a Q-and-A session with Gerald Bracey, a prominent voucher critic. He responded that the free market works for products but not for services. This is obviously untenable; we pay FedEx and UPS for services, just as we do when flying by commercial airliner.

28. For example, Andrew J. Coulson's *Market Education* (New Brunswick, NJ: Transaction Publishers, 1999) and John Merrifield's *School Choice Wars* (Lanham, MD: ScarecrowEducation, 2001) are two books that point out in detail why the school choice plans that have been adopted meet few, if any, of the conditions required for a free market.

29. For example, in Wisconsin, the state superintendent of public instruction vigorously opposed the Wisconsin voucher legislation and tried to undermine it after enactment.

30. Hess, *Revolution at the Margins*.

31. See Schumpeter, *Capitalism, Socialism, and Democracy*, for the classic statement of different kinds of competition.

32. Adam Smith, *An Inquiry into the Nature and Causes of the Wealth of Nations* (Oxford, UK: Clarendon, 1976), vol. 1, book 2, 27; vol. 5, book 1, 785.

33. See Moe, *Schools, Vouchers, and the American Public*, 344–397, 372.

34. See Schumpeter, *Capitalism, Socialism, and Democracy*, 84.

35. Albert O. Hirschmann, *Exit, Voice and Loyalty* (Cambridge, MA: Harvard University Press, 1970).

36. Amartya Sen, *Development as Freedom* (New York: Random House, 1999), 111–145. Emphasis in original. For a statement supporting universal vouchers in the U.S. situation, see Joseph Bast and Herbert Walberg, *Ten Principles of School Choice* (Chicago: Heartland Institute, 2004), 22–23. http://down loads.heartland.org/16856.pdf.

37. *Serrano v. Priest* 487 P. 2d 1241, 96 Cal Rptr. 601 (1971) (*"Serrano I"*); 557 P. 2d 929, 135 Cal Rptr. 345 (1976) (*"Serrano II"*).

38. *San Antonio Independent School District v. Rodriguez* 411 U.S.1 (1973).

39. William A. Fischel, "School Finance Litigation and Property Tax Revolts: How Undermining Local Control Turns Voters Away from Public Education," in *Developments in School Finance, 1999–2000*, ed. William J. Fowler Jr., NCES 2002-316. (Washington, DC: U.S. Department of Education, National Center for

Education Statistics, 2002), 108. See also Caroline M. Hoxby, *Local Property Tax-Based Funding of Public Schools*, Heartland Policy Study, No. 82 (Chicago: Heartland Institute, 1997). Hoxby argues that local property taxes provide incentives to residents and school staff, encourage people who value education to support their public schools, and enable the tax burden associated with schools to be more fairly distributed.

40. S. E. Murray, W. N. Evans, and R. M. Schwab, "Education-Finance Reform and the Distribution of Education Resources," *American Economic Review* 88 (1998): 789–812.

41. See Paul Hill, "The Costs of Collective Bargaining Agreements and Related District Policies," in *Collective Bargaining in Education*, ed. Jane Hannaway and Andrew J. Rotherham (Cambridge, MA: Harvard University Press, 2006), 89–109. In June 2006, the Fordham Foundation published a brochure entitled "Fund the Child: Tackling Inequality and Antiquity in School Finance" advocating "weighted school funding," a more detailed proposal based on Hill's suggestion. See also Hoxby, *Local Property Tax-Based Funding*.

42. Mancur Olson, "Comment," in *Constitutional Economics*, ed. Richard B. McKenzie (Lexington, MA: Lexington, 1984), 39.

43. Michael J. Petrilli, "What If Competition Doesn't Work?" *The Education Gadfly*, 4, December 15, 2006, 1–3.

# 10

---

## The Strategy and Tactics of School Choice

$A$ny discussion of school choice strategies and tactics should recognize the huge advantages of the public school establishment in opposing it. First, the establishment is unified behind measures likely to weaken support for public education. It overwhelmingly opposes school choice with the possible exception of public school choice. At the same time, the unions adamantly oppose privatization except when it is a union or teacher benefit, such as binding arbitration of grievances instead of litigation to resolve alleged violations of the contract. The above objectives are easily understood and do not clash with each other or with the interests of the teacher union allies; on the contrary, they are also important objectives for their allies, such as other public sector unions.

The school choice and reform coalitions face a much more difficult situation. Some want vouchers; others want tuition tax credits. Some want vouchers for equity reasons; others want them for free-market reasons. Many groups devote their resources to remedying one aspect of the status quo, such as excessive tenure protection, multiculturalism, merit pay, or sex education. Some support parental add-ons; others oppose them. Religious groups differ with each other and internally. With the exception of contracting out, the upshot is unified control with clear, internally uncontested objectives and ample resources on one side, and internally contested objectives without unified control or adequate resources on the other.

A major pro-choice mistake was acceptance of the idea that "school choice" must be supported by trial programs, to which the NEA and AFT attached every possible obstacle. This had the predictable result of focusing the school choice debates on underfunded, restriction-laden, small-scale school choice plans.[1] The proponents of school choice accepted, even advocated, the challenge of demonstrating that academic achievement in a myriad of small-scale, underfunded, nonprofit school choice plans under severe antimarket restrictions would be superior to outcomes in public schools.[2] Meanwhile, the public school establishment argued that school choice had to demonstrate its superiority in U.S. schools while they were doing their utmost to prevent or weaken any such demonstration.

In 1978 and 1993, the PTA national president was the nominal chairperson of the public school coalition opposed to vouchers. Under the PTA's governance documents, policies adopted by the National PTA are binding on its state and local affiliates; state and local PTAs cannot support a school choice plan opposed by the National PTA.[3] It is open to question whether a voucher campaign should be based primarily on an appeal to parents, especially when the most prestigious parent organization is adamantly opposed to vouchers. Furthermore, parents of young children are a declining percentage of the voting population, and most spend more to take care of their parents than their children.

The major voucher initiatives in 1993 and 2000 were in California and Michigan—the two states with teacher unions best able to conduct an all-out antivoucher campaign. It appears that these states were chosen because the main contributor to the voucher campaign lived in the state. In contrast, the unions take small amounts from thousands of members nationwide, and the funds can be spent anywhere.

Note also the tremendous union advantage in experience. All the data and records of previous campaigns are kept by the unions and are available to them for future reference and analysis. For example, the *NEA Action Plan for Opposing Vouchers* was based upon the Pennsylvania State Education Association's successful effort to defeat voucher legislation in Pennsylvania. The plan highlights the antivoucher arguments that have been effective regardless of the voucher proposal at issue. The arguments that have not been effective are also identified; they are to be mentioned to target groups but are not to be the focal point of the campaign. The plan points out that union officers should not be the formal leaders of antivoucher coalitions; presidents of organizations like the PTA and League of Women Voters should play this role. The ready availability of union facilities while their opposition must pay for and rely on ad hoc facilities is another underappreciated advantage of the anti–school choice forces. With the exception of public school choice, which is hardly a reform, the public school establishment opposes all of the versions of school choice. Its criticisms of school choice plans will be much the same, regardless of the versions on the ballot.

## MISLEADING ADVERTISING

Will parents be misled in a voucher system by advertising and fly-by-night schools? Of course, some will be misled—just as they often are when they vote for president and vice president, governor, lieutenant governor, two U.S. senators, members of the House of Representatives, state treasurer, mayor, members of the city council, tax assessor, members of the school board, members of the neighborhood advisory commission, or whatever. The assumption that parents who are supposed to know enough to choose among dozens of candidates for various political offices cannot choose from among two to six schools (the likely feasible number that they can consider) and that they can visit and discuss with friends and neighbors shows the superficial nature of this objection. Also, bear in mind that there are advisory services on stocks, bonds, colleges, cars, real estate, food, credit, air travel, and a host of other goods and services; such services will undoubtedly expand in K–12 education if schools are competing for customers.

The notion that most parents will visit several schools, assess teacher quality, review the curricular and the extracurricular program, and consult with guidance counselors is unrealistic. A small number of parents may do these things, and many students may benefit as a result, but the normal dynamics of a competitive system should be adequate. Unlike one-shot transactions like buying a car, buying educational services will be a repetitive process over several years. During this time, schools will point out the deficiencies of their competition.

The more schools compete for students, the more likely it is that even indifferent parents will be adequately informed about the positive and negative features of competing schools. That said, many children are currently left to the peer culture and television, without any guidance on the habits and attitudes essential for success in any endeavor. Most supporters of school choice realize this, but, fearful of saying anything that might weaken the case for parental choice, they merely repeat that parents know better than anyone else the kind of education that is in the best interests of their children. A more defensible rationale is that parents are more likely to make decisions in the best interests of their children than others are to make in the best interests of somebody else's children. Furthermore, the negative influence of some parents and homes is less likely in a competitive system because

- Indifferent parents get the benefit of knowledgeable, interested parents. When the latter check the school menu to make sure their children are getting a nutritious lunch, the children of the indifferent parents benefit.
- Competition helps to publicize poor school performance in ways that school boards would never do. School boards are supposed to represent the public interest, but they are also part of the producer complex. When the two roles conflict, as is inevitable, protection of their producer role usually takes precedence over candid reporting on their consumer protection role. Competing schools will not be so restrained in criticizing their competitors.
- External examinations will identify the students who are falling behind. Schools may try to spin the reasons, but competition will make this difficult.
- Schools are more likely to have an active outreach program for parents if their viability depends upon student retention.

Despite the foregoing considerations, the emphasis on parents may have been a strategic mistake by the school choice forces.

- Parents qua parents have no reason to oppose school choice, but not many feel strong reason to support it. Most do not see viable choices in existence and do not visualize the multiplicity of choices that would emerge in a free market.
- The National PTA is practically an adjunct of the NEA and is adamantly opposed to vouchers. In addition, its constitution and by-laws prevent any sudden changes in its policies, which are binding on its state and local affiliates.

- Turnover among parents interested in school choice for their own children renders it difficult to achieve knowledgeable, experienced leadership from parents and parent organizations.

The free-market view is that the consumers benefit from competition among the producers. The parties who pay for education (taxpayers) can be considered the consumers. Students are the third-party beneficiaries. The problem is that it is extremely difficult to organize consumers, especially if they are geographically dispersed, pay different amounts, and have different criticisms of what they are getting for what they pay.

Although voucher proponents usually frame their arguments in terms of parental rights, some libertarians advocate parental absorption of all the costs of educating their children. Such advocacy is probably counterproductive. Most parents or putative parents of young children will not support measures that would require them to bear the full cost of educating their children. Moreover, having parents absorb all the cost of educating their children is not essential to the development of a competitive education system; in fact, a competitive education system that reduces costs while increasing educational achievement is probably a condition precedent to having parents absorb a larger share of the costs of K–12 education.

## EQUALITARIAN STRATEGY AND TACTICS

Terry M. Moe has been the most explicit equalitarian on strategy and tactics. His comments on the subject include the following:

> There is really only one solution that is acceptable to the entire spectrum of voucher opponents, including groups like the teachers unions that have no intention of supporting any form of voucher program. That solution is *public* school choice—and especially, in more recent years, charter schools, which come closest (in principle) to offering the basics of a market-like system within the public sector. . . .
>
> For it is reasonable to suggest that, were public school choice to spread, Americans would come to think of choice as a familiar, normal, and even necessary part of their education system—and this would encourage them to see vouchers as a closely related form of choice that is just a short step away and not threatening or fraught with risk. It is difficult to argue that,

once public school choice is adopted, Americans will somehow draw the line. It is more likely that as the school system as a whole becomes more thoroughly built around choice and competition, and as this way of thinking and behaving becomes the norm, attitudes and beliefs will adapt—and so will views toward vouchers.[4]

Moe's contention that charter schools "come closest (in principle) to offering the basics of a market-like system within the public sector" may be charitably characterized as faulty economics. It relies on superficial similarities while overlooking several basic differences, such as the absences of prices and monopoly producers.

Elsewhere, Moe asserts that vouchers (and then only for students from poor families) will require decades to become commonplace.[5] In 2001, he thought that "the key development, which could happen within five years, but could take a decade or more, is that the NAACP and other civil rights groups will come around and support vouchers for the disadvantaged."[6]

Moe's argument that public school choice will lead to competition, and also to acceptance of choice in private schools, is contradicted by a wealth of evidence from 1987 to 2006. As a matter of fact, when Minnesota enacted the first open enrollment plan in the nation in 1987, the leadership of the antivoucher forces viewed it as the way to stop the movement for inclusive vouchers, and this is the way that the public school establishment still regards it.[7]

Also, only a very small percentage of students, especially minority students, transfer out of their districts when public school choice is a right instead of a school board option. This has been the case since Minnesota enacted the first state public school choice law in 1987. Factors underlying this outcome include these:

- The travel time, regardless of whether the school districts pay for it
- The inconvenience of conferring with teachers a longer distance from home
- Student difficulties in participating in extracurricular activities outside of their neighborhoods
- The difficulty of getting to or from school in case of emergency
- The social costs of attending school away from neighborhood friends, such as the difficulties of forming close relationships with students

and families not seen outside of school hours and the negative reactions in the students' neighborhoods to transfers outside of it
- The absence of compelling differences between public schools

Understandably, most out-of-district transfers in Minnesota and elsewhere have been for noneducational reasons. Public school choice elsewhere was enacted only *after* it became clear that it was not a springboard to school choice inclusive of private schools.

Only about 1 percent of the students eligible to transfer under NCLB have requested a transfer, even though transportation was provided and the Bush administration has spent millions to encourage students and parents to take advantage of their right to transfer. The reasons are substantially the same as they were in Minnesota in 1987 and the years thereafter.[8]

Ironically, the Minnesota law was adopted to prevent competition, not foster it. When Minnesota enacted Statute 12.335, subdivision 14 provided that "school districts shall not compete with one another for the enrollment of students." The Minnesota prohibition against school district competition for students grew out of competition to enroll athletes for high school athletic teams. The issue became so contentious in the state legislature that it was finally turned over to the state high school federation to resolve.

My view is that if inclusive school choice materializes in the United States, it will do so in spite of equalitarian strategy, not because of it. Public school choice will not pave the way for vouchers inclusive of private schools; the NEA, AFT, and PTA leaders who are urging public school choice as the way to prevent inclusive vouchers are much more realistic. Supporters of universal or near-universal school choice are not likely to accept a protracted strategy that does not have universal choice as an ultimate overriding objective.

## THE FREE-MARKET STRATEGY TO ACHIEVE INCLUSIVE SCHOOL CHOICE

As we have seen, Milton Friedman believed that free-market plans would be far more effective than public education in raising achievement and lowering the costs of education. In his opinion, their margin of superiority would be so great that less-than-ideal plans would still prove to be very worthwhile.[9] Friedman also believed that the public would not accept a voucher plan in the absence of a successful demonstration of their efficacy. This is why Friedman and the Friedman Foundation supported school choice plans that fell far short of free-market plans. Nevertheless, in November 2005, Friedman conceded that the school choice plans that had been adopted were not achieving the goals of the school choice movement.[10] Astonishingly, his comment did not attract much attention or lead to any publicized changes in Friedman Foundation strategy.

Friedman has predicted that one state adopting a free market in education would trigger a rapid, unstoppable movement toward a free market in education. Presumably, free-market strategy would be oriented toward identifying the states that might serve as breakthrough examples and preparing for the conflict that lies ahead in such states. Nevertheless, since it was founded in 1996, the Friedman Foundation strategy has been virtually indistinguishable from equalitarian strategy: praise for any development labeled "school choice," no matter whether means-tested or what its antimarket restrictions; exaggerations of the benefits or expected benefits of "restriction-laden school" choice plans; and failure to point out the critical differences between free-market and nonmarket plans.

The free-market critics of Friedman's strategy did not contend that free marketeers should never support nonmarket school choice plans. Their strategy would have supported some nonmarket school choice plans but (1) always pointing out why they were not free-market plans and (2) getting a commitment from leaders of the nonmarket plans to support steps toward a free-market plan, regardless of the outcome of their own plans. Had this strategy been followed, supporters of a free market would not have gotten bogged down defending ineffective school choice plans. Instead of defending the outcomes of nonmarket school choice plans, the free marketeers might have utilized the results to justify free-market plans. This strategy would have also avoided the futile and irrelevant arguments over whether public schools are as good as they used to be.

A basic premise of the free-market rationale is that it will lead to schools and technology and educational services that will be very different from the kinds available in existing nonprofit private schools. The comparisons between public school students and comparable voucher students utilizing highly restricted, means-tested vouchers are not relevant to comparisons of achievement or costs between public school students and comparable students in a free market system of school choice. The critics of an educational free market have drawn unfavorable implications about it from studies that are basically irrelevant to the desirability of a market system of school choice.


## A PRO-CHOICE CONSULTANT STRATEGY ON SCHOOL CHOICE

While school choice partisans disagree about strategy and tactics, Frank Luntz, a leading conservative political consultant, and Bob Castro emphasize that "any educational reform effort that is openly and specifically hostile to 'public education' will be opposed by a majority of parents no matter what the situation is in their local schools." Luntz and Castro go on to say that

> many in the school choice movement (Milton Freedman [*sic*] for one) are openly hostile to public education. I fear that even suggesting the use of pro–public school arguments will be looked upon negatively by choice advocates, but that is the only way to overcome the voucher/scholarship barrier. . . . If you are perceived right off the bat as being hostile to public education, per se, you will be dead in the water.[11]

Not surprisingly, the education establishment had embraced Luntz's tactical views long before he expressed them. In voucher controversies, the public school establishment's first line of attack is that vouchers will hurt the public schools. Usually, the criticism is phrased as "vouchers will drain funds that would go to our public schools."

Luntz's strategic advice is supported by the fact that U.S. schools frequently generate social capital in unique ways. In countries with national school systems, parents are much less active in school affairs, whereas in the United States, school events, especially athletic competitions, are frequently sources of community interest, loyalty, and support in ways that have no counterpart elsewhere.

The Luntz–Castro memorandum specifies four arguments for vouchers that are not politically effective:

- Vouchers appeal to the benefits of competition.
- Parents opposed to vouchers would change their views if they sent their children to poor schools.
- Voters are more willing to support vouchers out of compassion rather than anger.
- U.S. higher education, which is supposedly competitive, claims to be the best in the world.

Luntz's blunt analysis is an indictment of school choice strategy and tactics for the past fifty years. The public school establishment has implicitly agreed with his analysis for a long time, while the school choice forces appear to have done so only very recently, if at all.

## SCHOOL CHOICE AS A "CIVIL RIGHT"

In recent years, several supporters of school choice have referred to it as a "civil right." According to U.S. Secretary of Education Rod Paige, "The president and I believe education is a civil right—there should be equal access for all, not just the privileged few."[12] Paige's comments were made in the course of a discussion that pointed out that very few white students remained in the District of Columbia public schools, whose overwhelmingly black student population was at the low end of an achievement gap and high end of the per-pupil cost. The *Wall Street Journal* has also embraced the conclusion that school choice is a civil right; in its view, "from the vantage point of Brown, we can now see that vouchers have become the cornerstone for a fundamental civil right."[13] In a widely reviewed book, Abigail and Stephan Thernstrom assert that "this is a book about education. But it also addresses the central civil rights issue of our time; our failure to provide first-class education for black and Hispanic students, in both cities and suburbs."[14] Inasmuch as Abigail Thernstrom was a member of the U.S. Commission on Civil Rights at the time the book was published, her characterization indicates the widespread support for the idea.

As Luntz points out, presenting a political position as a "right" conveys the message that the policy advocated is essential, not merely desirable or reasonable or beneficial.[15] The civil rights argument for school choice is a recent add-on to the arguments made by Milton Friedman and the scholars and politicians who followed him. The rationale can be summarized as follows: Most parents choose to live near schools that they regard as beneficial for their children, 25 million in toto. Add 5 million in nonpublic schools and 2 million being home-schooled, the result is that most students already attend schools of choice. The fact that only low-income families cannot exercise school choice allegedly converts it into a civil rights issue.

The issue being addressed here is not a case of a government spending more for students of one race than for students of a different race, although that still happens. The issue is whether the government should equalize educational opportunity by spending enough on students from low-income families to equalize their educational opportunities with students whose superior opportunities result from their private expenditures. Indubitably, black and Hispanic children have the same legal right to attend private schools as white children, and their families have the same right as white and Asian families to move to the suburbs and better schools. Furthermore, the private schools are not discriminating against students on ethnic or religious grounds; the schools are merely exercising their rights by not providing their services to anyone who can't afford to pay for them. The black and Hispanic families lack the money, not the right, to enroll their children in private or suburban public schools.

It is interesting that an administration that has repeatedly proclaimed its opposition to judges who create rights should proclaim school choice to be a "civil right." The U.S. Commission on Civil Rights defines "civil rights" as "equal protection under law with respect to race, color, religion, sex, age, disability, or national origin."[16] If school choice is a civil right, it would be the first public service to be characterized as such in the absence of any invidious discrimination by government or private entities. If school choice is a civil right, why isn't medical choice for those who can't afford to pay for private medical services? As we have seen, "school choice" has a limitless number of variations. Which ones satisfy the civil rights rationale for school choice?

The liberal definition of freedom leads to the position that pregnant women don't "really" have freedom to have an abortion unless they have the means to pay for it, which many do not have. Thus liberals support government funding for abortions, whereas the conservatives adamantly oppose it. In the school context, the positions are reversed. The conservatives argue that the legal right to send your children to private school is meaningless if you can't afford it. And the liberals argue that the government should not support your legal right to send your child to a private school. The stark inconsistency within each group illustrates how interests trump principles in political campaigns—or that the principles never mattered in the first place.[17]

## TUITION TAX CREDITS

Tuition tax credits are an alternative to vouchers to effectuate a free market in education. It is an alternative that may have more favorable political prospects than vouchers in some situations. For instance, Democratic senator Daniel P. Moynihan of New York and Republican senator Robert W. Packwood of Orgeon introduced a tuition tax credit bill in 1978. The bill passed the House of Representatives but was defeated in the Senate by a 56 to 41 vote. A few years later, Moynihan commented that the liberal opponents to vouchers

> present immense problems for a person such as myself . . . who was deeply involved in this issue long before it was either conservative or liberal. And if it prevails only as a conservative cause, it will have been a great failure of American liberalism not to have seen the essentially liberal nature of this pluralist position.[18]

Nevertheless, Moynihan did not initiate any school choice plans after the defeat of the Packwood–Moynihan bill in 1978. Undoubtedly, one reason was the growing strength of the New York State United Teachers (NYSUT), which led the opposition to the Packwood–Moynihan bill and would have been a huge obstacle to Moynihan's reelection if he had not ended his active support for tuition tax credits.

In legislation on the subject, tuition tax credits sometimes provide credits for educational expenses in addition to tuition. This broader meaning is more useful, hence "tuition tax credits" will be regarded here as any legislation that provides tax credits or tax deductions for the expenses of elementary and secondary education.

The proponents of tuition tax credits claim the following advantages compared to vouchers:

- Tuition tax credits do not require a new bureaucracy. Taxpayers simply deduct the tax credits from their income taxes.
- Government involvement is minimal. Government does not receive any money or provide the funding for schooling.
- No new government program is needed. Compliance is mainly an IRS problem that does not generate social conflict. Regulations can minimize fraud or otherwise unacceptable private schools but should not be used to prevent competition to public schools.
- Tuition tax credits provide more flexibility in parental decisions on how much to spend for education. In voucher plans, the government contributions are established by government. Under tuition tax credits, parents who spend more for education receive larger government tax credits up to any limit in the legislation.

These would be significant advantages, but critics of tuition tax credits challenge all of them.[19] Furthermore, the fact that the poor do not file income tax returns on which they could use tuition tax credits would exacerbate the existing inequities in public education. A tuition tax credit for the costs of educating an autistic child might be worth tens of thousands to an affluent family and nothing to a poor family. Vouchers would be universal under most free-market plans.

Another major objection to tuition tax credits is that using the tax system to achieve social objectives usually has several unintended negative consequences. The tax system should be designed to raise revenue efficiently and equitably; adding social objectives further complicates a system in which unintended consequences are probable.

Tuition tax credits can be enacted by federal or state action or both. Understandably, the politics of tuition tax credits differ from the politics of means-tested vouchers. The latter are supported by economically disadvantaged minorities, who are often strongly opposed to tuition tax credits. The denominational groups that support denominational schools prefer tuition tax credits. Due to the emphasis on reducing the achievement gaps in large urban districts, vouchers are likely to be the basis of school choice plans in states with substantial black and Hispanic populations.

Although the educational aspects of tuition tax credits may be uppermost in the minds of parents, the fiscal and political aspects tend to dominate the legislative controversies on the subject. The fiscal impact would depend upon several factors but primarily the following:

- What is the amount of the tax credit, and is it available for expenses other than tuition?
- Who is eligible for the credit?
- Is the credit refundable to parents who do not pay enough in taxes to use the credit?
- How many children will transfer from public to private schools as result of the credit?

In practice, the impact would depend upon the interaction of these four factors. A credit that covers only a small fraction of the parental costs of private schooling would not be helpful to many parents. Furthermore, if private schools raised their tuition as the result of tuition tax credits, the effect of the latter would be to enhance private school revenues without lowering the costs to parents.

Insofar as tuition tax credits provide deductions for the expenses of public education, there would be a revenue loss from the parents of public as well as private school pupils. Obviously, more parents would receive a tax credit if it applies to the expenses of education in both public and private schools. If more school districts charge parents for discrete items, such as transportation, athletic uniforms, textbooks, and laboratory fees, tuition tax credits could gain more support than they have at the present time.[20]

The more pupils who transfer to private schools, the more we can reduce expenditures for public schools; clearly, however, the costs of public schools would not decrease in the same proportion as the decline in their enrollment. We pay teachers the same, regardless of whether they teach twenty-seven or twenty-eight pupils. It costs as much to heat a building with 250 pupils as one with 260 pupils. Nevertheless, this point is only a short-run argument against tuition tax credits or vouchers. Public schools adjust all the time to changes in enrollment, and when they do not, the reason is often poor management.

Because the impact of tuition tax credits will depend upon their specifics and the circumstances in which they are applied, it is difficult to assess their impact upon racial segregation in education. Nevertheless, the claim that vouchers or tuition tax credits would foster racially segregated schools is a weak reason to oppose them. Clearly, there is widespread ethnic segregation in public education, which is unlikely to be affected very much by school choice. Every metropolitan area already has ethnic communities that will continue to exist under any school system. We should not forget that private schools in the South demonstrated a greater acceptance of racial integration than public schools, both before and after the 1954 Supreme Court decisions that declared government imposition of racial segregation in public schools to be unconstitutional. The efforts to use vouchers in the 1950s and 1960s to maintain racially segregated schools were led by racist politicians, not private school officials. Regardless, contemporary civil rights legislation would preclude using tuition tax credits or vouchers to encourage racial discrimination in education.

The argument that poor parents would not benefit from tuition tax credits is not necessarily a valid objection to tuition tax credits. The Nixon administration tried to implement Milton Friedman's suggestion of a refundable income tax credit. If individuals did not have enough income to pay taxes, the government would pay these individuals as it does with housing vouchers. Refundable tuition tax credits would enable poor parents to choose the schools that would educate their children and would do so without creating a government bureaucracy; administration of the credits would be an IRS responsibility. Parenthetically, Friedman had proposed similar reforms of other government programs for the poor, such as housing vouchers instead of government-built housing for the indigent. Today, it is largely overlooked that refundable tax credits were defeated by the welfare bureaucracy—the agency established to serve the poor.[21] This fact underscores the possibility that the education establishment's opposition to school choice is more self-interested than it cares to admit.

## PRIVATE SCHOLARSHIPS

During the 1990s, private scholarships emerged as an alternative to both vouchers and tuition tax credits. The rationale was most fully spelled out by Andrew J. Coulson in 1999. In Coulson's analysis, both vouchers and tuition tax credits would continue to involve government in education in undesirable ways: "They perpetuate the church/state controversy and the regulation ratchet; they encourage lobbying for ever-higher scholarship amounts; and they set up an incentive structure conducive to fraud, corruption, and mismanagement."[22]

Coulson goes on to say, "But there is nothing inherent in the concept of scholarships that requires money to pass through the hands of bureaucrats."[23] As he points out, it was commonplace prior to the twentieth century for private funds to finance government projects. And as of the time (1999) that he wrote, there were approximately forty scholarship-granting organizations in the United States. Although they funded only a few thousand students per year, they could—or Coulson thought they could eventually—"raise enough money to educate all low-income children."[24]

Obviously, private scholarships would be utopian without some way to support education, especially the education of the economically disadvantaged. Coulson's solution to this problem points out that

- Elementary education costs much less than secondary education.
- Generally speaking, parents are more able to pay when their children are in secondary school.
- Private education would be much less expensive at all levels.
- Educational tax credits could greatly reduce the financial burden on parents.

Coulson's solution to the funding problem would give taxpayers an option: They could either contribute a certain amount to an approved scholarship fund or pay their education taxes. The tax revenues from taxpayers who did not contribute to a scholarship fund could be used for a nonsectarian government program that would function along with the private programs, or the states could distribute these funds according to the number of students.

In a break with Friedman, Coulson does not accept the idea that "programs for the poor are poor programs." First, he points out that after more than a century of public education, the gap in education between the rich and poor was as great as ever. Second, the controversies over means testing would be less likely to arise in voluntary private programs.

Coulson also favors nonrefundable tax credits, whereas Friedman supports refundable tax credits. Under Friedman's plan, the poor would receive refundable tax credits that would enable them to buy food, shelter, and other necessities, thereby abolishing the need for a welfare bureaucracy. Friedman is opposed to using the tax code to guide social policy, whereas Coulson is not necessarily opposed to this. Finally, Coulson rejects the arguments that the problems of education are largely in the inner cities and that government schools are essential for the preservation of our democratic society.

## PUBLIC SCHOOL CHOICE

Several conservative education policy analysts and political figures have suggested that public school choice has the potential to be a significant reform in public education.[25] For example, in January 1989, President Reagan and President-Elect Bush held a news conference on education. At the conference, President-Elect Bush announced that his top educational priority would be public school choice. This was supposed to be an unofficial but practical first step toward "real choice," that is, choice of any public or private school, and the Bush I administration sponsored four regional conferences to promote the idea before dropping it precipitately. While the Bush I administration was advocating public school choice to foster competition, the teacher unions were promoting it as a way to head off competition from private schools. The unions had it right from the outset.

On May 18, 1993, Secretary of Education Richard Riley announced that public school choice would be the Clinton administration's policy on school choice. With the blessing of the teacher unions, Riley announced a plan whereby districts would publicly grade their schools so as to make them accountable. This was hardly serious. First, where pupils were not achieving, school boards and school administrators would blame drug use, broken families, poverty, anything that was not the school board's fault to persuade communities that their public schools were not responsible for poor academic achievement. Second, if school boards did grade their schools, parental reaction would not be to transfer to the "good schools," which may be far away, accessible only by the family car that may be nonexistent, and filled to capacity. Instead, they will insist upon improvements in their neighborhood school. Third, the multiyear collective-bargaining contracts that govern class size and transfers would not allow significant differences in class size among district schools; if all classrooms were being utilized, increasing class size in the "A" schools and decreasing them in the "F" schools would be the only way to accommodate transfers. If more teachers were needed in the A schools, transfers were normally based on seniority, something that could not be changed until the contracts expired and then only after bruising and losing battles with local unions. The upshot was that if more teachers must be assigned to the A schools, the teachers in the F schools would be the ones who fill the vacancies; the fact that a school was rated as "low performing" or "unsatisfactory" had no implications for the quality of the individual teachers in the school. All might, and often did, have favorable evaluations despite low pupil test scores. And if class size in A schools must be increased to accommodate the transfers of students out of the F schools, the administration's policy would have the perverse effect of increasing class size in the A schools and lowering it in F schools—a strange way to reward the teachers in the A schools.

To summarize, public school choice differs from market competition in the following ways:

## Public School Choice

1. The same management controls the schools that are supposed to compete.
2. Parents locate near the schools.



3. There is no expansion of facilities to accommodate increased demand.
4. There is no price or cost competition.
5. There is no R and D to increase market share and profits.

## Market System

1. Different management controls competing schools.
2. Schools locate near the parents, just as department stores moved to the suburbs when their customers did.
3. There are increased facilities to accommodate increases in demand.
4. There are price and cost competition.
5. There is R and D to gain market share and profits.

6. Inefficient schools are propped up by government subsidies.
7. Most parents are confined to a school by choice of residence.

8. Government decides what information is made available to parents.

6. Inefficient schools must improve or drop out of the market.
7. Parents can purchase education from one of multiple competing schools.
8. Schools advertise to persuade parents to buy their services. Each school controls its public information campaign.

Drawing conclusions about school choice that do not take account of such basic considerations illustrates the naiveté of educational policymakers at the highest levels in both Bush administrations. The idea that choices offered by a public monopoly are a significant step toward a market system hardly requires criticism; public school choice has existed in several states and school districts for a long time without any movement toward options that include private schools. Actually, public school choice weakens the movement toward a competitive education industry, which is why the public school establishment is willing to accept it, even though it prefers not to bother.

Despite its demonstrated futility to effectuate educational improvement, Congress has continued to appropriate funds for promoting public school choice ($100 million in the 2006–2007 budget). Its failure to recognize the limits of public school choice illustrates the abysmal level of educational policy analysis in the Bush II administration.

## SCHOOL BOARD VOUCHERS OR SUPPLEMENTS

School board vouchers are a substantive as well as a strategic issue that merits serious consideration. Actually, the Southeast Delco, Pennsylvania, school board adopted the idea in 1988; it established a local voucher program that would have provided $250 for each kindergarten student, $500 for each student in grades one through eight, and $1,000 for high school students to attend a nondistrict public or private school. The board's purpose was to reduce the number of its pupils in order to avoid the necessity of building new schools. The district's efforts were challenged and held to violate the Pennsylvania Public School Code, and the decision was not appealed. Nevertheless, the idea is a good one that is widely applicable; for example, school districts in several states contract out instruction for special education students who they cannot handle effectively. Needless to say, school boards encounter union resistance if they try to contract out any work performed by unionized employees, but in some districts, local vouchers should be utilized regardless.[26]

Clearly, school boards that have retained their authority to "voucherize" their students have much greater authority to manage their districts. Just as the possibility of contracting out enabled carmakers to insist upon changes that led to greater efficiency, the same result would materialize in public education if school boards had the voucher option. Inasmuch as the decision to provide vouchers would be made by school boards, it would be difficult to argue that the legislation was tantamount to privatizing public education. Legislation that rendered voucher authorization a prohibited subject of bargaining would be legally sufficient in the bargaining-law states if not accompanied by a host of limitations, exceptions, and qualifications.

William A. Fischel argues that local or state "supplements" for students from low-income families could make a community more attractive to families with school-age children. The supplements would be payments in addition to the regular state aid payments per pupil but could be used only in a public school. The rationale is that the supplements would eliminate the objections to low-cost housing by taxpayers afraid that their property taxes would rise if low-income families with school-age children moved into the district; taxpayers would not be burdened with the extra cost of schooling for pupils from low-income families. In Fischel's view, the fact that most voters do not have children in school results in a major loss of political support under state and national voucher plans.[27] In districts with good schools, homeowners tend to vote for school taxes because good schools maintain or increase the value of their homes. This incentive is lost when the states fund public schools.

On the negative side, Fischel suggests that vouchers and supplements would probably lead to some loss of community cohesion. Both specialization and the dynamics of scale would result in many pupils attending schools outside of their community; spectator sports and activities based on community schools build social cohesion in ways that teams composed of players from different communities are less likely to achieve. This thought underscores the point that U.S. schools are not likely to go down the path of foreign countries that have adopted much more intensive academic routines.

Fischel's proposal is for a "supplement," not a voucher, for low-income children. His interest is in overcoming opposition to low-income housing by high-spending property-rich school districts. For this reason, Fischel is opposed to supplements for attending schools outside the district, public or private. Such supplements would lead to low-income opposition to school taxes; their children would not benefit because they would be enrolled in private schools or in public schools outside their district of residence.

In some situations, such as overcrowded public schools, school board vouchers would provide public school districts with needed flexibility in dealing with unions of school district employees. Instead of controversies with school district unions over split shifts, overtime, crowded classrooms, and inconvenient bus and lunch schedules, the school board might find school board vouchers a much better solution for everyone.

The political dynamics of such a plan would be problematic. School districts with declining middle-class areas might receive a tremendous boost from homeowners no longer worried about the possibility that public school decline would lower the values of their homes. Granted, small school districts would fear that vouchers would decimate their public schools, a major source of community cohesion. Nevertheless, while a variety of reactions to school board vouchers would result, the benefits would far outweigh the negatives in many districts. The existence of a local voucher plan might stimulate an influx of parents of modest means who would view local vouchers as insurance against declining schools. We should not overlook the fact, as the equalitarians did, that most children in poor families live in school districts with large numbers of middle- and upper-class families. To discourage neighborhood decline, the latter groups must have incentives to stay, and school district vouchers might provide the incentives. By doing so, they would also provide incentives for business as well as parents to support vouchers.[28]

School board supplements or vouchers usable only at public schools would be a better plan than the public school choice plans under NCLB — "better" for land use and urban development as well as for educational reasons. Such a plan would be a moment of truth for the proponents of school choice. Supplements or vouchers only for public schools would be a blow to the emergence of a competitive education industry and would weaken instead of strengthen private schools; still, equalitarians would probably support such a plan. Advocates of a free market would have to think again whether every "school choice" plan is a step toward a free market in education. The idea might split the school choice movement, which would have trouble adjusting to a school choice plan designed to protect instead of compete with public education.

## THE FUTURE OF SCHOOL CHOICE

The previous discussion has identified the basic flaw in equalitarian strategy. Because equalitarian school choice plans cannot deliver substantial educational improvement, they cannot generate the kind of public support required for effective school choice plans. In effect, Milton Friedman publicly asserted this in November 2005, despite the fact that the Friedman Foundation had supported equalitarian school choice plans since its establishment. Equalitarian plans have also created and strengthened various interest groups that are opposed to market-oriented school choice plans.

This is not to say that free-market supporters of school choice should have supported only free-market versions of it. This would have been as unrealistic as supporting only free-market plans; nothing of the sort is implied by the foregoing commentary. Instead, the strategy should have been to support nonmarket plans only on the basis of reciprocal support if the nonmarket plans failed to achieve agreed-upon benchmarks of educational improvement. Of course, the criticism of nonmarket plans should have been made privately, tactfully, and not accompanied by offensive "I-told-you-so" gloating over the failures of nonmarket plans.

When free marketeers accept supportive roles in nonmarket school choice plans, they should ensure that the relevant parties, especially media personnel who report on such matters, are well informed on the differences between market and nonmarket school choice plans. This is a common scenario in political negotiations; accepting a compromise does not necessarily lead to or require abandonment of a more effective position on the issues. As matters turned out, however, Friedman declined to adopt such a strategy despite repeated efforts to persuade him to do so.

The most important strategic issue is not how to convince opponents of school choice to support it. The critical issue is how to persuade supporters of school choice to coalesce around a school choice plan that has a reasonable chance of achieving more effective educational services at a lower cost. In the near future, any such development probably depends on whether the supporters of a free-market sector can reach agreement with social conservatives on a program of school choice that will meet the primary objectives of each group. Neither group can achieve its objectives without the support of the other.

The primary objective of the free marketeers should be a reasonable opportunity for a free-market system of school choice to demonstrate its superiority over other systems for delivery of K–12 educational services. In this context, "reasonable," requires a sufficient scale, adequate duration, universalistic vouchers, price competition, and avoidance of onerous restrictions on schools and parents intended to sabotage the effectiveness of the plan. The most difficult regulatory problem may be the duration of a free-market plan. The dynamics of free markets take time. Investors are not likely to invest in new services and facilities whose legal basis expires in a few years and which are under fierce political assault from the very beginning.

To many observers, agreement between the libertarian and social conservative forces in the Republican Party is the key to whether the party can regain a majority position. As will be evident, these groups disagree on a wide range of basic issues, educational and noneducational. Nevertheless, there is a compelling case for their agreement on the specifics of a school choice program. The highest priority of the social conservatives is a school system that supports religious values, conventional marriage and family structure, and an emphasis on patriotism and the Protestant ethic in education. A free market in education is not their highest priority, even in education, but they are generally supportive of it. Their support for public education has declined in recent years; evangelical Protestants have become a major supporter of private schools. As the public schools have become less supportive of their values, evangelical Protestants have become a major source of private schools, and this trend is likely to continue.

Like the free marketeers, the social conservatives are strongly opposed to government regulation of denominational affairs, including their schools. For a long time, evangelical Protestants were opposed to vouchers on the ground that vouchers would lead to excessive government regulation of their schools; we should not forget that the Pilgrims emigrated to the United States to avoid government regulation of religious affairs. Initially, evangelical Protestants refused government assistance for their schools. Subsequently, they concluded that if their schools declined government support while other schools did not, the competitive position of their schools would be eroded because the latter would be unable to provide services provided by their competitors. In short, free marketeers and social conservatives can agree on the importance of private schools and the dangers of government regulation of them and also on the importance of preserving a free economy.

To be sure, social conservatives and free marketeers differ on a host of educational and noneducational issues. For instance, social conservatives generally support the prohibition of same-sex marriage, whereas most free marketeers believe that government should not be involved in regulating adult living arrangements. Social conservatives typically support restrictive policies on immigration to the United States; free marketeers generally advocate policies that are much more hospitable to immigrants. Nevertheless, these and other major differences should not preclude their agreement on universal vouchers in a free-market version of school choice. Of course, it may be impossible for these groups to cooperate on school choice issues in view of their disagreements on other issues, but political pundits are already citing libertarian and social conservative cooperation as a key to the future of the Republican Party, hence the prospects for a competitive education system.[29]

## NOTES

1. John Merrifeld, *School Choice Wars* (Lanham, MD: Scarecrow Press, 2001), has the best discussion of this point.

2. Merrifield, op. cit., emphasizes this point.

3. Charlene K. Haar, *The Politics of the PTA* (New Brunswick, NJ: Transaction, 2002), 136.

4. Terry M. Moe, *Schools, Vouchers, and the American Public* (Washington, DC: Brookings, 2001), 381. Emphasis in original.

5. Moe, *Schools, Vouchers, and the American Public*, 382–383.

6. Terry M. Moe, "How Choice Will Prevail," *Hoover Digest*, no. 3 (2001), 12.

7. The data about public school choice in Minnesota and some of the language is taken from Myron Lieberman, *Public School Choice* (Lancaster, PA: Technomic, 1990).

8. Outside of Moe, the equalitarians have not proposed a strategy. I have characterized his strategy as "the equalitarian strategy" because of his prominence among the equalitarians, the fact that their activities are consistent with Moe's strategy, the absence of any criticism of it by other equalitarians, and the fact that Moe received a $25,000 award from the Fordham Foundation for his scholarly contributions to the school choice movement.

9. Milton Friedman, "Education: The Next Fifty Years," *The American Spectator* (November 2005), 18–20. Whether or not Friedman was right on this issue, his point of view illustrates Moe's error in portraying Friedman as an ideologue who would not accept any deviations from a free-market version of vouchers.

10. Friedman, "Education," 58.

11. Frank Luntz and Bob Castro, *Memorandum to Interested Parties*, Education and School Choice Findings (Luntz Research Companies, April 14, 1998), 1–2. Some of the text reads as if only one person is giving the advice, and I have attributed it to Luntz because some of the substance was published in his book *Words That Work* (New York: Hyperion, 2007).

12. Rod Paige, "Where's the Choice?" *Wall Street Journal*, July 29, 2003, A14.

13. "An Idea Has Consequences," Editorial, *Wall Street Journal*, May 17, 2004, A20.

14. Abigail and Stephan Thernstrom, *No Excuses: Closing the Racial Gap in Learning* (New York: Simon and Schuster, 2003), 1.

15. Frank Luntz, *Words That Work* (New York: Hyperion, 2007), 253.

16. U.S. Commission on Civil Rights, "Mission," www.usccr.gov, accessed February 18, 2006.

17. See Lance D. Fusarelli, *The Political Dynamics of School Choice* (New York: Palgrave MacMillan, 2003), 152. Fusarelli opines that the ultimate impact of the school choice movement may be the breakdown of union opposition to significant concessions on such matters as teacher tenure and merit pay.

18. Daniel P. Moynihan, "What the Congress Can Do When the Court Is Wrong," in *Private Schools and the Public Good*, ed. Edward McGlynn Gaffney Jr. (South Bend, IN: University of Notre Dame Press, 1981), 84.

19. For arguments favoring vouchers over tuition tax credits, see Joseph L. Bast, *Fiscal Impact of Proposed Tuition Tax Credits for the State of New Jersey*, Policy Study No. 96 (Chicago, IL: Heartland Institute, 2001); George A. Clowes, *GOP Can't Decide between Tax Credits and Vouchers* (Washington, DC: Ameri-

can Legislative Exchange Council, 2002); George A. Clowes, *Still No Consensus on School Choice* (Chicago: Heartland Institute, www.heartland.org/Article.cfm ?artId=16914&CFID=181272&CFTOKEN=58021248, accessed March 23, 2007, August 10, 2005). For a detailed argument supporting tuition tax credits over vouchers, see Andrew J. Coulson, *Market Education* (New Brunswick, NJ: Transaction, 1999); Andrew J. Coulson, *Forging Consensus* (Midland, MI: Mackinac Center for Public Policy, 2004).

20. Richard Vedder, "Market-Based Education: What Can We Learn from Universities?" in "Creating a Competitive Education Industry," ed. David Salisbury and John Merrifield, *Cato Journal*, 25, no. 2 (Spring/Summer 2005), 279–295.

21. See Daniel P. Moynihan, *The Politics of a Guaranteed Income* (New York: Random House, 1975). See also a remarkable discussion of the implications of the 1944 federal voucher program for veterans of World War II by David W. Kirkpatrick, "The WWII GI Bill: Exhibit A for School Choice," *School Report*, February 8, 2007, www.freedomworks.org/schoolreport/issues_template.php?issue _id=2727, accessed March 23, 2007.

22. Coulson, *Market Education*, 374.

23. Coulson, *Market Education*, 374

24. Coulson, *Market Education*, 374–375.

25. David T. Kearns and Denis P. Doyle, *Winning the Brain Race* (San Francisco: Institute for Contemporary Studies Press, 1989), 18; Moe, *Schools, Vouchers, and the American Public*.

26. For a brief analysis of the Southeast Delco case, see David W. Kirkpatrick, "School District Based Vouchers," *School Report*, July 21, 1999, www.freedom works.org/schoolreport/issues_template.php?issue_id=407, accessed March 23, 2007.

27. William A. Fischel, *The Homevoter Hypothe*sis (Cambridge, MA: Harvard University Press, 2001), 149–151, 155–156. For an earlier analysis of the negative effects of the shift from local to state funding, see Caroline M. Hoxby, *Local Property Tax-Based Funding of Public* Schools (Chicago: Heartland Institute, 1997).

28. In 1999, Pennsylvania Governor Tom Ridge proposed to allow local school districts to establish their own voucher programs, utilizing only local funds for the vouchers. Only "academically distressed" districts that had failed to improve for two years would be eligible to provide the vouchers. Ridge was unable to generate support for the proposal from either proponents or opponents of vouchers. Lance D. Fusarelli refers to Ridge's proposal as "bizarre" but offers no explanation for his pejorative. Fusarelli, *Political Dynamics of School Choice*, 133–134.

29. As this book was going to press, Utah enacted HB 148, a universal voucher bill. The amount of the voucher varied from $500 to $3,000 according to family income. If it withstands challenge, the Utah bill would be the nation's first universal voucher plan. Pupils already enrolled in private schools who are eligible for free or reduced-price lunch would be voucher eligible. Although HB 148 may well invigorate the entire school choice movement, both its survival and its consequences were uncertain when this book went to press. If middle-class families take advantage of the law more than low-income families, the political fallout from HB 148 may not be as encouraging as supporters of it anticipate; however, a sliding scale for either vouchers or tax credits could be an acceptable compromise between equalitarian and free market supporters of school choice.

# Part 4

## EDUCATION'S INFORMATION SYSTEM

One of the most enduring fallacies in American political culture is the idea that the merits of a policy are decisive in its reception by the public. Chapter 11 helps to explain this fallacy. Policy issues are presented to the public through media personnel who frequently do not understand them; in fact, the educational issues presented through mass media, such as newspapers, radio, and television, are often trivial while important issues are overlooked, often indefinitely. Interests frequently dominate media treatment; the interest group with the largest or most skillful media staff often prevails in publishing decisions by education reporters reviewing scores of news releases with only a small amount of space or time to provide the "news." Failure to take account of such considerations explains a great deal of policy paralysis.

Chapter 11 is devoted to a subset of media problems, to wit, the role of public intellectuals (pundits, columnists, "experts") in educational policy development. Chapter 12 shows that there is no accountability for even the most egregious mistakes coming from the most prestigious sources of educational information and policy leadership. On this issue, both the supporters of public education and its critics are often unreliable and will continue to be as long as there is no accountability for major mistakes on important matters. The good news is that this may be a fixable problem, even though no one or no organization is addressing it effectively.

# 11

## Education in the Media

**P**erhaps no other aspect of education has been as unstudied and as immune from criticism as the role of media. One overriding fact explains media immunity: Media have the last word, and it can be devastating. Others must often pay to have their views disseminated, but the media have unlimited access to the public at virtually no cost. One additional point is crucial. Public education issues are resolved in political markets, and the media play a pivotal role in such markets. This is especially true in large urban centers and states in which opportunities for face-to-face interaction with public officials are very limited. Those who criticize the media risk losing favorable treatment or receiving no treatment at all. Ordinarily, nothing is to be gained by it.

Individuals who do not work in media seldom realize the attention paid to nuance and connotation in media communications. For instance, union press releases never refer to anyone who "disagrees" with the union; instead, the critics are "right-wing extremists" who are out to destroy public education or the union. Agency fees are payments that must be made to a union in order to keep a job. The teacher unions refer to such payments as "fair share" fees; their critics refer to them as "coerced dues" or "payments to union bosses."

An NEA manual on media relations before, during, and after a strike is a revealing example of the importance of media. The manual provides carefully nuanced language for a variety of press releases and news conferences. Its underlying importance is its recognition that a teacher strike is a battle for public opinion—a very different happening than private sector strikes, which are usually economic conflicts.

The cumulative impact of the never-ending efforts to influence public opinion by any means possible renders thoughtful analysis extremely difficult. Analysis that recognizes valid points on all sides is squeezed out because the media ordinarily prefer conflict in reporting "news." The situation is further complicated by the fact that there are liberal dupes and right-wing extremists, even though Hillary Clinton's "right-wing conspiracy" deserves all the ridicule that conservatives have heaped upon it.

In any case, citizens who have work to do, families to take care of, and bills to pay cannot be expected to understand most public policy issues fully, when, as has been shown repeatedly, the professors and think tank experts whose job it is to understand them frequently do not. The difficulty in achieving public support for sound policies is that interests distort issues that most citizens could readily understand if they were not exposed to so many interest-driven statements about them.

Despite bipartisan political correctness, most citizens have little or no active interest in public policy issues. As Richard A. Posner points out, we are fortunate to live in a society in which most citizens can go about their business without getting involved in public policy matters. When young people were encouraged to "participate" in politics, the upshot was an interest group that sought more taxpayer absorption of the costs of higher education (which is the cause of, not the solution to, the high costs of higher education), lower age limits for drinking and voting, and policies that minimized the possibility of military service. In other words, one more interest group was added to the mix. Nothing wrong with that, but idealism was not evident in its participation.

A daunting problem in analysis of the media role in education is its enormous scope. There are thousands of newspapers and magazines, not to mention a large number of radio and television stations. It would be practically impossible to monitor all of these outlets; it would be prohibitively expensive just to sample them enough to generalize about the role of the media in education.

This chapter seeks to overcome these difficulties in the following ways. First, it provides an analysis of the membership, structure, policies, and programs of the Education Writers Association (EWA), the national organization of education reporters. Second, it quotes and comments on education reporting in the *New York Times* and the *Washington Post*. The rationale is that if the most prestigious and most influential newspapers reveal certain tendencies, there may be some basis to generalize about print media as a whole. Third, it relies upon examples of media failure in reporting on educational labor relations to illustrate a few basic tendencies in media reporting on education. The following section illustrates this point.

In collective bargaining, the NEA and AFT invariably propose binding arbitration of grievances. A "grievance" is a claim by a covered employee or the union that the school district has violated the contract. Some contracts define "grievance" more broadly, but the heart of the union proposal is that the terminal point of the grievance procedure should be final and binding arbitration by an impartial third party, usually from the American Arbitration Association (AAA).

Ordinarily, if a party violates a contract and refuses to acknowledge the fact or compensate others for the violation, the remedy for the injured party is to take the offending party to court, where an impartial third party (judge or jury) will hear the case and render a decision. The NEA and AFT assert that arbitration is a much faster and much less expensive way of resolving disputes over whether management has violated the contract. "Do you really want to force us to initiate a lawsuit to decide whether you gave a teacher only a twenty-five- instead of a thirty-minute duty-free lunch period?" the UniServ director will ask. "It isn't your interest or ours to be involved in litigation over these matters."

Essentially, binding arbitration of grievances is privatization. The unions argue that private resolution of claims of contract violations is superior to having the claims resolved through court proceedings, that is, governmental processes. The arguments made by the unions are that private dispute settlement is faster and more efficient than governmental resolution of them—precisely the same arguments for privatization that are made in other government services as well as in education.

Why do the NEA and AFT promote privatization of dispute settlement while simultaneously opposing privatization of teaching, transportation, food service, and several other services required by school districts? Judges and court personnel are not NEA or AFT members, nor is there any realistic possibility that they will be. In short, the NEA and AFT support privatization when it enhances union interests but oppose privatization when it affects them adversely. The union interest lies in maximizing its dues revenue, and this means maximizing its membership base. This forces the union to appeal for support from nonteaching personnel, and its appeal is simple: "Join the union and it will protect you against having your jobs contracted out," that is, privatized. It is a mistake to assume that privatization is tantamount to wage reduction, but that is the way the NEA and AFT want their members to think about it.

Obviously, if the real reason for NEA and AFT opposition were laid on the table, it wouldn't get anywhere; the union can't achieve its goals by conceding that it opposes privatization because it is bad for the union. Instead, the NEA and AFT have to camouflage the reason, and they do this by labeling contracting out as "privatization" and then demonizing privatization. The strategy often works because education reporters do not recognize the contradictions in the union position. And because the education reporters don't recognize it, many citizens don't recognize it either.

## THE EDUCATION WRITERS ASSOCIATION

The Education Writers Association (EWA) is the professional association of education reporters and editors. EWA's structure provides for four classes of membership: active, associate (including institutional), student, and benefactors (foundations). As of March 2006, EWA had 885 members, of whom 327 (37 percent) were associates. EWA's constitution provides that active members are journalists at editorially independent media—newspapers, magazines, radio, and television. "Associate membership is open to media representatives for education organizations and institutions, as well as educators, public information officers, education policy-makers, and others interested in the way education is reported."[1] In short, associate members are usually employees in charge of media relations by whatever title; their job is to achieve favorable mention of their organization in the media. In 2006, thirty-three NEA and AFT staff members had associate memberships, including fifteen from the national level and eighteen from state organizations. Thus, NEA and AFT staff constituted approximately 11 percent of the associate membership in EWA.

EWA's constitution provides that "all members shall be entitled to vote and hold elective office (As defined in Article IV) and shall be entitled to all other rights and privileges."[2] Article IV, Section 1.1 provides that the "elected officers . . . shall be a president, two vice-presidents and a secretary, who shall be elected annually. The president, one vice-president and the secretary shall be active members. One vice-president shall be an associate member."[3] Section 1.2 provides that

> The board of directors shall be composed of nine members: The president, two vice-presidents, secretary and immediate past president of the organization; and four members of the organization to be named by the president with the advice of the other officers. Seven of the nine members shall be active members. The president shall make every effort to select board members who represent the geographical and professional diversity in the membership.[4]

Thus associate members are assured of representation on the board of directors, and in view of their numbers, they probably exercise a de facto veto power over EWA policies that would disadvantage their employers. Inasmuch as associate members join EWA to promote their sponsoring organizations, it is hardly surprising that EWA is not a threat to any vested interests; on the contrary, EWA is essentially an establishment organization.

Liberal foundations are the main source of support for EWA. The absence of support from any conservative foundation is apparent immediately. Not surprisingly, EWA's educational and political orientation reflects this fact. For instance, the Buskin lectures are a once-a-year event at the annual meeting, given by persons who are deemed to have played an important role in education. The vast majority of the twenty-eight Buskin lecturers from 1976 to 2004 were liberal Democrats; only four were Republicans at the time of their lecture.[5]

EWA's conflict-of-interest policy includes the statement that EWA "will accept support from organizations if . . . EWA continues, over the full course of our work and activity, to observe journalistic standards with regard to balance of viewpoints and range of opinions."[6] The Buskin lectures clearly violate the policy. EWA's failure to consider certain critical issues, such as the often counterproductive educational role of unions, media, and foundations, also violates the spirit if not the letter of its policy on conflicts of interest.

EWA's officers are elected annually, and it has an executive director based in Washington. Its annual meeting is held in April in conjunction with a meeting by a major educational organization. A brief look at its 2002 meeting, the most recent one I attended, was typical. Senator Ted Kennedy was the Buskin lecturer. His lecture consisted of a scathing criticism of the Bush administration's education and tax policies and recommendations for much higher federal appropriations for education. Several liberal but no conservative organizations rented exhibit space ($500 for members, $600 for nonmembers, and $35 for the privilege of leaving materials on two tables overloaded with free materials).[7] A constantly recurring theme was the achievement gap between white and black or Hispanic students. More formal schooling and more funding to close the gap were widely urged but never questioned; affirmative action was taken for granted as desirable.

A lack of sophistication pervaded the presentations and discussion. Arthur Wise, the executive director of the National Council for Accreditation of Teacher Education (NCATE), pointed out that inner-city schools tended to be staffed by higher percentages of inexperienced teachers and less than fully qualified teachers. His suggested solution was more intensive training for beginning teachers. What Wise did not say, and what no one in the audience brought up, was that the lack of experienced teachers in inner-city schools is due largely to union contracts that give preference in transfers to vacant positions on the basis of seniority; the experienced teachers take advantage of these provisions to transfer out of inner-city schools. Understandably, Wise did not mention the fact that the NEA is the largest contributor to NCATE; the NEA contributed $850,000 to NCATE for 2003–2004 and budgeted $825,000 for 2004–2005 for expenses explicitly supportive of NCATE. This amount appears to be part of NEA's continuing support for NCATE, including Wise's $150,000 salary.[8] Obviously, Wise was in no position to publicly criticize the NEA or AFT at this or any other time.

The prevalence and effects of seniority in teacher transfers have been amply documented in the professional literature for almost fifty years. If the education reporters read even minimal books and articles on the subject, Wise's solution would have been dismissed out of hand.

Another panel emphasized the importance of good schools in business decisions to locate new plants. No panelist mentioned the fact that in recent years, seven foreign carmakers have established carmaking facilities in the United States at sites not known for their high-quality schools. The fact is that good schools follow, not precede, industrial development: The significant educational story in most industrial relocation decisions is the irrelevance of the quality of K–12 education.

## EWA'S *STANDARDS FOR EDUCATION WRITERS*

In its *Standards for Education Writers* (hereinafter, *Standards*), EWA first lists the skills that are needed. Education reporters need to be able to

- Size up a school
- Use computer spreadsheets and database programs
- Cultivate extensive sources
- Read a budget
- Interview students
- Analyze statistics, especially test scores
- Understand school politics

Each of these skills is followed by an explanatory paragraph, and then *Standards* turns to "Knowledge." The latter begins,

> The knowledge that would benefit reporters in their work is nearly without limits, stretching over a breadth that ranges from methods of teaching to school law and encompassing the curricula of the nation's schools and universities. . . . There are some areas of knowledge that are essential to anyone covering education with authority. Following is some of the terrain that education reporters can expect to travel. Though the scope of knowledge outlined below may seem daunting, education reporters can expect to learn much of this over time through their daily work; by reading *Education Week*, the *Chronicle of Higher Education*, *Phi Delta Kappan*, and other education news; and by attending regional and national seminars for education reporters.[9]

Education reporters should strive to know

| | |
|---|---|
| The big picture | The federal role |
| Accountability and reform | Specal education |
| Standards and testing | Technology and education |
| Racial and ethnic dynamics | Learning theory |
| Poverty and achievement | Instructional practices |
| Curriculum and textbook debates | Early childhood education |
| The teaching profession | Higher education |
| School leadership | School law |
| Middle and high school | School finance[10] |

This is futile advice. On most of these topics, there is a substantial body of literature that is increasing on virtually a daily basis. Reading this literature without knowing what to look for is largely a waste of time, or would be if a reporter spent the time required.

The superficial nature of the reading regimen recommended by the *Standards* is rather obvious. The *Kappan* is a monthly published ten times per year by an organization that has adopted defense of public education as its main objective. Reading it requires thirty to forty-five minutes per month. The *Chronicle of Higher Education* is a weekly that must have been cited for the benefit of reporters who cover higher education; not much of its content is of interest to reporters on K–12 education. *Education Week* carries one or two policy articles a week along with news about elections and appointments to high-ranking positions, legal and legislative developments, controversies between educational agencies, school district and educational crime, education conventions, and ethnic strife in school districts — whatever items its editors believe to be "news." At the same time, there was no mention of about 150 specialized education journals and a huge output of books and reports on a varied list of educational issues and developments.

The unrealistic nature of the *Standards* results from an industry structure that renders knowledgeable reporting very unlikely. Education reporters are expected to report on a multitude of events about which they have only superficial knowledge at best. Their reporting is dumbed down to their knowledge level and is further limited by the space and time requirements of the media.

A partial remedy would be assistance to reporters in identifying expert sources, but EWA's efforts on this possibility merely highlight its deficiencies. For example, its 2001 guide for education reporters lists ten sources on teacher unions. Four are employed as union officers or consultants; one is an NEA staff member in press relations. Only one of the ten, Michael Podgursky, professor of economics at the University of Missouri, has been a critic of the teacher unions. The list does not include anyone who has represented management in bargaining with teacher unions or anyone from organizations such as the Landmark Legal Foundation or the Evergreen Freedom Foundation or the National Right to Work Committee, which have demonstrated extensive knowledge about the teacher unions in extended litigation against them. As a member, I have attended four EWA conventions and received EWA program materials for several years. My fifteen minutes as a presenter does not require any change in my assessment of EWA programs.

Another EWA publication, *Covering the Education Beat*, includes a one-and-a-half-page discussion under "Teacher Unions." Aside from the minor errors, such as "AFT has its roots in the progressive movement of the 1920s" (the AFT was founded in 1916), consider the following statement: "With 80 percent of American teachers in one of the two unions and more than 60 percent of teachers covered by a collective bargaining agreement, widespread school reform could not go on without their agreement."[11] There are two major errors in this sentence. First, more teachers are covered by collective agreements than are members of the NEA and AFT. The second mistake is the statement that "widespread school reform could not go on without their agreement." Leaving aside the definition of "widespread," the intensity of union disagreement varies a great deal. Their refusal to agree to a reform does not necessarily mean that they prevent it from materializing. In situations to which the statement applies, one might think reporters would be advised to look into the situations. After all, reform would be practically impossible in most other industries if employees could block reforms that they oppose. One might suppose that education reporters would be very interested in how the unions acquired their veto power over reform, what reforms were blocked by the unions, and the political as well as the educational ramifications of union veto power over proposed reforms. Nevertheless, the EWA manual simply takes this alleged union power for granted without a hint of its implications.

Since 1965, I have received at least a few telephone calls every year from education reporters. Whatever the reason for a call, I always inquire whether the caller has read the contract between the school board and the teacher union. The contracts would often answer the questions I am asked, but none of the reporters had read the contracts.

## EDUCATION IN THE *NEW YORK TIMES*

Public education in New York City is an enormous enterprise. Its budget for 2003–2004 was $13.9 billion, and it employed 124,000 employees, of whom over 89,000 were teachers, paid over $5 billion for their services. Inasmuch as the basic rules governing the work of teachers are set forth in the contract between the UFT and the NYC Board of Education, one might assume that the *Times* would analyze it extensively. Surely, nothing on education would be more important to NYC readers than an analysis showing the rules and compensation governing the work of teachers and their implications for students, teachers, taxpayers, policymakers, and the general public.

Nonetheless, the *Times*, which employs ten reporters in its education department, has rarely published an in-depth analysis of the board's contract with the UFT or a comprehensive summary for parents, taxpayers, and other interested parties.[12] With rare exceptions, this point applies to newspapers elsewhere in the United States.[13] If the nation's leading newspaper with ten reporters covering education has rarely provided an in-depth analysis of the most important public document about the New York City's school system, it is not surprising that newspapers elsewhere ignore it also.[14] In fact, in my twenty-five years as a labor negotiator in public school districts, I never met an education reporter who had read the teacher union contract in the districts being covered. In EWA's manual on how to cover education, there is no suggestion that reporters should read the school district labor contracts, although teacher compensation consumes about half of all district expenditures.

## THE QUALIFICATIONS REQUIRED TO BE
## THE *NEW YORK TIMES* EDUCATION EDITOR

Since the 1960s, I have been convinced that the education editor of the *New York Times* holds the most influential educational position in the United States. Be that as it may, the *New York Times* is unquestionably the most influential newspaper in the United States. Consequently, the qualifications of its education reporters are of interest. Some light on the issue was provided by Edward Fiske, who became education editor in 1974 and held the position until 1991.

Fiske had started at the *Times* as a clerk and became a religion reporter and religion editor before his assignment as education editor. Commenting upon his appointment as education editor, Fiske said, "I was very good at dealing with dogma, so they kicked me over to education. There are no education courses worth taking, probably. Education isn't significantly different from covering any other beat—you learn what you have to know."[15]

Fiske's comments illustrate the culture of arrogance that goes with being a reporter for the *New York Times*. Presumably, good reporters can report on anything; it doesn't really matter whether the reporter knows anything about the subject about which he or she reports.[16] Of course, if a newspaper that adopted Fiske's view were honest with its readers, its education articles would be captioned, "Caveat: This article was written by a reporter who is learning what he needs to know to re-port on educational matters—we hope. Regrettably, there is no test of when the reporter knows enough for us to eliminate this caveat, but the editors hope that you will bear with us during this uncertain period of time."

"Knowing the subject" in the context of educational journalism pre-sumably means knowing the level of importance to be ascribed to various issues. Anything about Harvard is deemed newsworthy; for example, in 2003, the *Times* published articles on such significant topics as the resig-nation of a professor of black studies at Harvard to teach at Princeton and the proposal by a Harvard professor of economics to offer an alternative introductory course in economics. I have not read every *Times* article or column on education since 1956, but I have read most and do not recall the *Times* ever publishing an article on the following topics:

- Racial quotas in the NEA, the country's largest teacher union.
- The emergence of gay and lesbian caucuses as powerful interest groups in both the NEA and AFT and in public education generally.
- The reasons it is practically impossible to assess the outcomes of hun-dreds of billions spent for special education.
- The implications of the fact that there are teacher organizations that enroll more members than either the NEA or AFT in three states that have not enacted a collective bargaining law.

- The conflict in the school choice movement over means-testing for eligibility to receive vouchers and its implications for school choice.
- The implications of the fact that the NEA and AFT supported federal aid to denominational schools in the late 1940s.
- The National PTA's legal position that it is not an educational organization.
- How the National PTA, which was initially a mothers-only organization, became a political adjunct of the NEA.
- The UniServ system in the NEA.
- How the NEA reconciles federally required reports showing minimal political activity, while politicians and pundits, including a few at the *New York Times*, agree that the NEA is an extremely powerful political organization in elections at all levels of government.
- The expenditures for educational research and why the results have been so meager.

Reckless misstatements of fact show up in the *Times* treatment of education. Consider a column by Michael Winerip, an education columnist at the *Times*. The column was devoted to an Arizona mother who enrolled her children in three different charter schools, beginning in 2001. Referring to the teacher turnover in the charter schools, Winerip writes,

> But wait. Wasn't that supposed to be the beauty of charters? No unions, no tenure. Here in Arizona, America's most charter school–friendly state, a charter school principal doesn't even need a college degree. When it comes to education, Arizona's motto is: "Let the free market rule baby." When charters first appeared, they were touted as the free-market alternative to bad old public schools. . . . To lure students, charter school leaders often derided the bad old public schools and promised fast results, including sky-high test scores.[17]

As chapter 10 notes, although not actively opposed to charter schools, Milton Friedman, the acknowledged intellectual leader of a free market in education, has never regarded charter schools as an example of a free market in education.[18] The other leading supporters of a free market in education are highly critical of charter schools. For example, Andrew J. Coulson's *Market Education*, widely regarded as the most thorough statement of the free-market rationale for K–12 education, asserts,

> Though charter schools should yield some improvements in the quality of public school services, their effects are likely to be miniscule when compared to those of free and competitive markets. Charter schooling also fails to solve some of the most pernicious social problems caused by state-run education. . . .
>
> A system dominated by charter schools would thus loosen, but not remove, the straitjacket that has restrained the U.S. schooling industry since it was taken over by the state a century and half ago.[19]

Coulson continues for eleven pages, showing why charter schools are contrary to free-market principles and why they will not be effective.

University of Texas, San Antonio, professor John Merrifield is another leading advocate of a free market in education. In his 2001 book, Merrifield points out that

> charter schools will harm the private sector. The private sector's primary shortcoming is unequal access to resources, a problem that charter schools exacerbate by recruiting some of the children who would have attended public schools. . . . Like other versions of school choice that create few, if any, market conditions, charter schools could reduce the political feasibility of a competitive education industry. Though certainly an improvement over the status quo, charter schools are much more likely to be a major, perhaps permanent, detour than a step in the right direction. . . . Charter schools can be a detour, and a devastatingly bad one.[20]

The above excerpts should suffice to show the egregious falsehoods in Winerip's column. Clearly, Winerip's underlying objective was denigration of a free-market system of education; if he wanted only to criticize charter schools, he could have done that without a gratuitous and wholly erroneous criticism of a free market in education.

Winerip became the *Times*'s regular education columnist in 2002, and his last column in this capacity appeared July 12, 2006. The *Phi Delta Kappan*, a journal dedicated to protecting public education from vouchers, comments, "Many of us were stunned and dismayed when the *New York Times* dropped Richard Rothstein as its education columnist. He is still missed. For a while, various *Times* reporters wrote each Wednesday's column, but then the paper settled on Michael Winerip. It was a great choice."[21] The praise might be well deserved if a flagrant disregard for easily obtainable facts isn't a criterion.

Not everything about education in the *Times* reflects Winerip's orientation; for example, in an editorial supporting NCLB, the *Times* perceptively notes that the critics of NCLB were divided between those who wanted the law to work better and those who wanted the law "to go away."[22] Nevertheless, the *Times* constitutes a major obstacle to public understanding of the critical issues in education because its education staff lacks the experience and the knowledge to identify or assess critical education news and issues. Instead, it relies on "experts," preferably from Harvard or Stanford, who usually have their own agendas on these matters.[23] To be fair, however, my comments do not take into account what matters the education staff may have been directed to cover or any rejections of articles they may have submitted.

Not surprisingly, expertise in a field is not required to editorialize about it in the *New York Times*. The editorial and op-ed pages of the *Times* are the responsibility of an editor and deputy editor. These two pages include the editorials, letters to the editor, and the op-ed page opposite the editorial page. The two editors are assisted by a sixteen-person full-time editorial board. The only editor or member of the editorial board with a professional background in K–12 education taught three years in New York City elementary schools; he joined the *Times* as a news clerk in 1977 and, as of October 2005, was the senior editorial writer on foreign affairs. One board member with a PhD in psychology is listed as specializing in "Education, Race and Culture" with no showing of professional experience or scholarship in education. Most members of the editorial board had careers in journalism or writing prior to service on the editorial board.[24]

The liberal bias in the *Times* is often reflected in subtle ways. For instance, a recent analysis of four articles in the *Times* and three in the *Washington Post* referred to research by Jack Jennings, the founding head of the Center on Education Policy (CEP). The *Times* article referred to Jennings and CEP as "nonpartisan" or "independent" without revealing that Jennings had been a highly influential Democratic staff member of the House Education and Labor Committee from 1967 to 1994 and that his policy recommendations since 1994 typically support Democratic positions.[25]

# EDUCATION IN THE *WASHINGTON POST*

The *Washington Post* brings to mind the business mantra "Location, location, location." The *Post* has taken advantage of its location to become widely read by government officials and national educational organizations and the thousands of foreign embassies and consulates, lobbying organizations, think tanks, and national television and radio networks located in the Washington area.

Education is not very prominent in the *Post*, and when it is, education in the District of Columbia, Maryland, or Virginia is often the subject matter. Nevertheless, with unparalleled access to the U.S. Department of Education, the education components of Congress and the executive branch of government, and a wide array of national think tanks and denominational organizations, education coverage in the *Post* enjoys unparalleled opportunities for good reporting on education. A statement about the role of teacher unions by a long-time *Washington Post* and *Newsweek* education reporter, Jay Mathews, should dispel any such expectation. Mathews's take on the teacher unions is as follows:

> Many education reporters don't spend much time looking at the unions because we don't think they have much to do with what happens in the classroom. . . .
>
> I have been a full-time education reporter for only six years. For many years before I got this job, while doing other things for the *Post*, I became very interested in the mysteries of teaching that led me to write two books on high schools in my off-hours and spend a lot of time during the day sitting in classrooms when my editors thought I was doing something else. During my two decades so far as a school room habitué, *I cannot think of a single instance in which the NEA or the AFT have had a significant impact on what was happening in class*. There have been occasional strikes and sometimes teachers have bickered over union policies. But the difference between good teachers and bad ones, effective lessons and ineffective ones, has never had much to do with the instructor's commitment to the union or *the language of their labor contract. The best educators I know have confirmed this in hundreds of conversations.*[26]

Any observer who has spent as much time in unionized school districts as Mathews did would have seen incompetent teachers because the contract renders it prohibitively difficult to dismiss teachers, substitute teachers because the contract provides excessive leave with pay for several dubious reasons or no reason at all, students who need help but can't get it because the contract allows teachers to leave after pupils are dismissed, teachers who have inadequate subject matter preparation because the contract allows salary credit for any courses chosen by the teachers no matter how little they contribute to teacher competence, and so on.

The fact that Mathews never found anything in the contracts that impacted the classroom may be true, but one has to wonder what teacher union contracts Mathews read, his sophistication about education, and the identity of the "best educators" who confirmed his conclusions in "hundreds of conversations." In any case, Mathews's contention that the teacher unions do not affect what happens in classrooms is appalling.

The *Post* sponsors Live Online, an online discussion program usually moderated by *Post* reporters. Lois Romano, a *Washington Post* reporter, was assigned to write an article about NCLB. After Romano's article appeared, the following online discussion took place.

> *Washington Post* staff writer Lois Romano discussed her story on the "No Child Left Behind" Act and a new study that shows little improvement in students' scores since its implementation. . . .
>   Lois Romano: Good morning everyone. Just a note about myself. I have been at the *Post* for twenty years and only recently started covering education. I have covered politics, however, for years. I will do my best to answer your questions.[27]

The naiveté in the *Post*'s coverage of education can be frustrating. For example, the complete text of a 2006 article is as follows:

> ### Teachers' Payday
> Teachers win students' accolades and admiration and put up with their smart mouths and bad attitudes. They often spend their summers on their own pursuits but also spend an average of $443 a year of their own money on supplies and other student needs.
>   Even though their profession is held in high esteem by most Americans, many won't remain in it. Almost one in five new public school teachers leaves the profession in the first year and nearly half leave within five years, the National Education Association estimates.

Why are teachers skipping out on a job that has regular hours, summers free, and a chance to make a difference? Their pay, which teachers and their unions say doesn't measure up.

Nationwide, a high school teacher earned an average $48,980 in 2004—less than an insurance agent or a statistician, according to federal figures. A first-year teacher in suburban Washington earns about $40,000.

So on this National Teacher Day, instead of getting another coffee mug, perhaps they want a little more in the pay envelope. Or at least help paying for construction paper, extra books, and ink jets.[28]

The $443 figure was taken from an NEA study that is inherently improbable and has never been confirmed by any independent research.[29] In my experience negotiating hundreds of teacher union contracts in six states, reimbursement for teacher expenditures or a petty cash fund were never proposed by union negotiators, but all districts provided cash for supplies needed immediately.

Media articles that allege that low pay is the reason for high teacher turnover invariably say nothing about the jobs actually taken by teachers after their teaching positions. We know that low pay is not the reason for a sizable amount of teacher turnover: Pregnancies, moving outside the district employment area, and going to graduate school illustrate this point. One has to assume there is no reliable evidence that a majority quit because of low pay. If there was evidence that showed a substantial number of teachers left teaching for higher-paying positions, the teacher unions would be spending some of their $2 billion a year telling us about it.

Scholars who have studied media treatment of education have expressed conclusions that are more critical of it than mine. For example, Richard Phelps, who conducted a detailed study of media treatment of testing, concludes that

- Journalists talk mainly to advocacy groups; they rarely read the scientific journals that are supposed to deal with the issues objectively. The advocacy groups naturally welcome any opportunities to get coverage for their views.
- Journalists rely on the most convenient sources. For example, when they receive a publication that has a cover letter, a report, and

an executive summary, they have most of what they need—or think
they need.

- Journalists frequently call for the evidence they need to support their
  own nonexpert conclusions.
- "Balance" is often achieved by citing disagreements on trivial matters.[30]

Phelps's conclusions say nothing about "liberal" or "conservative" bias,
whereas my conclusion is that there is a liberal bias in most education reporting. This difference is less than meets the eye. The liberal bias in the
press is not deliberate. Eighty-nine percent of K–12 students are in public
schools. Because reporters covering K–12 education naturally devote
most of their attention to public education, the educators they like and respect will be overwhelmingly from public education. Their reportorial
bias in favor of public education is not a deliberate but an unintended consequence of their training and daily work.[31]

In my view, education reporters and editors are an intelligent group, but
their training, experience, and conditions of employment do not equip
them to inform their readers about the important education developments
at the local, state, or national levels. Superintendents and teachers agree
with this conclusion. In 1997, Public Agenda published a study of how
three groups viewed the education press: 500 members of the public, 303
superintendents and teachers, and 269 education reporters and editors.[32] In
addition to an opinion poll, the study included focus groups and one-on-
one interviews and appears to have been conducted as carefully as is reasonably necessary for a study of this kind. In brief, only one in nine respondents was confident of the educational expertise of education
reporters. This result is probably close to the reality if the reporting does
not require sophistication on educational policy issues.

## HOW CAN MEDIA TREATMENT
## OF EDUCATION BE IMPROVED?

Regardless of one's opinion of the quality of media treatment of education, the question of how to improve it merits attention. The following
suggestions on this matter admittedly do not address all the dimensions of
the problem, but they would cost very little and could go a long way to
remedying the most glaring weaknesses in education reporting—the lack

of knowledge about education among education reporters and editorial writers, their heavy reliance on "experts" with dubious qualifications, and the absence of any accountability for poor performance.

Basic improvement in education's information system requires candid analysis of these questions:

- What interest groups are the most and least adept at utilizing media successfully?
- What safeguards, if any, exist to avoid conflicts of interest in education reporting? For example, do the employers of education reporters promulgate and enforce any restrictions on reportorial work by parties with a stake in favorable treatment in the media? Do reportorial organizations?
- What books, journals, reports, and blogs do education reporters and writers read?
- To what extent are education reporters capable of assessing education research?
- What are the dominant career patterns of education reporters?
- To what extent is educational coverage initiated by an external source, such as a news release?
- Do education reporters read and fully understand the labor contracts in the school districts that they cover?

The current approach to improvement is for the EWA to choose topics and ask foundations to support one- to two-day seminars on them, with reportorial expenses subsidized through the grants to the sponsoring organization. EWA (for instance) then sends out notices advising its members about the program and inviting applications and requests for assistance when appropriate. EWA officers and staff invite the presenters, who are often paid from the grants to support the seminars. Reading materials are not provided or even recommended beforehand, nor is there meaningful follow-up on whether reporters understood or utilized the presentations at these "seminars." A university that followed these practices would rightly be perceived as providing bogus seminars.

Philanthropic foundations should support different approaches to the deficiencies in media coverage of education. In one, the content of education reporting in publications would be analyzed for a specific period of time, such as six months or a full year. The importance of the content, its technical quality, and other criteria would be utilized to assess the coverage. Because what appears in print may be due to several factors beyond the control of the education reporters, the evaluations of the content would not necessarily reflect the competence of the reporters themselves.

Another approach would be to test reportorial knowledge and capability directly. Can reporters understand educational research without outside assistance? Have they read and understood the leading publications on educational policy and practice? There is no technical barrier to testing reporters on such issues. Granted, there are difficult obstacles to overcome, but various approaches can be utilized to address them. If a significant number of editors was willing to consider the test results in employment decisions, the practice may spread rapidly. Another possibility would be to pay reporters for taking the tests at EWA or education conventions. One can anticipate reportorial objections to such testing, but they would be even less defensible than teacher objections to teacher testing.

Still another possibility is for an entity to provide reporters with periodic analyses of educational issues and developments accompanied by bibliographies, follow-up questions, and caveats. This effort could be followed up by reviews of reportorial content and interviews with reporters to assess its effectiveness. One way or another, reflexive praise for media personnel in education as a means of maximizing favorable treatment must be supplanted by a critical approach by an entity that does not depend upon favorable treatment in and by the media.

Editorials and op-eds in leading media should also be monitored on the basis of relevant criteria, such as the importance of their issues and their accuracy with respect to empirical issues. The fundamental change required is to abandon the idea that nothing can be done to remedy the deficiencies in media treatment of education. Most school officials will continue to try to curry favor with media personnel, but the emergence of an entity dedicated to critical review and analysis of media treatment of education may possibly bring about some improvement in both educational news and commentary.

## INFORMATION TECHNOLOGY AND EDUCATIONAL BLOGGERS

Although mass media treatment of education can be improved in other ways, information technology (IT) may have the most potential to overcome the deficiencies of education's information system. Undoubtedly, IT has rendered access to information and policy analysis less expensive, much faster, and more convenient, but this may strengthen the forces supporting the status quo more than the forces seeking to change it.

Clearly, the Internet can provide ongoing opportunities for an unlimited audience to become well informed on factual and policy issues at a minimal cost. The potential also exists to provide productive interaction between the producers and consumers of information and policy analysis on every dimension of education, at a pace that was hitherto unimaginable.

Here again, the heavy hand of the status quo is apparent. Established organizations have websites that disseminate organizational views and news more effectively than they did previously. There are more than one hundred blogs devoted solely to education and countless others that include education within the scope of their operations. By and large, the sources of educational information and analysis that were dominant in conventional print media are dominant on the Internet. As is generally the case with conventional media, the parties who utilize the Internet rely on supportive websites for data and analysis. Nevertheless, the huge savings in cost and time from using IT render it possible for individuals to elicit and to interact with a much broader range of data and policy analysis. For instance, any interested party can find criticism of my publications or the amounts and recipients of NEA and AFT political contributions or the track record of public intellectuals on education. The impact of capabilities such as these in conjunction with practical objectives and strategies may have an enormous impact on education. The roadblock is not the cost or the time required to make reliable information and policy analysis available. It is the cost, mainly in time, of identifying the high-quality blogs. The impact of IT remains to be seen, but clearly it has enormous potential to affect educational policy in the United States.

## NOTES

1. Education Writers Association, "Membership and Benefits," www.ewa.org/desktopdefault.aspx?page_id=116, accessed March 25, 2007.

2. Education Writers Association, "EWA By-Laws," Article II, Section 1.3, www.ewa.org/desktopdefault.aspx?page_id=8, accessed March 25, 2007.

3. Education Writers Association, "EWA By-Laws," Article IV, Section 1.1.

4. Education Writers Association, "EWA By-Laws," Article IV, Section 1.2.

5. Author survey, but the party affiliation of most was apparent.

6. E-mail exchange with Lisa Walker, executive director, EWA, March 26, 2007. The two-page policy statement addressed concerns that may arise over EWA's efforts to broaden its sponsorship, participate in broader collaborative relationships, and accept advertisements for its annual meeting brochure and newsletter. Note that the policy statement applies to EWA, not to its members in their occupational roles.

7. These are the 2005 rates. The Friedman Foundation and the Koret Task Force, a joint project of the Hoover Institution and the Koret Foundation, rented booth space at the 2005 convention in St. Petersburg, Florida.

8. NEA, *Strategic Plan and Budget, Fiscal Years 2004–2006* (Washington, DC: National Education Association, 2004), 14. It is impossible to know from the budget lines how much of this amount goes directly to NCATE and how much is spent by NEA for NCATE activities, but the NEA contributed $850,000 to NCATE for 2003–2004.

9. Education Writers Association, *Standards for Education Writers* (revised final draft) (Washington, DC: EWA, n.d.), 3.

10. Education Writers Association, *Standards for Education Writers*, 1–9.

11. Education Writers Association, *Covering the Education Beat* (Washington, DC: EWA, 2001), 124.

12. Nonretrievable letter to the author from the *New York Times*, 2005.

13. I say "rare" because copies I have not seen may have published the contract or a summary. EWA's recommendations to education reporters do not include analysis of the contract between the teacher union and the board of education, although the contracts spell out the rules under which about half of district funds are spent.

14. Actually, the New York City Board of Education negotiates labor contracts with several unions, and publishing all of the contracts is not feasible, although there may be sections in all that are newsworthy. The main contract with the UFT is too long (2,005 pages in 2004) to be published in its entirety.

15. Amy Stuart Wells, *A Study of Education Reporting in American Newspapers* (MS thesis, College of Communication, Boston University, 1986), 18.

16. Fiske and his wife, a professor of education at Duke University, wrote a book about education in New Zealand. The book purported to show that the results of a voucher system in New Zealand led to grave doubts about the desirability of a market system in education, but its authors did not understand the basic features of a market system.

17. Michael Winerip, "When It Goes Wrong at a Charter School," *New York Times*, March 5, 2003, A23.

18. Nor did Friedman explicity oppose charter schools (see pages 226–228).

19. Andrew J. Coulson, *Market Education* (New Brunswick, NJ: Transaction, 1999), 340.

20. John Merrifield, *The School Choice Wars* (Lanham, MD: Scarecrow, 2001), 34–35. This is the best book on the deficiencies of charter schools from a free-market perspective.

21. "The Golden Apple Awards," *Phi Delta Kappan* (October 2003), 151.

22. "Stand Firm for Educational Fairness," *New York Times*, April 22, 2005, A24.

23. After this chapter was written, *Education Next*, an education journal, carried an article on Winerip's biased, error-filled reporting. None of the examples in the article are included in this chapter. The article confirms two points in this chapter. See Andrew J. Rotherham, "No Distortion Left Behind," *Education Next* (Winter 2005), 68–71. Rotherham was diector of education policy at the Progressive Policy Institute, a liberal think tank.

24. "The *New York Times* Editorial Board," www.nytimes.com/ref/opinion/editorial-board.html, accessed October 26, 2005. The educational policy expertise of individuals can be assessed without regard to their formal training and experience; the expertise of groups cannot ordinarily be assessed this way. Theoretically, everyone in the group might have the required expertise despite the lack of formal training or experience in the subject, but the possibility becomes more remote as the size of the group increases. It is not credentialism to question the educational expertise of the seventeen-member *New York Times* editorial board on the basis of their minimal education and experience on the subject.

25. Greg Forster, "Donkey in Disguise," *Education Next* (Summer 2006), 77–81.

26. Jay Mathews, "A Closer If One-Sided Look at Teacher Unions," *Washington Post*, February 25, 2003, A27. Emphasis added. Reprinted by permission.

27. Lois Romano, *Washington Post* Live Online chat, October 20, 2005, www.washingtonpost.com/wp-dyn/content/discussion/2005/10/19/DI2005101901959.html.

28. Vickie Elmer, "Teachers' Payday," *Washington Post*, May 9, 2006, D2.

29. NEA Research, *Status of the American Public School Teacher* (Washington, DC: NEA, 2003).

30. Richard Phelps, *Kill the Messenger: The War on Standardized Testing* (New Brunswick, NJ: Transaction, 2003), 147–214, especially 157–159. Phelps's analysis of the *Washington Post* and other media coverage of testing is more critical and comprehensive than the discussion here.

31. Although published before this book was completed, Richard A. Posner's essay on the media supports the analysis in this chapter in far more depth. See Richard A. Posner, "Bad News," *New York Times* book review, July 31, 2005, 1, 8–11.

32. Public Agenda, *Good News, Bad News: What People Really Think about the Education Press* (New York: Public Agenda, 1997).

# 12

## Credence Goods and the Accountability Gap

Accountability is a subject of mind-numbing confusion in education. One reason is the lack of definitional agreement. In this book, accountability is a state of affairs when we know who did what, and the actor is subject to disciplinary or remedial action by specified parties for failing to act appropriately. If we do not know the actor, we cannot hold anyone accountable; similarly, if the actor is invulnerable to negative consequences for his or her actions, there is no accountability. However, to distinguish actual from formal accountability, two additional questions must be answered. First, what corrective or disciplinary action is reasonably possible? And second, who has the power to hold the actors accountable? The answers to these questions are essential to assess the extent of accountability in any given situation.

A weaker concept of accountability equates it with transparency. For example, the supporters of public education assert that the private schools that accept vouchers would not be accountable because taxpayers cannot examine the financial records of private schools. Consequently, tax revenues would allegedly be spent in ways that avoid oversight by public officials. In contrast, public officials and presumably the public allegedly do have access to public school financial records.

Accountability in public education is an administrative and a political process. If you object to a school policy, you can protest to the principal or the superintendent. If you are still not satisfied, you can appeal to the school board, and, if still unsatisfied, you can try to elect supportive school board members into office.

Several problems are inherent in this concept of accountability. Because of the plethora of interrelated local, state, and federal legislation, it may not be clear what legislative or executive body or officials should be held accountable for what happens at the school or district level. In response to criticism, school administrators and school boards frequently assert that "our hands are tied" by federal or state legislation.[1] It is usually too expensive and time consuming for citizens to assess this response, but if it is valid, accountability may be a hopeless quest. Citizens can vote for only a few state officials and legislators and five (two senators, a member of House of Representatives, and president and vice president) at the federal level. In order to hold legislators accountable, citizens must know how they voted and their reasons, a task that is much too arduous for most voters. Furthermore, legislator positions on other issues are usually more important to voters than their educational positions.

Even at the school board level, accountability is usually too attenuated to be of any practical use to most parents and taxpayers. The individual's vote very rarely matters, and if voters elect board members only from their own area of the school district, the board as a whole is not subject to the will of the electorate as a whole. In districts in which school board members have staggered terms of office, the board members who are being held accountable may not be up for reelection for three or four years. Furthermore, school board elections commonly attract less than 5 percent of the electorate when held separately from general elections. Consequently, the teacher unions, which are usually well organized and funded for school board elections, enjoy decisive advantages over voters who must organize an ad hoc constituency for their cause.

Individual parents may have strong opinions on who should be accountable for what, but parents cannot put board members in office, fire or hire school administrators and teachers, evaluate teachers for personnel decisions, or take corrective action regarding school district personnel who fall short for one reason or another. Individuals must form or be part of organized groups that share the same objectives and ability to act on educational matters, and such entities do not exist in most school districts. Where they do exist, they are usually teacher unions and PTAs, which are political adjuncts of the teacher unions. Even where the structure of accountability in public education is clear, the obstacles to utilizing the structure are insuperable for most parents.[2]

## ACCOUNTABILITY IN THE CLASSROOM

Accountability implies several reciprocal relationships. For instance, if principals are accountable to school management for the academic outcomes in their schools, teacher–principal relationships must be consistent with the principal–school management ones. Hospitals, factories, and military services illustrate the basic point: Accountability to higher levels usually requires accountability at lower levels.

At the teacher–principal level, public education is drastically deficient on the required consistency. When teachers are asked, "To whom are you accountable and for what?" the answers, even in the same school, reveal striking diversity, as do the answers at other levels. Teachers often respond that they are accountable to pupils or to parents but do not mention accountability to principals. The mechanics of accountability show the same unstructured diversity. As Charles Abelmann and Richard Elmore summarize their research on accountability, "in most cases, teachers and principals viewed external accountability systems like the weather—something that might affect their daily lives in some way, something they could protect themselves against, but not something they could or should do much about."[3]

One reason for this disconnect between teachers and principals is that there is no bottom line in education. Test scores are rejected as too simplistic, but the public school establishment has yet to accept other criteria that would make teacher–principal accountability feasible.

## ACCOUNTABILITY AND CONSERVATIVE LEADERSHIP

Who, if anyone, should be held accountable for the failure to recognize and limit the negative consequences of teacher unionization, and what consequences, if any, have the responsible parties experienced as a result of their failures to rise to the occasion? To answer these questions, let us review what public intellectuals say about the teacher unions and collective bargaining in public education.

In his thought-provoking book on public intellectuals, Richard A. Posner defines a *public intellectual* as "a person who, drawing on his intellectual resources, addresses a broad though educated public on issues of a political or ideological orientation."[4] Posner then argues as follows:

- Contemporary public intellectuals are mainly academics and think tank staff who do not risk their jobs or reputations by errors of prediction or assessment. Absent any risk when they are mistaken, they have become irresponsible in their analyses, predictions, and assessments of social policy.
- The mistakes of public intellectuals are excused because they are read mainly for their entertainment value or because they support the policy positions of readers who seek confirmation, not challenges to their beliefs. What they say and write is not intended to be tested.
- Their predictions and assessments over time are not monitored or readily available in one place because nobody really cares what they have to say. When it does matter, as in the case of stock market analysts, their errors are pointed out.
- For the most part, public intellectuals are not very influential.[5]

How well does Posner's analysis hold up with respect to the conservative public intellectuals on K–12 education? Before answering this question directly, let me explain why the focus is almost entirely on the conservatives.

The liberal side of educational policy is dominated by the public school establishment, especially the teacher unions. Liberal policies reflect the needs of this establishment; there is no traction for liberal intellectuals who oppose the public school establishment on any major educational policy. There are liberal public intellectuals such as John Goodlad, Ted Sizer, and Deborah Meier, who write books and articles, make speeches, and receive awards, but their policymaking influence is insignificant compared to the influence of the teacher unions.[6] Before his death in 1997, AFT president Albert Shanker was the leading public intellectual on education, but Shanker's influence was based upon his role as AFT president and senior vice president of the AFL-CIO, as well as his advertorials in the Sunday *New York Times* Week in Review.

The public school establishment is opposed to more accountability in the existing system. Consequently, the forces promoting it are largely conservatives. Our task here is to see how conservative educational policy leaders related to teacher unionization. The issue to be explored is *not* the contemporary views of the parties on union issues; with the exception of Diane Ravitch, it is their views on these issues before Republican teacher union power metastasized in the early 1990s.

## JOHN E. CHUBB AND TERRY M. MOE

The most widely read and highly praised book on education policy in the 1990s was *Politics, Markets, and America's School*, and coauthored by John E. Chubb, an economist at the Brookings Institution, and Terry M. Moe, a political science professor at Stanford.[7] Although published in 1990, the authors had held the point of view discussed in the book for several years before its publication.

Chubb and Moe recommend the following concerning the teacher unions:

> Teachers will continue to have a right to join unions and engage in collective bargaining, but the legally prescribed bargaining unit will be the individual school or—as in the case of the district government—the larger organization that runs the school. If teachers in a given school want to join a union or, having done so, want to exact financial or structural concessions, that is up to them. But they will not be allowed to commit other schools or teachers to the same things, and they must suffer the consequences if their victories put them at a competitive disadvantage in supplying quality education. Similarly, if teachers at district-run schools want to remain unionized, their decisions will not apply to any other public schools in the district.[8]

This recommendation reveals a failure to understand the basics of collective bargaining. First, a bargaining unit consists of the positions that are covered by the contract. It is not "the larger organization that runs the school"; it is not an organization of any kind. Unit determination is a decision on what position holders are eligible to vote in the representation election and are covered by the contract if there is one. For instance, are part-time or substitute teachers in or out of the bargaining unit?

Union membership is usually irrelevant to the composition of the bargaining unit. The Chubb–Moe recommendation provides that teachers in a given school should have the selective right to opt out of a districtwide bargaining unit. Any such right would lead to chaos in school district labor relations.

Suppose the teachers in New York City vote overwhelmingly for a district-wide bargaining unit, but a majority in 100 of its approximately 1,573 existing schools vote for a school-based unit determination. Chubb and Moe would obligate the district to bargain with the representatives of these one hundred schools, overriding the preference of the overwhelming majority of the city's teachers.

Due to deaths, retirements, and transfers, support for bargaining or choice of exclusive representation in a particular school would frequently change from year to year. Keeping up with petitions for a different union or going from no representation to representation or vice versa would be an administrative nightmare in which large numbers of teachers would be represented by unions they did not want or not represented by a union they did want. These consequences sometimes materialize under the existing legal framework of collective bargaining but not on the scale that would result from the Chubb–Moe recommendation.

If the teachers with bargaining rights are perceived as getting concessions that other teachers did not, the latter would surely choose to bargain collectively. If the teachers with bargaining rights failed to achieve more favorable terms than the teachers without bargaining rights, the former would quit the union. Knowing this, their unions would never settle for the same or less than teachers in non-union schools or schools organized by a different union. Policymakers would have to be brain dead to support a system that led inevitably to such conflict.

Bear in mind that management and the public also have a stake in how school district bargaining is structured. In bargaining, management usually prefers the smallest feasible number of bargaining units so it will not be whipsawed by unions trying to get a better contract than other unions have negotiated. Remember that in New York City, the NEA affiliates wanted three bargaining units (elementary, junior high, and senior high school), but the consultant, University of Pennsylvania professor George Taylor, recommended and the school board agreed to only one. In contrast, Chubb and Moe proposed that each school, perhaps one thousand at the time, constitute a separate bargaining unit.

Chubb and Moe ignored the virtual certainty that teachers in most schools would choose a districtwide union to bargain for their schools, and the district- or divisionwide union would propose the same agreement at each school. They would succeed at getting it at union-dominated schools, and the pressures on others to accept the same contract would be irresistible.

Who would exercise managerial authority under the Chubb–Moe proposal? Obvious possibilities are (1) the principals, (2) the school district central office, and (3) a governing board of some kind at each school. There would be major problems with each of these alternatives. In any event, the Chubb–Moe recommendation would have required drastic changes in every state bargaining law, every school district contract, every regulatory structure, every state and national NEA and AFT affiliate, and every state labor relations agency over the opposition of all of these entities.

Unfair labor practice charges, hearings, impasse procedures, and litigation would undergo huge increases, not only because of the huge number of bargaining units, but also because many of the judicial and regulatory precedents built up since 1961 would no longer be applicable. In short, the Chubb–Moe recommendation was utterly impractical and revealed a failure to understand the basics of collective bargaining.

## DAVID T. KEARNS AND DENIS P. DOYLE

David T. Kearns, the former CEO of Xerox Corporation who became deputy secretary of education in the George H. Bush administration, and Denis P. Doyle, a pro-union conservative education analyst, coauthored *Winning the Brain Race: A Bold Plan to Make Our Schools Competitive*. The "bold plan" was public school choice, and the other recommendations were just as pathetic. On the subject of teacher unions, Kearns and Doyle say:

To many outside the schools, modern teachers' unions appear to be part of the problem. We are convinced they are part of the solution. Teachers, particularly those in large bureaucratic systems, will need representation to help them restructure their profession. Teachers' unions are the biggest single institutional stakeholder in public education. They have the most to gain or lose in the success or failure of the future school, and we are confident that they will help lead the way. . . . If you want to see one version of the future, look to Xerox's old home town, Rochester, New York. There the teachers' union president, Adam Urbanski, and the superintendent, Peter McWalters, have negotiated a contract that can only be described as remarkable. Indeed, it may be the most important collective bargaining agreement in the country since World War II.[9]

In the real world, the superintendent and school board who agreed to the contract that Kearns and Doyle praised so highly were fired or voted out of office, and even the Rochester local refused to renew its supposedly pioneering provisions when the contract expired.

## CHESTER E. FINN JR.

Chester E. Finn Jr. is undoubtedly the most influential conservative on educational policy who is not currently in government service.[10] Finn is a ubiquitous presence in the educational scene. He is intelligent, hard-working, thoroughly knowledgeable about the Beltway scene (he was assistant secretary of education in the Reagan administration, 1985–1988), and able to pay scholars to pursue lines of inquiry in which he is interested, to publicize persons and issues of interest, and to place his friends in mid-level but important government positions. Furthermore, Finn is an excellent speaker and participates frequently in forums with other policy leaders. Last but not least, nobody works harder at stroking the media, an inexpensive but extremely effective tactic in achieving media recognition. Finn is mentioned in the media more often than any public intellectual specializing in education.[11]

Prior to the mid-1990s, Finn was a strong union supporter. In 1977, he was a signatory to a pro-union advertisement critical of the National Right to Work Legal Defense Foundation (NRTWLDF), a nonprofit organization dedicated to protecting employees from union abuse that "derives operating funds from employer sources."[12] Of course, no mention could have been made in 1977 of Finn's "operating funds" from the anti-union, employer-funded Olin Foundation, which awarded Finn's projects $1.204 millon from 1982 to 1998.[13]

> The following quotation from Finn's 1991 book is even more revealing: Unionism per se does not alarm me. Nor do many of the stances and positions that unions take. There aren't a dozen issues, foreign or domestic, on which I have any large quarrel with Albert Shanker, for example. That's why, a couple of years back, I felt comfortable joining his AFT (as an associate member).[14]

At the time Finn made this statement, Shanker was the senior vice president of the AFL-CIO. The AFL-CIO policies in effect when Finn declared his broad agreement with Shanker included the following:

## The AFL-CIO supported
- An unlimited scope of bargaining
- A ban on permanent replacement of striking workers
- Minimum wage equal to 50 percent of average wage
- A thirty-five-hour work week
- Triple pay for overtime
- The Davis–Bacon Act
- Government-supported childcare
- Federal loan guarantees for shipbuilders
- Taxation of capital gains like other income
- Government funding for American flag vessels
- Higher levels of government-subsidized housing
- Universal healthcare
- General revenue funding for Social Security
- A total ban on goods made with child labor
- Statehood for the District of Columbia

## The AFL-CIO opposed
- A right-to-work law
- Subminimum wage for youth
- U.S. airlines contracting out work to foreign airlines

- Exports of Alaskan gas and oil
- Contracting out government work
- Privatization of the postal service
- English as the official language of public agencies

Shanker seldom, if ever, disagreed publicly with any AFL-CIO position, and he frequently expressed support for its positions and leaders in his advertorials in the Sunday *New York Times*. According to Finn's longtime colleague Diane Ravitch, Shanker "was never afraid to say what he believed, no matter how unpopular it made him. He was never afraid to stand up for principle, no matter how much it annoyed others."[15]

Obviously, the AFL-CIO positions were an AFL-CIO wish list, the antithesis of policies commonly associated with conservatives. When coupled with Shanker's leadership of the opposition to vouchers, tuition tax credits, contracting out, alternative certification, restrictions on the right to strike, and his failure to maintain the subject matter emphasis in NBPTS, Finn's claim to a wide area of agreement with Shanker while maintaining his prestige among conservatives is remarkable.[16] I do not know whether this wide area of agreement included Shanker's participation in labor espionage during the 1961 representation election in New York City, but Shanker's participation had been public information since 1985.[17] As Selden (Shanker's supervisor during the representation election) makes clear, I was completely surprised by the information and even more surprised that Selden would publicly boast about it. Of course, Shanker knew better.

Only two years after his statement of solidarity with Shanker, Finn appears to have concluded that the teacher unions were an obstacle to reform, but he did not explain his reasons. In 1998, his explanation was that he had been naive about teacher union matters; however, his failure to offer any reasons for his new position on teacher unions suggests that either his initial views or his epiphany or both were opportunistic.[18]

## DIANE RAVITCH

Second only to Finn, Diane Ravitch is the most cited public intellectual on educational matters. On May 12, 2005, the *Wall Street Journal* published Ravitch's highly critical op-ed about New York City mayor Michael

Bloomberg and school district chancellor Joel Klein. Bloomberg and Klein had been engaged in bargaining with the United Federation of Teachers (UFT) over a two-year period that did not result in a contract. Two days after her op-ed was published, Ravitch received the UFT's John Dewey award. In accepting the award, Ravitch praised the UFT as follows:

> Right now, New York City's teachers need the UFT more than ever. It is the only counterforce to an autocratic style of management. Right now, it is the sole agency that will speak up for teachers, parents, and others who have a different point of view. The lesson of history is as clear today as it was in 1916: Teachers need their union. And so, I might add, does the public. The challenge in the immediate future is to protect your right to think and act as professionals and as free men and women. For this, you must once again turn to your union.[19]

If the UFT is "the sole agency that will speak up for teachers, parents, and others who have a different point of view" from Mayor Bloomberg, one has to wonder what happened to the ACLU, NAACP, GLSEN (Gay, Lesbian, and Straight Education Network), United Parents Association (UPA), Manhattan Institute (MI), denominational and business organizations, and the editorial departments of the *New York Times*, *New York Daily News*, *New York Post*, *Village Voice*, *Wall Street Journal*, *New York Magazine*, and so on.[20]

Ravitch also coauthored a March 2004 op-ed in the *New York Times* with Randi Weingarten, president of the UFT.[21] The article attacks New York City mayor Michael Bloomberg for getting a school board that serves "at the pleasure of the mayor" instead of for set terms. The article includes such inanities as "There is a good historical reason for having a wall between schools and electoral politics." Ravitch's idea that there was or is or should be a "wall between schools and electoral politics" must have been read with puzzled looks in the NEA, which has explicitly declared that "every education decision is a political decision."

These conservatives were not solely responsible for the conservative failure to cope with union issues; it is at least arguable, however, that if they had been knowledgeable critics or had just remained silent on the topic, American education would be in better condition than it is today. This conclusion contradicts Posner's argument that public intellectuals are not very influential; however, note that Finn, Ravitch, and Kearns held high-ranking policy-making positions in the U.S. Department of Education during the Reagan and first Bush administrations: deputy secretary of education (Kearns); assistant secretary of education (Finn, Ravitch); and chairman of the governing board, National Assessment of Educational Progress (Finn).

All of the discussed individuals (except Kearns) are or were affiliated with think tanks or organizations that disseminated their views nationally. Although one might argue that they did not exert much influence individually, their collective influence was undoubtedly significant.

Harvard professor Caroline Hoxby is frequently cited by equalitarians to support restriction-laden school choice programs. In 1996, she concluded a letter to the *Wall Street Journal* this way:

> While my study tells us what happens to the average school when it unionizes, unions surely help students in some schools. That is why I do not advocate "union busting." A union that enhances its school's productivity has nothing to fear from such reforms; it will be rewarded for helping students. Only unions whose activities hamper students will be reined in.[22]

Presumably, Hoxby would not say "I am opposed to Social Security reform because the system we have helps some senior citizens"; most social policies benefit some of their intended beneficiaries even when the policies are indefensible. The implication that teacher union reform is limited to "union busting" is fallacious, as are the statements about unions that enhance productivity. And if choice among public schools "really does act as a check on unions," one has to wonder why the NEA and AFT are more than willing to advocate it.

## EDUCATION AT THE HERITAGE FOUNDATION

The Heritage Foundation is perhaps the most influential think tank, liberal or conservative, in the country. Founded in 1973, Heritage has almost 200,000 donors annually, the broadest base of support for any U.S. think tank. Its support in 2006 ranged from 58 Founders (donors of $100,000 or more to 280,000 others who contributed less than $100,000.[23] As Heritage sees it,

> Since Day One, Heritage's primary audience has been those who govern — the people who make policy decisions in Congress and the executive branch. In Washington, half of the battle in turning your ideas into battle is "getting in the room" with them. Led by Vice President Michael Franc, Heritage's Government Relations Department got our experts 'in the room' virtually every day in 2003. It lined up Heritage experts to give formal testimony in critical Congressional hearings. Even more importantly, it arranged for our experts to conduct more than 500 briefings for members of Congress, administration officials, and Capitol Hill staffers. These weren't chatty, get-to-know-you-sessions, either. This was serious business.[24]

Although reaching those who govern is Heritage's highest priority, its marketing of conservative ideas and policies exceeds that of any think tank. It has arrangements with newspaper, radio, and television networks to provide columns or speakers; table 12.1 shows the growing presence of its staff in various media outlets.

**Table 12.1.  Getting Heritage's Message Out**

TV Appearances
    2001: 405
    2002: 688
    2003: 1,100
Radio Appearances
    2001: 868
    2002: 1,144
    2003: 1,418
Commentaries Appearing in Major Print and Online News Outlets
    2001: 645
    2002: 673
    2003: 907
Visits to Heritage.org
    2001: 2.7 million
    2002: 3.0 million
    2003: 3.6 million
Visits to Townhall.com
    2001: 13.0 million
    2002: 15.0 million
    2003: 25.0 million

*Source:* Heritage Foundation, *Creating Solutions, Getting Results,* (Washington, DC: Heritage Foundation, 2004), 24.

During 2001, the Heritage Foundation was cited by 81 media sources in 159 new items on education. In addition to the citations in news items, Heritage staff had fifteen op-eds on education published and were radio or television guests seventeen times during the year. These are impressive figures inasmuch as education is not a high priority field at Heritage. It published 35 studies on education during 2001 out of a total of 684.

The Heritage education staff usually consists of a senior policy analyst, who shares one or two research assistants with other senior staff; however, there is a crucial difference between education and other fields of Heritage interest. For example, in foreign policy, Congress and the executive agencies of the federal government are the critical policymaking, funding, and implementing levels of government. In public education, however, the federal government is not the major policymaker and pays only 7 percent of the costs. Even when the federal government does make educational policy, it must rely on states and school districts to implement them. A focus on Congress and the Department of Education is not a good fit with the realities of educational policymaking; clearly, any effort to utilize the federal government to establish and implement policy on how 93 percent of education funding is spent will encounter a host of problems.

## POLICY EXPERTS:
## THE INSIDER GUIDE TO PUBLIC POLICY EXPERTS

The Heritage Foundation annually publishes *The Insider Guide to Public Policy Experts*. The *Guide* is characterized as "the Definitive Directory of the Conservative Public Policy Community." The preface states that the *Guide* is "envisioned as the single source reference to 'the best and the brightest' thinkers and policy organizations throughout the United States and around the world."[25]

The 2005–2006 edition of the *Guide* includes 149 experts on "education unions and interest groups." These numbers are impressive, but each individual listed in the *Guide* is responsible for identifying his or her areas of expertise. Unfortunately, not everyone can be trusted to avoid exaggerations of his or her expertise. Consider an article coauthored by Kirk A. Johnson, who became a Heritage policy analyst in 2003. Johnson has been listed in the *Guide* since 2005 as an expert on "education unions and interest groups." In that year, Johnson coauthored an article on collective bargaining contracts in Michigan school districts that includes the following comment:

Limit Exclusive Bargaining Representative Clauses
More than 500 contracts contain a separate provision by which the school board agrees not to negotiate with any other teacher organization.

In other words, if a school board wished to contract with a math, science, or professional teacher organization for the purpose of professional development for its staff members (a term of employment), it would first require the union's permission. School boards should remove exclusive bargaining representative clauses that require such permission before employees can explore opportunities with other professional organizations.[26]

First, even if the clause that requires the school board to refrain from negotiating with anyone except the union were removed from the contract, the school board would still have a statutory duty to negotiate only with the union for all members of the teacher bargaining unit. Second, the duty "not to negotiate with any other teacher organization" would not necessarily preclude a school board from contracting with any other entity on professional development. Tens of thousands of employers, including a large number of school boards, have retained the right to employ parties not in the bargaining unit for services provided by members of the bargaining unit.

Understandably, Heritage's critics do not share its favorable view of Heritage staff. An Arizona State University (ASU) study says about Krista Kafer, the Heritage senior education policy analyst from February 2001 to May 2005:

According to her Heritage Foundation biography and an article in *Roll Call*, Krista Kafer graduated from the University of Colorado with a B.A. in history in 1994. She then worked for the Colorado chapter of the National Right to Life Committee, Rep. Dave McIntosh (R-IN), and Rep. Bob Schaffer (R-CO), as well as Sen. Bob Dole's 1996 presidential campaign. According to the *Washington Post*, she joined the Heritage Foundation in the spring of 2001. It appears that Krista Kafer has never studied or worked in education.[27]

A similar lack of educational background is evident among prior Heritage analysts in education since 1990.[28] Only one appears to have had any graduate work in education or labor relations or employment as a public or private school teacher for more than a year or two. The ASU study underscores the fact that Heritage educational policy advice is a "credence good"; it is advice that consumers cannot test. Consumers accept or reject it on the basis of the reputation of the source. It is Heritage's reputation, not the staff members', that persuades others to accept the Heritage staff recommendations on education. The fact is, however, that education is not a high-priority policy area at Heritage. Its educational policy analysts have lacked the training and experience normally associated with expertise. For an organization that serves as a major employment agency for USED in Republican administrations and dispenses advice on education to U.S. presidents, members of Congress, governors, and other educational policymakers, the lack of educational expertise among the Heritage educational policy experts is a troubling deficiency.

## THE ACADEMIC MYSTIQUE: HARVARD EDUCATION PRESS AND THE AMERICAN ENTERPRISE INSTITUTE[29]

Statements by university professors and individuals with doctoral degrees from Harvard University are often credence goods, but consider a 2006 book published by the Harvard Education Press, a publishing unit affiliated with Harvard University.[30] The book is a collection of chapters written by professors at leading universities and policy analysts at prestigious think tanks, such as the American Enterprise Institute (AEI). One chapter is coauthored by Frederick M. Hess and Andrew P. Kelly. Hess has an MA and PhD in government from Harvard University and is director of education policy studies at the American Enterprise Institute (AEI), one of the most influential think tanks in Washington. In addition to his appointment at AEI, Hess is executive editor of *Education Next*, an education policy journal sponsored by the Hoover Institution, Harvard University's Program on Educational Policy and Governance, and the Fordham Foundation and supported by several foundations. Kelly is described as a Dartmouth graduate who worked as an "educational policy researcher" at AEI before enrolling as a graduate student in political science at the University of California, Berkeley. Because he is the senior author and for editorial simplicity, I shall refer to Hess as the author.

My comments follow the italic quotations from Hess's chapter in *Collective Bargaining in Education*.

*"Critics assert that teacher contracts usurp managerial authority."*[31]

*"Perhaps most intriguing, we ask whether contracts constrain district management as some ardent union critics have suggested, or whether these constraints have resulted in part from the arbitration, operational routines, timid district leadership, or contract implementation."*[32] It would be difficult to think of a labor contract that did not "usurp managerial authority" or constrain management in some way—why would a union agree to such a contract? Management would be guilty of an unfair labor practice for insisting on such a contract. "The arbitration process" may be grievance arbitration or arbitration of the terms of the contract. Each of these kinds are further categorized as "binding" or "advisory," "final and binding," or just "binding." To which does "the arbitration process" apply?

*"CBAs are the contracts that govern the relationship between any group of employees and its employer. In the case of teacher collective bargaining, the two parties are the local teachers union and the school district."*[33] To some extent, CBAs govern the relationships between unions and the employees they represent; for example, contracts typically govern the dues deduction process and union and employee rights in grievance procedures. "The two parties" are not necessarily "the local teachers union and the school district." Teachers in the bargaining unit can choose a regional, state, or national union or an organizing committee (or probably even an individual in some states) to represent them in collective bargaining.

*"In states with mandatory collective bargaining, employers must collectively bargain with organized employees."*[34] Not necessarily. The district is obligated to bargain with the exclusive representative even though no teachers are members of it or of any other union. Employees can be "organized" (members of a union) but lack bargaining rights.

*"Unorganized employees may seek to organize a bargaining unit as follows. . . . An organization seeking to represent the employees must petition the state agency, be approved by the agency, and win a majority vote of employees in a certified election."*[35] In most states, the required majority is of the employees voting in the election, not a majority of the employees in the bargaining unit. Winning a majority vote of members of the bargaining unit is a condition precedent to being certified as the bargaining agent. In the nine states that allow collective bargaining in the absence

of a bargaining law, there is no state agency to certify any of these matters, and even in the states with a bargaining law, school boards sometimes bargain with uncertified teacher unions when certification is regarded as a mere formality.

*"In a few states, such as Texas, state law stipulates that districts may* not *collectively bargain. In Texas districts where teachers have organized and selected a representative, districts typically negotiate with teachers through a process called 'exclusive consultation.'"*[36] Only 6 of approximately 1,200 Texas school districts have "exclusive consultation." Six out of 1,200 is hardly typical.

*"The laws define which employees will be bound by the contract, . . . how teachers who wish to collectively bargain can choose a representative, how bargaining takes place, how disputes will be resolved, the legality of teacher strikes, the legality of payroll deduction of dues or agency fees, and the scope of the bargaining process."*[37] There are at least five errors in this statement:

1. The recognition clause in the contract or the certification by the Public Employment Relations Board (PERB) defines who is covered by the contract.

2. The union and the school board, not the law, determine how bargaining takes place (place, time, frequency, ground rules, requests for information, treatment of agreements, publicity, and much else).

3. The laws do not define how "disputes" will be resolved; the parties at the table do that. The bargaining laws usually define how *impasses* are to be resolved. An impasse is a situation in which one or both parties asserts that bargaining on *any* item is futile. These assertions are usually submitted to the PERB, which does not necessarily agree that the parties are at impasse. If the PERB does not agree, the parties must resume bargaining.

4. In some states, judicial decisions or attorney general opinions, not statutes, have resolved the legality of teachers strikes.

5. In the states without a teacher bargaining law, the school board and union must agree on the scope of bargaining since there is no penalty for refusing to bargain. In states with a bargaining law, the statutes generally define the scope of bargaining in very general terms, and the PERB decides whether a specific issue is within the scope of bargaining; however, its decisions are subject to legal challenge.

*"A CBA is a legal contract laying out the rights and obligations of teachers and the school board."*[38] It is astonishing that the statement does not refer to the contractual rights and obligations of the union, which, as previously noted, is one of the two parties to the contract.

The previous examples are only a partial list of the erroneous and misleading statements in just the first four pages of Hess's thirty-four-page chapter; continuing in this vein would be belaboring the obvious, but one additional statement sheds considerable light on the entire chapter: *"Despite the importance of arbitration, the process has largely escaped either scholarly or journalistic attention."*[39] In 1994, the Cornell University Press published a 1,336-item bibliography on arbitration.[40] The bibliography explicitly excludes

- General studies of labor law and labor relations
- Most publications that treat arbitration as part of a larger topic, such as labor law or labor relations
- Newspaper articles, editorials about arbitration, book reviews, and articles in journals and periodicals that specialize in current developments, such as *Legal Times*
- Publications on alternative dispute resolution
- Arbitration outside of North America, with a few exceptions
- Studies of arbitration in foreign languages
- Articles less than four pages
- Articles at the introductory level

The 1,336 items include 27 under "Schools" and 52 under "Public Sector," but a majority of the remaining items appear to be relevant to arbitration in K–12 education. The arbitration items listed under "Schools" cite nine different journals. Inasmuch as the bibliography was published in 1994, the number of entries might well have doubled since then.

Professional organizations that focus on arbitration include those listed in the following paragraphs.

## The American Arbitration Association (AAA)

Founded in 1926, AAA has a national office in New York City, thirty-four offices in the United States and Europe, and fifty-nine cooperative agreements with institutions in forty-one countries. It resolves about 14,500 labor-management disputes annually; in 2002, its members resolved a total of 230,255 disputes through arbitration, mediation, fact-finding, and other forms of dispute resolution. AAA publishes *Arbitration in the Schools*, founded in 1970.

## The Labor and Employment Relations Association (LERA)

Founded in 1947, LERA includes 3,000 members with a professional interest in employment relations. Members can choose to be associated with two sections, including collective bargaining, dispute resolution, labor and employment law, labor markets, labor economics, labor unions, labor studies, and worker–employment relations. LERA publishes an annual research volume, a quarterly newsletter, proceedings of the annual conference, a biannual magazine, *Perspectives on Work*, a monthly newsletter entitled *LERA Labor and Employment Law Newsletter*, and a membership directory. All of the publications deal with arbitration from time to time. There are fifty local chapters throughout the country, and the national office is based at the University of Illinois, Champaign–Urbana. LERA members categorize themselves as either "practitioners" or "academics," and over 60 percent are academics; however, a large number of academics are also employed as arbitrators, and a smaller percentage of practitioners are part-time faculty members.

## National Academy of Arbitrators (NAA)

The National Academy of Arbitrators (NAA) is a professional, honorary association devoted to arbitration of labor-management disputes. NAA includes a Committee on Public Employment Disputes Settlement; several other committees deal with one or more facets of arbitration in public employment. The academy includes seventeen regional offices as well as a Research and Education Foundation. Membership includes a substantial number of university personnel who are evaluated partly on their research.

This incomplete survey does not include scores of books on labor arbitration and innumerable articles on the subject in journals, such as law reviews and labor law journals. Actually, the output of the Cornell University Press and the Bureau of National Affairs, the two largest publishers of books and journals on labor relations and labor arbitration, would have sufficed to discredit any alleged lack of scholarly and journalistic attention to arbitration.

First, we can safely say that the public, policymakers, and media will continue to rely on credence goods; it is unavoidable as a practical matter. Second, this reliance is often egregiously unwarranted. Third, this is not a problem that can be solved by governments, which are among the most flagrant sponsors of flawed data and are the least likely sources of data on government mistakes and failures. Better credence goods are essential and feasible, but they are not likely to emerge from heavy contributors to the educational morass.

What explains the policy debacle on education that emerges from think tanks, liberal as well as conservative? The dynamics of think tank funding differ markedly from the dynamics of funding for higher education. In the latter, criticisms of one's oeuvre are not usually a threat to a professor's job or compensation. The professors have tenure, and future funding is usually assured. As a result, criticism of professors is seldom threatening. In contrast, most think tanks must constantly raise funds. In this context, criticism is perceived as a threat to organizational and personal survival. The result is much less criticism of think tank products by analysts in think tanks of the same or similar broad policy orientation. Such criticism could easily spill over into mutual assured destruction; it is safer for liberal think tanks to be critical of conservative ones and vice versa. Thus without any formal treaty or agreement, there is a striking absence of criticism among think tanks that appeal to the same funders.

## ACCOUNTABILITY IN PUBLIC INTELLECTUAL WORK

From the preceding discussion, we can conclude that public intellectuals on educational issues (including this author) should be regarded cautiously. They are not always mistaken, but they are mistaken often enough on critical issues to warrant much higher standards for assessing what they have to say. As long as no negative consequences follow even egregiously mistaken credence goods, better educational policies are improbable. Better policies require improvements in the market in which educational policies achieve professional and public approval.

Richard A. Posner suggests some actions that can be taken to improve this market. First, it should be possible to review all of the contributions of public intellectuals and education reporters without exhaustive search procedures. This calls for making all the publications and presentations of these groups available on one website. Second, public policy should require disclosure of any income received for public intellectual work. This requirement should apply especially to professors and think tank experts. Third, universities and think tanks should require their faculties to post their nonacademic writing, testimony, and public addresses, other than work that is readily accessible. Each year, the content on their websites should be printed out and made accessible and copies deposited in major university libraries.[41]

I suggest that think tanks set aside a certain percentage of their grants for independent evaluations of the major projects that they fund. The amounts may be geared roughly to the amounts of the grants, but ideally the independent evaluators should be chosen by lot from a list of tough-minded evaluators who do not accept other kinds of employment. The independent evaluators would assess the research and policy issues raised by the grant and point out any deficiencies in the final product. The evaluation reports would be available on the Internet, along with a rejoinder by the project officials and possibly a rejoinder by the independent evaluators. The evaluators should be prohibited from accepting paid employment from parties whose work they have evaluated for at least a year after their evaluative work.

The good news is that information technology has made it possible to achieve levels of accountability in educational policy leadership that were hitherto unattainable. Fortunately, no legislation is required, nor does it necessarily matter that most public intellectuals, education policy analysts, and reporters will not welcome accountability any more than the educational establishment does. There are dozens of philanthropic foundations that have the resources to bring about a higher level of accountability among the media, universities, and think tanks, even if their personnel are opposed to independent evaluation of their own projects or publications. Such evaluation might foster safer, more conservative philanthropy, but the results in the absence of any accountability are not impressive.[42]

A fallacy to be avoided is the idea that having heads roll will solve anything. It will not be helpful to replace one group of unaccountable pundits, public intellectuals, reporters, or government officials with a different group of unaccountable actors. Removal of incumbent policy and government leaders, even if it were possible, would not matter in the continuing absence of accountability for egregiously misguided efforts to inform or influence public policy on educational issues.

The educational morass illustrates a major weakness of democratic representative government: its vulnerability from interest groups that give a higher priority to interest group welfare than the public interest. There is no support among producers for restricting this freedom, but organizing consumers would be extremely difficult. Without endorsing any particular solution to the problem, we can say that the escalating costs and stagnant results of public education require a solution in the near future. It must be emphasized, however, that support for education is a problem because of its magnitude, not because education presents any special problems of principle.

In 1993, I asserted, "The promarket forces will have one ineradicable advantage in the years ahead. That advantage is the inherent futility of conventional school reform."[43] Clearly, the advocates of basic change have not been able to capitalize on this advantage since 1993. No basic fix-it or replace-it change has been implemented, while a plethora of policy failures have been recycled as revolutionary reforms, especially by parties seeking to justify their grants and awards from philanthropic foundations and the government, by politicians seeking to gain or remain in public office, and by public intellectuals playing to their galleries. Since 1988, Democratic and Republican administrations have each controlled federal educational agencies for approximately eight years; neither effectuated any significant improvement in our educational situation.

Is this outcome only to be expected because the resources employed to protect the status quo are greater than the resources devoted to changing it? This is plausible, but it is not the explanation for the absence of basic change. The conservatives are fond of saying that the basic reform issue is not more spending; it is how educational funding is spent. Unfortunately, the same principle applies to conservative expenditures to achieve educational improvement. Whether conservatives will face up to this reality remains to be seen.

## NOTES

1. For a discussion of this point, see David Tyack and Larry Cuban, *Tinkering toward Utopia* (Cambridge, MA: Harvard University Press, 1995), 76–80.

2. Paul T. Hill, Christine Campbell, and James Harvey also contend that there is no way to enforce accountability in public education. Their concept of accountability differs from mine, but the practical implications of their views are the same. See Paul T. Hill, Christine Campbell, and James Harvey, *It Takes a City* (Washington, DC: Brookings, 2000), 22–23.

3. Charles Abelmann and Richard Elmore, *When Accountability Knocks, Will Anyone Answer?* (Philadelphia: CPRE, University of Pennsylvania, 1999), 41.

4. Richard A. Posner, *Public Intellectuals: A Study in Decline* (Cambridge, MA: Harvard University Press, 2001), 17–40. Posner's conclusion that public intellectuals are not very influential is not shared by other public intellectuals. In 1980 Frederick Hayek contended that "the attempts to appeal to the mass by propaganda in which they can sometimes be interested are futile. No system or systematic propaganda can undo the effects of the preaching of three to four generations of journalists, teachers and literary people who have honestly believed in socialism. It is only through that class we can hope to influence majority opinion" (Letter, F. A. Hayek to Antony Fisher, January 1, 1980).

5. Posner, *Public Intellectuals*, 83–166.

6. The term *academics* includes policy experts working for think tanks.

7. John E. Chubb and Terry M. Moe, *Politics, Markets, and America's School* (Washington, DC: Brookings, 1990).

8. Chubb and Moe, *Politics, Markets, and America's School*, 224.

9. David T. Kearns and Denis P. Doyle, *Winning the Brain Race: A Bold Plan to Make Our Schools Competitive* (San Francisco: Institute for Contemporary Studies Press, 1989), 44, 62–63. After Doyle, Shanker, and I had taped a program on Ben Wattenberg's talk show on September 16, 1994, Doyle told me that he regarded Shanker as the only "educational statesman" of our time. In 2002, Kearns informed me orally that he no longer agreed with the benign view of teacher unions in the book.

10. Finn's success in achieving favorable attention in prominent media is a textbook case on how to do it. He and Diane Ravitch established the Educational Excellence Network in the early 1980s. Its monthly publication was supposed to consist of the most outstanding policy and research studies in K–12 education. Within a short time, the content was mainly newspaper articles, frequently from the *New York Times*, *Washington Post*, and *Washington Times*. According to *Education Week*, through the Fordham Foundation, Finn "contracted

with the Editorial Projects in Education (EPE), to conduct an 'influence study' of the persons, organizations, sources of information, and studies that have had the most impact on education in the past decade. Mr. Finn, the foundation, and the *Gadfly* made the top ten lists, but not Fordham's reports." Still, two feature articles in *Education Week* are an excellent return on the investment. See "Finn Basks in Role as Standards-Bearer," and "Think Tank Takes the Plunge," *Education Week*, December 20, 2006. The study ranked the NEA as the seventh most influential educational policy organization after the American Federation of Teachers (sixth) and Achieve, Inc. Mistakes of this magnitude tend to confirm the media analysis in chapter 11.

11. Richard A. Posner, *Public Intellectuals: A Study in Decline* (Cambridge, MA: Harvard University Press, 2001), 168, 194–206.

12. Ad Hoc Committee for Labor in a Democratic Society, "Labor: A Force for Democracy and Human Rights," advertisement, *Commentary*, 64, no. 4 (October 1977).

13. Information received from the Olin Foundation, Summer 2005.

14. Chester E. Finn Jr., *We Must Take Charge* (New York: The Free Press, 1991), 90.

15. Diane Ravitch, "A Tribute to Albert Shanker," *New Leader*, March 3, 1997.

16. Was Finn unaware of AFL-CIO policies when he announced his broad agreement with Shanker's views? I will let Finn answer this question.

17. See David Selden, *The Teacher Rebellion* (Washington, DC: Howard University Press, 1985), 56–58.

18. Finn, letter to the editor, *Commentary* (March 1998), 4. Finn concludes his letter by asserting that the merger of the NEA and AFT will result in a "single giant union that will be even more of a menace. On this, I believe, Mr. Lieberman and I are in full agreement." We are not in "full agreement" and may not be in agreement at all. As long as the NEA and AFT are separate organizations, reporters who want an alternative to a statement or point of view expressed by an NEA or AFT spokesman will call someone from the other organization. If merger materializes, they are more likely to call a conservative teacher organization for a different point of view. More importantly, several state and local defections from the NEA were virtually certain if merger materialized, hence an NEA–AFT merger would probably have been desirable from a conservative standpoint.

19. United Federation of Teachers, press release, May 16, 2005.

20. From 1985 to 1999, the John M. Olin Foundation, a philanthropic foundation noted for its opposition to unions, awarded Ravitch $2,490,659. This amount included $1.250 million awarded to the New York University Center for Education and Civil Society from 1994 to 1997. Joseph Vitteritti was a coproposer of this grant. From 1990 to 2002, Ravitch received $810,000 for Olin Fellowships

at New York University. From 1982 to 1998, projects directed by Finn received $1,024,400 from the Olin Foundation. All of these grants were awarded to 501(c)3 organizations and covered a variety of expenses. What is interesting about these grants is that over the years, the Olin Foundation has contributed to the National Right to Work Committee and its foundation, perhaps the two organizations that have done the most to restrict union power in both the public and private sectors.

21. Diane Ravitch and Randi Weingarten, "Public Schools, Minus the Public," *New York Times*, March 18, 2004, A27.

22. Caroline Hoxby, "Unions' Effects on Schools," *Wall Street Journal*, October 31, 1996, A23. Chubb, Moe, Finn, Ravitch, and Hoxby constitute half the members of the Koret Task Force on Education, a group of ten conservative public intellectuals active on education issues. Supported by the Hoover Institution and the Koret Foundation, task force activities consist of issuing policy statements that are published in various media.

23. *Annual Report, 2006* (Washington, DC: Heritage Foundation, 2007), 26–27.

24. President and chairman Edwin J. Feulner, *Creating Solutions, Getting Results* (Washington, DC: Heritage Foundation, 2004), 22.

25. John Hilboldt, Bridgett G. Wagner, and Kelli Fulton, eds., *Policy Experts: The Insider Guide to Policy Experts* 2003, 16th ed. (Washington, DC: Heritage Foundation, 2003).

26. Kirk A. Johnson and Elizabeth Moser, "Reform Collective Bargaining," *Government Union Review*, 21, no. 1, 26–27.

27. Eric Haas, Alex Molnar, and Rafael Serrano, *Media Impact of Think Tank Education Publication* (Tempe: Arizona State University, 2001), 4–5. Contrary to the ASU study, Kafer did have some experience on education issues, having worked for two members of Congress on a variety of issues, mainly educational ones according to Kafer.

28. The period from 1990 to 2005 covers the tenure of the last five Heritage senior educational policy analysts and overlaps with fifteen of my nineteen years of residence in Washington.

29. Nothing in this section should be interpreted as a criticism of the Harvard University Press, which is a different affiliate of Harvard University.

30. Jane Hannaway and Andrew J. Rotherham, eds., *Collective Bargaining in Education* (Cambridge, MA: Harvard Education Press, 2006). The Harvard Education Press is not part of the Harvard University Press, which is also affiliated with Harvard University.

31. Frederick M. Hess and Andrew P. Kelly, "Scapegoat, Albatross, or What?" in Hannaway and Rotherham, *Collective Bargaining in Education*, 53.

32. Hess and Kelly, "Scapegoat, Albatross, or What?" 55. Emphasis added.

33. Hess and Kelly, "Scapegoat, Albatross, or What?" 55. Emphasis added.

34. Hess and Kelly, "Scapegoat, Albatross, or What?" 55. Emphasis added.

35. Hess and Kelly, "Scapegoat, Albatross, or What?" 55. Emphasis added.

36. Hess and Kelly, "Scapegoat, Albatross, or What?" 55. Emphasis added.

37. Hess and Kelly, "Scapegoat, Albatross, or What?" 56. Emphasis added.

38. Hess and Kelly, "Scapegoat, Albatross, or What?" 56. Emphasis added.

39. Hess and Kelly, "Scapegoat, Albatross, or What?" 85. Emphasis added.

40. Charles J. Coleman and Theodora T. Haynes, *Labor Arbitration: An Annotated Bibliography* (Ithaca, NY: Cornell University Press, 1994).

41. Posner, *Public Intellectuals*, 387–400.

42. The School of Education at Arizona State University (ASU) and the Public Interest Center at the University of Colorado have established the Think Tank Review Project (TTRP) to monitor the educational policy research sponsored by think tanks. An explanatory note asserts that think tank policy statements are very influential and hence should be subject to scrutiny, a position obviously endorsed here. Nevertheless, TTRP is a flagrant example of intellectual hypocrisy. The poor research conducted by think tanks is miniscule compared to the huge quantities of such research emerging from colleges and universities. Furthermore, many think tank staff were professors immediately prior to, after, or concurrently with think tank employment. For example, I have been employed full-time by eight universities and three think tanks, not counting frequent part-time employment among both types of institutions. Moving from academe to think tank positions and vice versa is a frequently recurring pattern of employment in the United States. Not surprisingly, TTRP's research considered to date has been devoted to research conducted by conservative think tanks. As the previous chapters demonstrate, there is much to criticize in the research by conservative think tanks, but the Think Tank Review Project is merely a new cover on a liberal garbage can.

43. Myron Lieberman, *Public Education: An Autopsy* (Cambridge, MA: Harvard University Press, 1993), 315.

# Appendix

## The Public School Establishment

| Organization | Eligibility for Membership | Total Number of Members | Total Revenues or Budget |
| --- | --- | --- | --- |
| American Association of Colleges for Teacher Education (AACTE) | Institutional Four-year degree granting U.S. institutions that house schools, colleges, and departments of education. Affiliate: Entities with a mission directly related to education, especially educator education including four-year foreign universities, two-year colleges, state boards of education and regents, research laboratories, education organizations, and for-profit companies with an education mission and interest. | 789 institutional, 34 affiliate as of 2005 | $5.7 million as of 2005 |
| American Educational Research Association (AERA) | Regular: Eligibility requires satisfactory evidence of active interest in educational research, as well as professional training to at least the master's degree level or equivalent; graduate students, professors, government agencies, staff of policy organizations, and companies doing business in the K–12 market. | 24,483 as of June 2006 | $7.3 million as of 2004 |
| American Federation of Teachers (AFT) | Teachers; paraprofessionals; school-related personnel; local, state, and federal employees; higher education faculty and staff; and nurses and other health care professionals. | 1,300,000 as of 2006* | $214 million (2005–2006) |
| Association for Supervision and Curriculum Development (ASCD) | Superintendents, supervisors, principals, teachers, professors of education, and school board members. | 175,000 as of 2006 | $58,910,757 as of August 2005 |
| Children's Defense Fund | N/A | N/A | $21.4 million (2006) |
| Council for Exceptional Children (CEC) | Teachers, professors, parents, and private school officials interested in special education. | 40,000 as of 2007 | $8.7 million (2006) |
| Council of Chief State School Officers (CCSSO) | Public officials who head state departments of education in 49 states, DC, 5 extrastate jurisdictions, and DoD Education. | 56 school chiefs as of June 2006 | $43,662,618 (FY 2005) |
| National Association of Elementary School Principals (NAESP) | Elementary and middle school principals, professors of elementary education, and companies selling goods and/or services to elementary school market. | 30,000 as of June 2006 | $9,823,000 (2004–2005) |

| Organization | Description | Membership | Budget/Revenue |
|---|---|---|---|
| National Association of Secondary School Principals (NASSP) | Middle and secondary school teachers, professors of secondary education, and companies selling goods and services to secondary school market. | 30,000 (2006) | $23.9 million as of (2005–2006) |
| National Education Association (NEA) | Public school teachers, higher education faculty, education support professionals, retired educators, and college students studying to become teachers. | 2,800,000 as of 2006* | $279 million (2006–2007) |
| National Parent–Teacher Association (PTA) | Parents, teachers, school administrators, representatives of companies selling plans for PTA to earn income, and other business representatives. | 6,000,000 as of 2006* | $12 million (2006) |
| National School Boards Association (NSBA) | All state board associations, although a few are temporarily out of membership status due to nonpayment of dues. Also, about 2,400 local school boards that must also be members of their state school board associations. | 2,393 local boards, 48 state school boards and associations, and the Virgin Islands as of 2007 | $22 million |
| People for the American Way (PFAW) | N/A | | |
| Phi Delta Kappa | Open to professional educators and other individuals and institutions committed to the purpose of the association, which is primarily protection of public education. | 56,955 as of June 2006 | $7,346,618 as of June 2006 |

*Notes:* N/A = not applicable or not primarily a membership organization. Rounding of numbers usually done by source of information. *Self-reported but challenged by various sources.

The above list is illustrative, not definitive. For example, it does not include NEA's fifty-three state affiliates, some of which, like the California Teachers Association (CTA), are extremely influential organizations in their own right. The listing also does not include philanthropic organizations that are major sources of funding for think tanks active on K–12 issues and projects oriented toward public elementary and secondary education. Also, higher education faculty are not included although an integral part of the education establishment. Furthermore, several national organizations are more influential, at least on certain issues, than the organizations listed.

Membership and budget are not always realistic guides to influences. CCSSO has only fifty-six members, but it has more influence than many organizations with many more members and revenues. Also, there are difficult problems of overlapping membership, but listing all would be a mistake in the other direction. For example, organizations like the National Council for Social Studies includes many NEA and AFT members but also many who are not union members.

# Index

Abelmann, Charles, 274
*Abood v. Detroit Board of Education*, 149–51
accountability: 272–98; and American Enterprise Institute, 287–92; and John E. Chubb, 276–78; definitions, 272–74; and Denis P. Doyle, 278–79; and educational research, 51–53; and Chester E. Finn Jr., 279–81; and Heritage Foundation, 283–87; and David F. Kearns, 278–79; and Terry M. Moe, 276–78; and pay for performance, 6–9; of principals, 274; of professors, 274–76; of public intellectuals, 274–94; of school board members, 162–64; of teacher unions, 164–66; of teachers, 274; of think tanks, 274–94
achievement gap, 1–2, 86, 95, 229, 254
advanced placement (AP), 19–20
AFL-CIO, xiv, xvii, 136, 160, 178, 182, 276, 280–81, 296

Age Discrimination in Employment Act, 173
agency fees, 149–51, 182, 249, 289
Allen, Jeanne, 139–40
alternative certification, 76–79, 281. *See also* certification; teacher education
American Arbitration Association (AAA), 178, 251, 290–91
American Board for Certification of Teacher Excellence (ABCTE), 79–82
American Economic Association, 78
American Enterprise Institute (AEI), 56, 200, 207, 287
American Federation of Teachers (AFT), xiv, xvii, 136–78, 226, 276, 280–82, 296; affiliation with AFL-CIO, 280–81; and charter schools, 30–33; merger with NEA, 296; and privatization, 251–52, 281. *See also* AFL-CIO; National Education Association (NEA); Shanker, Albert; teacher unions
Americans with Disabilities Act, 173

# About the Author

**Myron Lieberman** was born in St. Paul, Minnesota, the fourth child of immigrants from eastern Europe. After attending public elementary and secondary schools in St. Paul, he received a BS in law at the University of Minnesota before entering military service for three and a half years, mainly in the South Pacific. He was discharged in 1946 as a staff sergeant to accept a position with the Civil Intelligence Section, GHQ, U.S. forces in Japan. He received a BSE from the University of Minnesota in 1948, taught one year at Humboldt High School in St. Paul, and became a graduate student and teaching assistant at the University of Illinois, receiving his MA in 1950 and a PhD in education in 1952. His full-time employment in higher education included service at the University of Oklahoma, Yeshiva University, Rhode Island College, City University of New York, Ohio University, and the University of Pennsylvania. From 1962 to 1969, Dr. Lieberman also served as an expert witness and consultant to the NAACP Legal Defense and Education Policy Fund, Inc., in cases in Alabama, Arkansas, and Mississippi, and to the U.S. Department of Justice in Louisiana. He was instrumental in persuading colleagues nationwide to assist the Fund in its challenges to government-imposed racial segregation.

Author or coauthor of eighteen books and scores of articles on educational policy issues, Dr. Lieberman has been an invited presenter in Australia, Canada, and Switzerland, as well as scores of universities and professional organizations in the United States. From 1977 to 1988, Dr. Lieberman served as the chief school board negotiator in hundreds of school board contracts in Arizona, California, New Jersey, New York, and Rhode Island.

An avid tennis player into his senior years, Dr. Lieberman was Minnesota state high school champion in 1936 and was a three-year letter winner at the University of Minnesota, from 1938 to 1941, and holder of over forty junior and senior titles in the north central states.